THE INNER CIVIL WAR

George M. Fredrickson

The Inner Civil War

NORTHERN INTELLECTUALS AND THE CRISIS OF THE UNION

with a New Preface

UNIVERSITY OF ILLINOIS PRESS

Urbana and Chicago

for my Mother and Father

Illini Books edition, 1993
© 1965, 1993 by George M. Fredrickson

Originally published by Harper & Row, Publishers, New York

Printed in the United States of America
P 5 4 3 2 1

This book is printed on acid-free paper.

Library of Congress Cataloging-in-Publication Data

Fredrickson, George M., 1934–
    The inner Civil War : northern intellectuals and the crisis of the
Union / George M. Fredrickson; with a new preface. — Illini
Books ed.
        p.   cm.
    Originally published: New York : Harper & Row, 1965.
    Includes bibliographical references (p.   ) and index.
    ISBN 0-252-06274-4 (pb : acid-free paper)
    1. United States—History—Civil War, 1861–1865.   2. United
States—Intellectual life—1783–1865.   3. United States—
Intellectual life—1865–1918.   I. Title.
E468.9.F83   1993
973.7'15—dc20   92-36773
                                                                CIP

CONTENTS

Preface to the 1993 Edition   vii

Preface to the First Edition   xv

Prologue   1

Part I

Roles and Rehearsals: The 1850s

1   Prophets of Perfection   7
2   Conservatives in a Radical Age   23
3   The Impending Crisis   36

Part II

The War as Idea and Experience, 1860–65

4   Secession, Rebellion, and Ideology   53
5   The Spirit of '61   65
6   "This Cruel War": The Individual Response
      to Suffering   79
7   The Sanitary Elite: The Organized Response
      to Suffering   98
8   The Meaning of Emancipation   113
9   The Doctrine of Loyalty   130
10 The Martyr and His Friends   151
11 The Strenuous Life   166

Part III

The Legacy

12 The Twilight of Humanitarianism   183
13 Science and the New Intellectuals   199
14 The Moral Equivalent of War   217
                                Notes   239
                                Index   269

PREFACE TO THE 1993 EDITION

ORIGINALLY PUBLISHED MORE THAN A QUARTER OF A century ago, *The Inner Civil War* is reissued on the assumption that it still has something to contribute to the ongoing search for the meaning of the greatest crisis in the nation's history. Despite all that has been written about the Civil War since 1965, it remains the standard account of the effect of the conflict on the intellectual life of the North. The continued historiographic relevance of this book is suggested by the fact that Phillip Paludan cites it several times in *A People's Contest* (1988), the volume in the New American Nation Series that sums up the North's Civil War experience.

The book has survived despite a veritable revolution in the writing of American history since its first appearance. In 1965, the traditional focus on the thought and action of elite white males had not yet been challenged by a "new social history" that shifted the angle of vision from elites to ordinary people, including women and minorities. In certain obvious ways, *The Inner Civil War* was rooted in the historiography of the 1950s and early 1960s, the era in which its author came of age. As an undergraduate at Harvard in the mid-fifties and a graduate student in the early sixties, I studied with Perry Miller among others. From Miller, I learned a reverence for what he called "the life of the mind"—the self-validating exercise of intellect among the most articulate members of society. But from Miller's magisterial work *The New England Mind: From Colony to Province* (1953), I also learned that sophisticated thought does not exist in a vacuum but constitutes a response to historical change. Just as Miller's covenant theology could not withstand the shock of colonial New

vii

England's transformation from cutting edge of the reformation to
provincial trading society, the radical individualism that I found
to be the dominant ante-bellum intellectual style succumbed to
the resurgent institutionalism or organizationalism encouraged
by the Civil War experience.

If *The Inner Civil War* was partly an outgrowth of an older
historiography that made much of the ratiocinations of intellectual elites, it was also affected by some of the tendencies of the
sixties that soon transformed the writing of American history.
My own preoccupation with the cultural and political significance of racism was clearly beginning to emerge, especially in
chapters 8, 10, and 12. Although the coverage of women's responses seems inadequate by contemporary standards, female intellectuals are not ignored or patronized; the fact that *The Inner
Civil War* deals with them at all was somewhat exceptional for the
time. But clearly there is no sense in which the work contributed
to "history from the bottom up." The book has survived, I would
think, because even the most zealous proponents of the New Social History would be hard put to deny that there is some value in
knowing about elites, if only because their thought and behavior
has important consequences for the lives of plain folk. If social
history is regarded as the history of social classes or status groups,
The Inner Civil War has implications for this field of study. It
focuses on what in sociological terminology might be described
as an upper-class intelligentsia and describes how it was transformed, partly as the result of its war experience, from a demoralized gentry without a clearly defined social role into a self-
confident modernizing elite. My insight into this process has
influenced the work of such subsequent historians and social scientists as Peter Dobkin Hall and Stephen Skowronek. (See Hall's
Organization of American Culture and Skowronek's *Building a New
American State,* both of which appeared in 1982).

As a book about the meaning of the war, *The Inner Civil War*
contributes to a sense of the conflict as a catalyst for American
modernization. In fact, the book's most enduring contribution
has been its use of the experience of intellectuals in the Civil War
as a window to view the "crisis of values" that attended the transformation of the United States from an individualistic society of

small producers to the organized, bureaucritized, and "corporate" America that was partially envisioned during the war and in place by 1900. More specifically, it argues the conflict helped to modernize the outlook of some who shaped the dominant thought and opinion of the post-war years. (Following Max Weber, whose ideas I had not fully absorbed at the time I wrote the book, I would now define the essence of modernizing thought as a commitment to bureaucratic rationality.) At times, the book may somewhat overemphasize the war experience itself as a cause of this transformation. What it really shows is a kind of elective affinity between certain modernizing attitudes encouraged by the social and economic developments of the mid-to-late nineteenth century and modes of thought directly inspired by the opportunities and necessities of the conflict. Certain older American ideas and values came to seem dysfunctional as the Union embarked on what Allan Nevins called "the organized war" (*The War for the Union,* 4 vols., 1959–71). Scientism, "realism," organizationalism, and a commitment to national or centralized authority (public or private) may have had some basis in the culture of the late ante-bellum period, but in 1860 the proponents of romantic individualism were still in the saddle. Long-term, apparently irresistable trends of industrialization and urbanization clearly favored the new world view, but it probably would not have triumphed so quickly and decisively had it not been for the catalyst of a total war for national consolidation.

Besides being about the impact of the Civil War, this book is also a study of American intellectuals. The question that arises, and that the text does not satisfactorily answer, is how to justify the selection of this particular group of intellectuals for treatment and the claim that their responses give us insights into the larger process of cultural transformation described above. Today, I find myself slightly embarrassed by the rather glib assertion in the original preface that "the few who have a genuine interest in ideas and a powerful urge to find meaning in their experience are able to tell us more about a crisis of values, with its inevitable confusion and ambivalence, than the many who avoid difficult issues and are content to speak in outdated cliches." What we would now call an elitist canon may have been at work here—a sense

that those whom the standard intellectual and literary histories of
the day regarded as important figures were indeed the people we
should pay the most attention to if we wanted to get the deepest
insights into the American mind. In practice, I included some
intellectuals (such as the Reverend Henry W. Bellows and
Josephine Shaw Lowell) who were not at the time I wrote considered significant contributors to American thought, for the simple
reason that I found them saying interesting and revealing things
about the meaning of the crisis, playing important roles in
organizing and motivating the Northern war effort, or applying
the lessons of the war to the problems of post-war America. But I
clearly had not reflected enough on who precisely was doing the
thinking I was analyzing and why they had the kind of importance I had accorded them.

My point of departure was Stanley Elkins's contention, in
a relatively uncontroversial chapter of his otherwise highly con-
troversial book *Slavery* (1959), that "the closest thing to an intellectual community in the [ante-bellum] United States" was
the group of transcendentalists who orbited around Emerson
in the vicinity of Concord, Massachusetts. I was also powerfully
influenced by Elkins's incisive categorization of their basic
viewpoint on the relation of the individual to society as "anti-
institutionalist" and his perception that they shared this radical
individualism with the Garrisonian abolitionists. My research,
however, uncovered a number of significant pre-war dissenters
from anti-institutionalism—a group of writers and professional
men who disparaged Emerson and the abolitionists and affirmed
their conservative commitments to established institutions and
collective authority. Several of them lived in Boston, and others
had strong ties to the Brahmin social and intellectual elite. I may
have followed Elkins a bit too closely in giving clear ascendency
to the anti-institutionalists as late as the 1850s, but the debate
between radical individualists and conservative collectivists evi-
dently had not been resolved in favor of the latter by the time of
the firing on Fort Sumter. It would take the war to make the
conservatives modernize their thinking and thus be in a position
to exert cultural authority during the Gilded Age. I was not
writing so much about the American mind or even the mind of

the North, however, as about a further episode in the history of the New England mind that Perry Miller had begun. In terms of local geography, it might almost appear that I was writing about a debate between Concord and Boston and showing how the Civil War contributed to Boston's triumph. My net was actually cast wider than Boston and its suburbs; it caught some Connecticut Yankees and quite a few representatives of "New York intellect." But the New England focus and flavor is evident; several of my New Yorkers had New England origins or connections.

I do not believe that this admission detracts greatly from the importance of the work. In line with Elkins's assertion about the transcendentalists, I would argue that the closest thing to an intellectual community in the United States during the Civil War era was precisely the group of old-stock New Englanders and their close associates, many of whom combined high social status with intellectual interests and accomplishments, who are in fact at the core of this study. They were not simply a "community of discourse" but also a community in a more literal social sense— almost, one is tempted to say, a social circle or set. To an astonishing degree, they knew each other face-to-face as well as on the printed page. Their interconnections are suggested by personal letters revealing, for example, that Henry Lee Higginson returned from military service to steal the object of Francis Parkman's affections or that the young William James looked on enviously as Charles Russell Lowell and Josephine Shaw Lowell paraded on horseback in Newport before Charles left to follow the example of his celebrated brother-in-law, Robert Gould Shaw, by dying heroically in battle. Of course not everyone in the study fits this upper-class New England/New York profile. Walt Whitman and John Wesley Powell, to take two prominent examples, came from very different backgrounds, and their thinking gives some sense of a larger America.

In sociological terms, however, I was principally writing about the most articulate segment of the old Northeastern upper class, an elite that had its economic basis in the mercantile wealth of the early republic. Highly educated (most had graduated from Harvard or Yale), predominantly Unitarian in religion, and sequentially Whig, Republican, and Mugwump in politics, they were, more than any other upper class that has existed in the United States, drawn to letters and intellectual activity. This unusual dedication to the life of the mind may stem in part from the extensive intermarriage in early nineteenth-century Boston of rising merchant families with other families known not for their worldly success but for their long lines of clergymen and Harvard graduates. This union of new wealth and old learning gave rise to the Brahmins of New England. The discourse of intellectuals who were born into—or assimilated by—this distinctive social group should not be reduced to an expression of particular class or status interests, but as this study shows, it was clearly conditioned by them.

This group is historically important for several reasons. First, and most obviously, it produced a lion's share of the most widely read and admired authors of the mid-Victorian period in the United States. Its imaginative writing and criticism gave rise to the "genteel tradition" that dominated American letters between the 1850s and 1890s. To a considerable extent, the Northern middle class as a whole looked to the Brahmin writers for its standards of taste and high culture. Second, this elite provided much of the leadership for the non-partisan or Mugwump reformism of the late nineteenth century. Its shift from anti-slavery (mostly of a moderate sort) to civil service reform and the struggle against urban machine politics signaled a conservative turn on the part of "the cultivated classes" of the Northeast, an affirmation of order and efficiency at the expense of the transcendent individualism and social humanitarianism that some of them had espoused during the sectional conflict.

It is insufficient, however, to write off "the best men" of the Gilded Age as nostalgic patricians who, after their flirtation with Emersonianism and abolitionism, simply harked back to the deferential society of the early republic. As the book suggests, and as Peter Dobkin Hall and Stephen Skowronek have argued more explicitly, they actually contributed much of the personnel and many of the ideas to the emerging cultural and political establishment that would lead the United States into the twentieth century. The institutional side of the intellectual developments described in the last chapters of *The Inner Civil War*—the growth of scientism, professionalism, and the ideal of "useful citizenship"—was the proliferation of non-profit corporations and voluntary associations from within which the educated elite could exert cultural authority. By 1900, modern universities, professional associations, hospitals, cultural institutions such as art museums and symphony orchestras, and a range of charitable or philanthropic organizations became loci of elite power and influence. Professional competence was the new basis of cultural authority, and the children of Civil War–era Brahmins (and others who were admitted on the basis of achievement and acculturation to their relatively open ranks) used their access to the best higher education that the nation offered to acquire the requisite qualifications. A few of their number, such as William James and the neo-abolitionist John Jay Chapman, regretted the new commitment to institutions and bureaucritization, but for the most part this allegedly "displaced" elite effectively modernized itself and embarked on a new career of cultural responsibility that would make people from their world enormously influential until at least the middle of the twentieth century.

The Inner Civil War argues in effect that the "collective trauma" of the struggle for the union reshaped the attitudes of this New England–based, educated elite and helped prepare it for a new modernizing role. The book, therefore, is not really so much about a few deep thinkers or unusually sensitive souls who understood what everyone else missed about the meaning of the war as about how the representatives of an educated elite took a great leap forward and landed on their feet. Those who sensed the tragedy or unfulfilled expectations of the war—truly great souls like Whitman, Melville, and William James—have their say, but they do not define the cultural future that is adumbrated in these pages.

As people who live in the shadows of the modern elitism (often called "meritocracy") that the Civil War intellectuals helped to legitimize, we may well question their legacy because of its hierarchical features and look back nostalgically on the seemingly more egalitarian world of small-producer democracy and antinomian radicalism that existed in the 1830s and 1840s. But we need to remember that African-American slavery was thriving at the time and in fact played a central role in creating that world, for its democracy was premised on racism, and its individualist radicalism was in part the protest of a New England elite against the unholy alliance of mass politics and black subjugation that sustained the national power of a rival Southern elite. Democracy without racism and reform without elitism may not be beyond the capacity of American culture, but from the Age of Jackson to the present, populist egalitarianism and the high-minded pursuit of justice for minorities have been in conflict more often than they have coincided. Hence the importance of Wendell Phillips in *The Inner Civil War*. He remains one of a handful of mainstream American reformers who synthesized the struggles against racial caste and economic privilege. In our own time, Martin Luther King, Jr., moved in the same direction before he was cut down. The fact that there have been so few others who have made this connection in a vital and creative way exposes some deep contradictions in our culture that American intellectuals need to think hard about. Today there are intellectuals on the left who argue that the pursuit of racial equity must be subordinated to the struggle against economic inequality among whites. Phillips, as presented in these pages, provides an example of how to combine multiculturalism—an idea that his image of a processional America of diverse races and cultures remarkably anticipated— with a commitment to the liberation of working people of whatever race from economic injustice. We desperately need an updated version of his broad and humane vision of America's possibilities.

PREFACE TO THE FIRST EDITION

HISTORIANS HAVE DEVOTED A FULL CENTURY TO STUDYING the Civil War. This massive scholarly effort has resulted in a thorough and detailed examination of the military and political aspects of the conflict. The social and economic side has received less attention, but has scarcely been neglected. But this interest in the clash of armies, the efforts of statesmen, or the triumph of one economic and social system over another—the public story of great happenings—has not been accompanied by a comparable concern with the thoughts and feelings of those who lived through the upheaval and reflected on its meaning, for themselves and for the nation. In our efforts to capture the meaning of the Civil War, we have paid too little attention to what it meant to thoughtful contemporaries in terms of their own ideological, philosophical, and aesthetic interests. This book is, first of all, an attempt to describe the "inner" Civil War of the Northern intellectual.

Inevitably, however, I was led to confront the larger question of how this experience affected the development of American thought. Although the war period has often been described as a "watershed" in intellectual and literary history, no real effort has been made to see exactly how, why, and to what extent the war itself acted as a catalyst for intellectual change. To offer some answers to this question, I have taken several prominent or representative Northern intellectuals and sought the correlation between their response to events and the transformation in thought and values which took place during the war. I have come to the conclusion that the collective trauma which polarized the nation's energies, thoughts, and emotions for four long years had consequences for the history of ideas which were comparable to its well-known political and economic effects.

I have limited myself to the Northern scene because most of the celebrated writers and thinkers of the period were Northerners, and because the North won the war and shaped the values of the postwar era. I have chosen to center on a relatively few individuals rather than constantly and systematically sampling a very wide range of Northern opinion because of some basic assumptions about intellectual history. I am convinced that the few who have a genuine interest in ideas and a powerful urge to find meaning and coherence in their experience are able to tell us more about a crisis of values, with its inevitable confusion and ambivalence, than the many who avoid difficult issues and are content to speak in outdated clichés.

I have also found that the best way to relate the life of the mind to historical change is to seek the relation of intellectual development to the flow of experience and the facing of particular challenges. Since an analysis of this kind required a fairly detailed record of thoughts and reactions, I have had to rely most heavily on the response of those who felt the need to commit themselves fully and frequently on the meaning of the war and its relation to their deepest concerns as intellectuals.

In the preparation of this book, I have of course contracted many debts. I wish to thank the staffs of Harvard's Houghton Library, the Massachusetts Historical Society, the Yale University Library, the New-York Historical Society, and the New York Public Library for their assistance in my research. My greatest obligation is to Professor Donald Fleming, who encouraged me to undertake the project and provided his invaluable advice and criticism at every step of the way. I also wish to convey my deepest thanks to John L. Thomas, who listened critically to my ideas as they were being developed, read the manuscript in its entirety, and made several important suggestions for improvement. William R. Taylor and Albert Gelpi also read the manuscript and gave me the benefit of their suggestions and evaluations. A final word of loving thanks goes to my wife, Hélène, whose constant help and encouragement speeded the work along and made the whole undertaking more enjoyable.

G.M.F.

Cambridge, Massachusetts
April 1965

THE INNER CIVIL WAR

PROLOGUE

". . . THE CIVIL WAR MARKS AN ERA IN THE HISTORY OF THE American mind," wrote Henry James in his life of Hawthorne. Writing, as he was, fourteen years after Appomattox, James could not fail to be aware that something had happened to "the national consciousness," that the "great convulsion" had "left a different tone from the tone it found." In describing this change, James had recourse, like so many later observers, to the Eden myth. The American, it seemed, had "eaten of the tree of knowledge"; he had gained from his war experience "a certain sense of proportion and relation, of the world being a more complicated place than it had hitherto seemed, the future more treacherous, success more difficult."[1]

If one takes this statement as a point of departure and seeks to define in more precise terms the impact of the war on American ideas and values, one finds that James was right enough about the importance of the war in intellectual history, but strangely wrong in viewing Nathaniel Hawthorne as a representative American responding to the crisis.

As James presents Hawthorne, he was a classic American innocent, at home only in "the broad morning sunshine" of a prosperous, optimistic, and uncritical society. Like other ante-bellum Americans, he had a "superstitious faith in the grandeur of the country, its duration, its immunity from the usual troubles of earthly empires." Then the war came, and Hawthorne could not face up to this unexpected holocaust. He was "horrified and depressed by it; it cut from beneath his feet the familiar ground which he had long felt so firm, substituting a heaving quaking medium in which his spirit found no rest." "Such," James con-

1

cludes, "was the bewildered sensation of that earlier and simpler generation of which I have spoken; their illusions were rudely dispelled. . . . This affair had no place in their scheme, and nothing was left for them but to hang their heads and close their eyes."[2]

No one can deny that Hawthorne was disturbed and depressed by the Civil War. Where James went astray was in suggesting that Hawthorne had a typical ante-bellum mentality and that consequently his response to the war was characteristic of "that earlier and simpler generation." The fact was that Hawthorne's reaction was unique; he was the only notable writer or thinker who took a detached and critical view of the Union cause. Elsewhere in the intellectual community, there was nothing but the most fervent devotion to the Northern effort; for as Merle Curti notes in *The Growth of American Thought:* "Almost all the leading men of light and learning exemplified ardent patriotism."[3] Hawthorne refused to go along with the rest precisely because he was not the archetypical prewar American that James would make him out. As a matter of fact, Hawthorne had always regarded the uncritical optimism of his contemporaries with ironic detachment. Everywhere in his works was an interest in original sin and a recognition of the dangers of excessive pride, which reflected a sense of human fallibility hopelessly at odds with the ante-bellum belief in the perfectibility of man.

When the war broke out, Hawthorne was greeted with a spectacle, not of confused and cringing innocence, but of militant, self-righteous innocence. It was the optimists, the believers in an ideal American destiny, who rallied to the standard, believing that the war would be a short cut to national perfection. They were joined, paradoxically enough, by *ideologues* of the opposite persuasion—the archconservatives who had no faith in popular government as advocated by the Declaration of Independence, but found to their liking the undemocratic discipline of war. Only Hawthorne remained the ironist, calling into question all the exalted hopes and pretensions. In July 1862, he published an article in the *Atlantic* which was so critical of Northern ideology that the editors found it necessary to answer it almost point by point in the form of footnotes, lest the patriotism of the reading public be undermined. In suggesting that the war might not have all the good results that were being promised, Hawthorne wrote: "No human effort, on a grand scale, has ever yet resulted according to the purpose of its projectors. The advantages are always incidental. Man's accidents are God's purposes. We miss the good we sought and do the good we little cared for." Incensed, the editors replied with a fine example of wartime self-righteousness: "The counsels of wise and good men are often coincident with the purposes of Providence; and the present war promises to illustrate our remark."[4]

Hawthorne's most devastating comment on what his contemporaries were doing and saying came in a letter to a British correspondent in which he showed his awareness of the cross-purposes and confusion which underlay the apparent unanimity of the "wise and good men" of the North. Recalling with some amusement that Napoleon III had announced a few years before that France was going to war for "an idea," Hawthorne went on to show that the Americans had now outdone the French; they had gone to war for several ideas. As a result, he wrote, "we seem to have little, or at least a very misty idea of what we are fighting for." Not only were the North and South seeking different objectives, but even within the North there was more than one version of what the conflict was all about. Of the many voices, "All are thoroughly in earnest, and all pray for the blessings of heaven to rest upon the enterprise. The appeals are so numerous, fervent, and yet so contradictory, that the Great Arbiter to whom they so piously and solemnly appeal must be sorely puzzled how to decide."[5]

Hawthorne died in 1864, too early perhaps to know which of the conflicting aims had come to dominate the Northern mind and certainly too soon to see how the plans of Northern "projectors" had gone awry or how "man's accidents" had become "God's purposes." It is possible now, with the perspective of a full century, to see fully what Hawthorne glimpsed, and to describe how the unanticipated twists and turns of history made the Civil War truly "an era in the history of the American mind." To do this, however, we must take leave of Hawthorne and examine the reactions and experiences of those prominent and representative intellectual figures who were not only carried along by the passions of the time, but saw in the war the relief of their frustrations and the fulfillment of their hopes.

PART I

Roles and Rehearsals: The 1850s

1

Prophets of Perfection

THERE WAS A STRANGE SENSE OF EXPECTANCY IN ANTE-BELLUM America, a feeling that the millennium, if not at hand, was fast approaching. This intuition was not limited to members of those chiliastic sects which proclaimed the imminent wrath of God; for there was a less specific but more pervasive millennialism which looked hopefully on the American future as the fulfillment of divine promise. This cosmic optimism had a secular as well as a religious basis. The ideals of the Declaration of Independence combined with the hopes of enthusiastic men of God to foster a bold vision of national perfection. Nothing stood in the way, many believed, but those inherited institutions which seemed devoted to the limitation and control of human aspirations, such as governments, authoritarian religious bodies, and what remained of traditional and patriarchal forms of social and economic life. And in America all institutions were at the mercy of public opinion. As one observer put it, "Institutions, as we are accustomed to call them, are but pasteboard, and intended to be, against the thought of the street."[1] If the people could be sufficiently aroused or uplifted, all or most of the traditional agencies of authority could be cast aside, to make way for *man himself* in

7

his natural perfection, free for the first time in history from the burden of privileged classes, oppressive governments, and outworn creeds.

A glance at the American scene in these years reveals that "the perfectibility of man" was more than a utopian cry. It was a basis of action on many fronts. When Carl Schurz, a young German radical, arrived in the United States in the early 1850s, he was awe-struck by manifestations of the American faith in an unruled populace. "Every glance into the political life of America," he wrote, "strengthens my convictions that the aim of a revolution can be nothing less than to make room for the will of the people —in other words, to break every authority which has its organization in the life of the state, and, as far as is possible, to overturn the barriers to individual liberty. . . . Here in America you can see every day how slightly a people needs to be governed. In fact, the thing that is not named in Europe without a shudder, anarchy, exists here in full bloom."[2]

The democratic "anarchy" seen by Schurz was the result of a ferment which began in the 1820s and 1830s, when the Jacksonians first declared war on "privilege" in all its forms. Riding a wave of democratic and egalitarian sentiment, the Jacksonians demanded a national repudiation of the old idea that certain "aristocratic" elements had a vested right to public office and official favors. The Bank of the United States, which was regarded as privilege incarnate, became the specific point of attack, and, when Jackson destroyed it, he opened the way for an economic system which relied on unrestrained individual initiative rather than on inherited wealth and charter rights. Many, however, wanted to go further. Those who were not content with popular elections and a free economy—for white males only—pointed out that women and Negro slaves were also members of the human race. The principle of equality, these reformers argued, compelled the abolition of slavery and the end of legal support for the traditional patriarchal family. The assault on privileged institutions did not spare even the church. Revivalists like Charles Grandison Finney shocked religious conservatives by emphasizing individual piety at the expense of ecclesiastical organization and authority. But Finney made others follow his example. In an evangelical age, the minister, like the politician, was forced to derive his power from an emotional rapport with his followers rather than from the dignity of his office.

What many ante-bellum Americans seemed to be striving for was a society of free individuals, operating without institutional restraint. To the modern mind, such a society seems almost inconceivable, a contradiction in terms; and Stanley Elkins, one of the most perceptive modern students of ante-bellum Northern social thought, has found it necessary to use the negative term "anti-institutionalism" to sum up the aspirations of the period.[3] But anti-institutionalism was more than a vague and utopian way of thinking. It was also an adaptation to what was actually happening in America. Traditional forms of social control were in fact breaking down, not so much from the trumpet blasts of reformers as from the natural conditions of a capitalistic society in the state of rapid economic and geographical expansion. The social class, the family, the church, and the state, for better or worse, were losing their hold over the individual, their ability to dictate opinions and conduct in the interest of an ideal of community. Revivalism and reform can be seen as a response to these conditions. If man was not to be governed, he must be taught to govern himself. God's grace or his own awakened conscience would have to take the place of external authority.

The weakening of hierarchies, the sweeping egalitarianism of the age, posed a particular problem for the intellectual community. As writers, clergymen, and philanthropists, the intellectuals were concerned with abstract ideals and values. But they were also concerned with something more mundane—their own role in society. Before the Jacksonian era, intellect had been closely identified with the "culture" of an upper class and had implied an active role in society and politics. Men like Jefferson, Hamilton, Madison, and the Adamses had been leading intellectual figures as well as men of the greatest social and political stature. The presidential campaign of 1828, however, had loosed a rabid anti-intellectualism upon the American political scene. John Quincy Adams' broad culture, his scientific and literary interests, had been turned against him; and his image as an effete intellectual had contributed to his crushing defeat by Andrew

Jackson, "the natural man" from the West. In driving class privilege from the seat of authority, the Jacksonians seemed to have driven out intellect as well.[4]

The egalitarianism of the times constituted a threat not only to the power and prestige of patrician intellectuals, but to any concept of an educated leadership—even Jefferson's proposal for an aristocracy of talent and virtue would have been badly received in this "age of the common man." The intellectual seemed to have a choice of evils: He could admit that he had no special claim to prominence and sink anonymously into the democratic ranks, or he could wage an apparently hopeless battle against the new forces, attempting to shore up the collapsing institutions that formerly provided positions of prestige and authority. The fact that most intellectuals subscribed in a general way to the democratic philosophy seemed to favor the first alternative. But in considering the role of the scholar in an egalitarian society, some thinkers were driven irresistibly to face a deeper issue—the ultimate question of the proper relation of the individual to any society. What in fact *is* the basis of social obligation, they were led to ask. Such radical questions suggested a way out of the dilemma. One could define social obligation in a manner that would allow the intellectual to repudiate not only traditional authoritarian institutions, but also those voluntaristic social and political organizations which denied him recognition. By denouncing the political party and the benevolent society along with the privileged class, the positive state, and the established church, he could call attention to himself as the ultimate embodiment of American individualism.

This new and radical posture for "The American Scholar" was first proposed by Ralph Waldo Emerson in his celebrated address of 1837. In his own career up to this time, Emerson had embraced precisely the role that democratic America seemed determined to impose upon its intellectuals. After resigning from the Unitarian ministry in 1832, he had retired to private life in Concord. In "The American Scholar," however, he revealed that his withdrawal was really a victory. For the scholar or "man thinking" nothing could be better than privacy and detachment; by turning inward upon himself, he would find "a more illustrious mon-

archy . . . than any kingdom in history." In terms of the intellectual climate, Emerson was arguing that anti-institutionalism
carried to its logical extreme was radical individualism. Private
life was a better springboard to self-realization than any public
career, because true individuality could be found only by turning
away from all forms, traditions, and institutions, even from the
new democratic organizations which were peculiar to American
life. "In silence, in steadiness, in severe abstraction," the scholar
was to hold himself aloof from the "ephemeral" political and
social controversies which agitated his fellow citizens. Justifying
this retreat from all worldly office and responsibility was Emerson's transcendentalist belief in intuition as the origin of truth—
a doctrine which offered the solitary man direct access to God or
"the Oversoul." "Self-culture" was more rewarding than the fulfillment of social responsibility, because "the main enterprise of
the world . . . is the upbuilding of a man." Emerson's scholar
could actually be that man; his eminence could come from the
fact that he was the ideal American, fulfilling in a unique way the
American promise of the free individual.[5]

This Emersonian style of intellectuality has been well defined
as "radical egoism."[6] But if the scholar was an egoist, he still had
one kind of responsibility. He was not permitted to keep his
wisdom for himself; he was obliged to preach the truth that he
had found, or, more accurately, to show others how to find the
truth for themselves. His function was "to cheer, to raise, and to
guide men by showing them facts amidst appearances."[7] His
influence, of course, would be completely spiritual, for he could
speak as the representative of no institution. Beyond contemplation and the utterance of general truths, the scholar also had a
need for physical activity: "Action is with the scholar subordinate,
but it is essential."[8] There is a characteristically American respect
for manliness and physical energy in Emerson's writings, even a
respect for practical men. The retiring scholar could admire his
opposite—the statesman, general, or entrepreneur. Basically, however, "action" for Emerson did not mean the taking of responsibility; rather than a means of accomplishing a worldly task, it
was another aspect of "self-culture," a way of reading the universal economy through the symbols of work.

Before the 1850s, Emerson followed his own dicta and, in general, held himself aloof from public controversy. He refused to become directly involved in any of the reform movements agitating American society. Although he shared the reformers' belief in the perfectibility of man, he preferred to look for perfection within the single individual rather than in society as a whole. This detachment was reinforced by what Stephen E. Whicher has described as Emerson's sense of "duality," his recognition that the divine intuitions could not generally be reconciled with the brute facts of experience.[9] As Emerson wrote of this "double consciousness" in "The Transcendentalist," a lecture of 1842, ". . . the two lives, of the understanding and of the soul . . . really show very little relation to each other . . . one prevails now, all buzz and din; and the other prevails then, all infinitude and paradise; and, with the progress of life, the two discover no greater disposition to reconcile themselves." Recognizing this dualism, one could hardly hope to transform the world overnight; for the moment at least, perfection could be found only in the inner life of the soul. Involvement in reform movements was actually dangerous because it could warp or domesticate the sublime intuition. Since "Each 'cause', as it is called, . . . becomes speedily a little shop . . . ," Emerson chose to live in the open air, free of all commitment and responsibility.[10]

Emerson may have had no program beyond "self-reliance," but his influence was far-reaching. Most directly inspired was the motley group of transcendentalists which thrived in the vicinity of Concord in the 1830s and 1840s. Among them was the orphic Bronson Alcott, whose inspired way of speaking was at times too celestial for Emerson himself, and Margaret Fuller, who viewed the emancipation of woman as more a matter of spiritual development than of passing or repealing legislation. Henry David Thoreau, whose secession from society and responsibility was far more dramatic and thoroughgoing than that of Emerson, was the most impressive of the group. His sojourn at Walden, a radical experiment in self-contained living, was meant to show the world the fatuity of all its cooperative enterprises.

There was, however, one wing of the transcendentalist movement which balked at the extreme individualism of Emerson and his immediate disciples. In the 1840s, a number of transcendentalists who were troubled by no sense of "duality" made the Emersonian view of man the basis of a demand for the immediate and radical reform of society. Emerson understood what these reformers were getting at. He approved of their "keener scrutiny of institutions and domestic life" and the examples they provided of the "withdrawal of tender consciences from the social organizations." He recognized in them his own "intuition that the human spirit is equal to all emergencies, alone." Yet he feared that their attack on particular evils and their tendency to band together would lead them astray from the primary task of individual self-renovation.[11] For men like George Ripley, William Henry Channing, and Theodore Parker, however, a man had no right to spend all his time in "self-culture" while surrounded by a threatening array of social problems. It was proper for the scholar to withdraw from corrupt institutions, but if he did so, he had a responsibility beyond the pursuit of his own eternal interests; he must make a real effort to set the human household in order.

By the late 1840s, the leading exponent of this view was Theodore Parker, Unitarian minister of the Twenty-Eighth Congregational Society of Boston. Parker had begun as a religious rather than a social radical. Stimulated by Emerson's Divinity School Address of 1838, Parker had gone on to frame a powerful theological defense of Emerson's view that religious faith is not a matter of external evidence, but comes solely from a direct intuition of God. Parker denied the divinity of Christ, the authority of Scripture, and the sanctity of the church as a corporate body and a set of rituals. The origin of faith was in "certain great primal intuitions of human nature, which depend on no logical process of demonstration, but are rather facts of consciousness given by the instinctive action of human nature itself"— namely (1) "the instinctive intuition of the divine," (2) "the instinctive intuition of the just and right, a consciousness that there is a moral law," and (3) "the instinctive intuition of the immortal."[12] The trouble with Emerson, according to Parker, was that he was so taken up with the first intuition that he had never really gone on to the second. As Parker noted in a critical essay of 1850, Emerson's strong sense of an immediate relation to God was regrettably accompanied by "a certain coldness in his ethics. He is a man running alone and would lead others to isolation, not society."[13]

It was the second great intuition, that of moral law, that led Parker into reform. His consciousness of "the just and right" made him feel a personal responsibility for the conduct of society, and he became active in prison reform, the temperance movement, feminism, and ultimately threw all his energies into the anti-slavery cause. Yet his attachment to a number of particular movements did not mean that he departed radically from the anti-institutional ideal, as set forth by Emerson and Thoreau, however much he deplored their love of isolation. Since all the institutions he confronted fell under the stern judgment of his moral sense—and he undoubtedly set standards to which no human institutions could possibly conform—Parker was not in fact working within institutions at all but was standing outside and calling for their radical reconstruction on *a priori* moral grounds.

Many followed Parker's path from Emersonian individualism to universal reform. By the 1850s, a number of young Unitarian ministers who had first learned the meaning of a religious life by reading or hearing Emerson had become avid followers of Parker—members of the coterie that Emerson called condescendingly "the 'fraternity' people." One of the most interesting of this group was Moncure Conway, the only Southerner of his generation to be swept along by the transcendentalist movement. Conway was not a man of genius like Emerson and Parker, but his commitment to the beliefs of his time was so profound and complete that his career is worth examining. His *Autobiography,* one of the great intellectual documents of this period, reveals much about the passions and enthusiasms of the generation of reform-minded transcendentalists that came on the scene in the 1840s and 1850s.

Conway came from a prominent Virginia slaveholding family and had been raised in an atmosphere of Methodist piety. What he called his "first conversion" took place in 1848 when he was sixteen. It was a typical camp meeting crisis, with the trip to the "mourners bench," the agony of conviction, and the public testimony of faith. Two or three years later, Conway began to read Emerson, who provoked his "second conversion." Southern Methodism laid so little emphasis on theology that Conway could read the essays of the first and second series without seeing anything that conflicted with his orthodox religious beliefs. He felt at the time that the Emersonian doctrines of "the personal character of spiritual life, the soul finding the divine in the solitude of individual life, the mission ordained for every human being" coincided perfectly with the Methodist doctrines of "miraculous conversion, the inward witness of the Spirit, progressive sanctification, and the divine 'call' to the ministry." This was more than the error of an untrained mind. Emersonianism and revivalism, with their common emphasis on the individual and his subjective experience, were manifestations of the same ethos. It was Emerson, Conway would claim, who made him decide to become a Methodist minister. As he recalled his sentiments at the time: "O that I could be even in a small way able to uplift fainting hearts and guide the groping as that great spirit has uplifted me . . ."[14]

By 1853, Conway had discovered that transcendentalism was not really compatible with Methodist Christianity, and he headed for the Harvard Divinity School to train for the Unitarian ministry. There he allied himself, under the general leadership of Parker, with ministers like James Freeman Clarke, David A. Wasson, John Weiss, and William Henry Furness. He became, in other words, a recruit to the "fraternity" men, caught up in their enthusiasm for social reform and millennial vision of the American future. One result of his new associations was that he began to look on slavery with new eyes. He had read *Uncle Tom's Cabin* when it first came out in 1852 and dismissed it as irrelevant to his own experience of slavery in Virginia. By 1855, his heightened sense of the possibilities of human perfection and happiness led him to recall "every ugly incident connected with negroes that I had seen since childhood" and to conclude "that Mrs. Stowe's book was a photographic representation of things going on in States farther south." The reformer's hope for the collective regeneration of humanity had no place for the slave auction.

In the years that followed, Conway became increasingly militant on the slavery issue. In 1856 he was dismissed from his pastorate in Washington, D.C., because he openly advocated the peaceful separation of the sections to free the North from the guilt of slavery. His repudiation of the social system of his native South led to an estrangement from family and friends. This was very painful to him—but what a consolation his transcendental vision of the future: "Alas, what a burden should be on me to become an antagonist of these beloved companions of my early youth! But ah, what sustained visions shone beyond the portal so painfully entered! There lay America freed from chains, slavery, strife; there mankind enlightened, woman emancipated, superstition no more sundering heart from heart, war ended, peace and brotherhood universal. O Morning and Night, serene on my portal, is not the time at hand when World-Soul shall harmonize with Oversoul?"[15]

For Conway and others like him, transcendentalism had ceased to be a license for the American scholar to withdraw to his study or take to the woods. It had become a mandate to preach millennial reform, both as a general principle and as the basis of an attack on particular evils. The intellectual had no right to the solitary enjoyment of his intuitions. He had to reshape society in conformity with his inward sense of human perfection. This interest in reform, however, did not mean a willingness to work for human betterment in practical, institutional ways. Overt political activity and pressure for legislation were rejected in favor of the moral reform of individuals through a direct appeal to conscience. In the final analysis then, the reform-minded transcendentalists differed from the Emerson who preached self-renovation only in their belief that it was possible to perfect the individual piecemeal, by getting him to cast off one sin at a time, and in their emphasis on human solidarity as a nobler ideal than "self-reliance."

II

It is not surprising that reform-minded transcendentalists like Parker and Conway ended as active supporters of the most radical

antislavery elements. From their respective beginnings in the
1830s, transcendentalism and the abolitionism of William Lloyd
Garrison had shared some fundamental beliefs about the individual and his relation to society. Both called on the individual
to free himself from corrupt institutions and demonstrate his
ideal integrity.[16] Beginning in 1831, issue after issue of Garrison's
Liberator made an unqualified appeal to conscience, demanding
that Americans ignore all political and institutional considerations
and immediately purge themselves of the great national sin of
slaveholding.

Garrison's relation to the abolitionist movement as a whole
resembled Emerson's position among the transcendentalists. He
was the leading spokesman of the cause, but his uncompromising
doctrines made it difficult for him to work with others in cooperative endeavors. His harsh invective, his refusal to consider
methods other than moral agitation, and his attempt to link the
antislavery movement to Christian perfectionist theories of universal reform brought dissension and division to the organized
abolitionist movement of the 1830s and 1840s. When Garrison
publicly burned the Constitution, called for the dissolution of the
Union to purify the North, or consigned to oblivion all American
institutions because they contributed to the maintenance of slavery,
he gave voice to the most extreme and insistent anti-institutionalism of the day. Although a professed Christian, he came to attack
all of the denominations because of their compromising stand on
slavery. Some of his followers even developed the habit of dis-
rupting religious services to make an appeal to all true Christians
to "come out" of the "proslavery" churches.[16] In tone and underlying philosophy, however, the Garrisonians differed from the
transcendentalists. Rather than a union of "the World-Soul" and
"the Oversoul," they anticipated a more Biblical millennium.
They resembled the radical sects of Christian history in pro-
claiming that a return to the pure doctrines of the Sermon on the
Mount would bring perfection on earth. As might be expected,
they were "nonresistants," who refused to countenance the use
of force in any form—which meant that they relied exclusively
on "moral suasion" as a method of reform. Without the episte-
mology of the transcendentalists, they had arrived at the same

result—a belief that the individual should not sully himself by using power or taking responsibility for the conduct of society.

By the 1850s, the leading spokesman for the radical abolitionists was Wendell Phillips, a Boston patrician who had been recruited by Garrison in 1836. Phillips, one of the great orators of the day, brought an uninhibited version of the antislavery message to lecture platforms throughout the North. No uncompromising pacifist or "nonresistant" like Garrison, Phillips regarded "moral suasion" as more a useful tactic than a divine commandment. This tactical sense was reflected in his concept of the role of the agitator in American society. Phillips understood that the basically conservative, slow-working nature of American democracy required agitation from outside the arena of political compromise to start the wheels turning in the direction of necessary reform. His address on "The Philosophy of the Abolition Movement" in 1853 demonstrated that he had not so much an *a priori* quarrel with all institutions as a sense that important American institutions like the church and the political party had a weak and dependent nature, a susceptibility to control by powerful property interests, which made them useless as direct avenues of radical reform. It was this understanding of the institutions of his time that led Phillips to the agitation of the masses as the best method of creating antislavery pressure in the community.[17]

There were risks involved in this program. Arousing an uninstitutionalized public opinion could lead to mass hysteria and a breakdown of law and order. Phillips was ready to take these risks because he had a sublime vision of what *might* be achieved, of the America that could result from the abolition of slavery and the achievement of equality. In an address of October 1859, he explained his own "idea of American nationality" by telling the story of a man in Milwaukee who had tried to have the body of his Asian wife cremated "according to the custom of her forefathers" and had been forced by a mob "to submit to American funeral rites." Pressure for cultural conformity, as much as Negro slavery, was incompatible with Phillips' "idea of American Civilization." His view of the America that ought to be was not the picture of Protestant, middle-class uniformity—New England "writ large"—that it was to many of his contemporaries, including abolitionists. He favored instead a vast diversity of "all races, all customs, all religions, all languages, all literature, and all ideas" protected by "noble, just, and equal laws" from denying each other's rights. To symbolize his vision, Phillips asked his audience to visualize Trajan's column in Rome, on which the emperor is represented as "leading all nations, all tongues, all customs, all races." America should also be a great procession, including "both sexes, all creeds, and all tongues" marching together in equality. Phillips would refer again the following year to the United States of his dream as "one glad, harmonious, triumphal procession," composed this time of "old and young, learned and ignorant, rich and poor, native and foreign, Pagan, Christian, and Jew, black and white."[18]

This processional image of a pluralistic society, blending, as it did, the promise of the Declaration of Independence with the Biblical millennium, was at the heart of Phillips' consciousness and explains why he devoted his life to championing the rights of minorities. To make the nation a microcosm of the world, free from all narrowness of country, caste, or class, in which men could follow many paths in freedom, was so broad and inclusive a task that freeing the Negro could only be a part of it, though an important part. Phillips was the most impressive example of the kind of reformer who stood outside of institutions, not because he had given up on all forms of human society, but because he cherished a social ideal which was, in its essential nature, an application of the best American values to the greatest American necessities.

III

If the anti-institutional impulse of the age was given philosophical, religious, and moral expression by the transcendentalists and abolitionists, it became the basis of a political creed in the thought of Jacksonian intellectuals like George Bancroft and the early Orestes Brownson. Although influenced by transcendentalism, Bancroft and Brownson rejected individualism and moral reform and turned to mass democracy as a means of sweeping away the vestiges of traditional authority because they believed that the common man in his natural, untutored state was a direct recipient of the divine message. It was their misfortune, however, to be saddled with the Democratic Party, an organization which was more a conglomerate of interests, seeking concrete advantages, than the pure expression of an ideological current. As it became clear in the 1840s that the party of Jackson was becoming a self-perpetuating conveyer of patronage and power, some of the Jacksonian idealists grew restive. By the 1850s, the party as such had lost the backing of many of its early ideological supporters, and the stage was set for Walt Whitman, a Jacksonian editor turned poet and prophet, to put forth a nonpolitical, noninstitutional theory of mass democracy and, more than that, to dream of combining democracy, transcendentalism, and humanitarianism —to make a generalized anti-institutional creed for America.

Whitman's quasi-mystical concept of democracy clearly emerged in the wake of his disillusionment with democracy as a purely political movement. As the editor of the *Brooklyn Eagle* in 1846, Whitman had been quite certain that "democracy" meant the Democratic Party. His editorials had acclaimed the national policy of expansionism and "manifest destiny" and vigorously supported the Jacksonian governor of New York, Silas Wright. The extent to which the young Whitman was a good party man and not a visionary democrat was seen in his endorsement of Wright's policy of using troops to put down the "antirent rebellion," a genuine popular uprising against the antiquated and oppressive system of patroonship in upstate New York. By 1856, however, Whitman was through with parties and rejoiced at the collapse of the Whigs and disorganization of the Democrats which had resulted from the slavery controversy and the growing sectionalism of politics. Although as a "free-soiler" he had some sympathy with the aims of the Republicans, he now denied on theoretical grounds that there was any value in an established system of political parties. All parties would inevitably go the way of the Democrats, who had betrayed their inner spirit by placing more reliance on the party as an institution or organization than on democracy as a spiritual force. The fact was that organized politics with its deals and compromises, its tendency toward centralized control, could never be an adequate expression of the free and tumultuous American spirit that Whitman was trying to capture in *Leaves of Grass*. In "The Eighteenth Presidency," an unpublished pamphlet of 1856, Whitman asked the question, "Are not political parties about played out?" and answered that "they are, all round. America has outgrown parties, henceforth it is too large and they too small."[19]

The parties had to be rejected, Whitman argued, because they had been taken over by a class of professional politicians, a swarm of self-seekers which had been spawned by the nation's "backyards, bed-houses, and bar-rooms." These men, who had become a ruling elite, the American equivalent of the Old World aristocracy, could not represent democratic aspirations because "their hearts have not been touched in the least by the flowing fire of the humanitarianism of the new world, its best glory yet, and a moral control stronger than all its governments." Whitman did not propose any practical alternatives to the political party for the expression of the general will; he had the anarchist's faith that formal government can be replaced by the spontaneous action of the people. He differed from the moral reformers in his radical democratic belief that the people did not need to be reformed. There was already enough of "the flowing fire of humanitarianism" to dispense for the most part with reform movements as well as with governing institutions. His "final aim," he wrote in his lecture notes of this period, was "to concentrate around me the leaders of all reforms—transcendentalists, spiritualists, free soilers —We want no *reforms,* no *institutions,* no *parties*—We want a living principle as nature has, under which nothing can go wrong."[20]

The vision of a nonpolitical democracy, a spontaneous mass movement—"a living principle"—expressed in "The Eighteenth Presidency" was appropriately the view of the poet who published "Song of the Open Road" in the same year—not only one of the great claims in literature for the autonomy of the soul, but also the major poetic expression of the anti-institutional impulse in American life. When he wrote that "from this hour I ordain myself loos'd of limits and imaginary lines" to take to "the open road," Whitman spoke for the desire of many Americans to free themselves of institutions, the past—all accumulated baggage—

and "light out for the territories" where self-fulfillment sup-
posedly awaited them.

In their different ways, Emerson, Parker, Conway, Garrison,
Phillips, and Whitman spoke for the dominant American belief
that the individual could find fulfillment outside of institutions.
As a corollary of this doctrine, they believed that the intellectual
or exceptional man of thought and feeling should assume no
narrow or specific role, no socially recognized vocation, but must
take it upon himself to be a representative man, embodying the
national ideals, whether as solitary individualist, millennial reformer, or poet of democracy. As prophets of perfection, these
men were fully capable of sounding the depths of American
idealism.

2

Conservatives in a Radical Age

THE ANTI-INSTITUTIONALISTS WERE, APPROPRIATELY ENOUGH, men who had no fixed place in the community and no institutional loyalties.[1] Most of them had in fact conspicuously seceded from organized society by repudiating an inherited or assumed social role. As we have seen, Emerson was an ex-minister, Conway an ex-Southern slaveholder, Whitman an ex-editor and politician, and Phillips an ex-Boston Brahmin. There were, however, important intellectual figures who had not seceded, either in fact or in spirit, from institutions. Men with an allegiance to well-established organizations or coherent social groups had a stake in the preservation of the traditional forms of social control. For some who had remained ministers, professors, or class-conscious patricians, the anti-institutional view represented the height of folly, and, what was more, a threat to the maintenance of a regulated community life. To avert social and moral "anarchy," they called for a *greater* stress on the value of institutions, and, in some instances, for the acknowledgment of an intellectual elite which would provide conservative leadership in thought and opinion by being in some way "established," like the clergy of the past. By asserting that man was a social animal, a fallible

23

creature in sore need of traditional guidance, they made no immediate impression on a generation of individualists, but they did suggest the possibility of a genuine dialogue on the meaning of America.

One way to open such a dialogue was to claim that America was not a promise of freedom but a specific set of inherited institutions. This was the argument of Francis Lieber, professor at South Carolina College (later at Columbia) and the outstanding American political theorist of the period. From the time he arrived from Germany as a political exile in 1827, Lieber defined himself as a champion of the American way of life. But for Lieber America was not a utopia in the making; it was a particular system of government which had received the blessing of history and experience. His classic work, *On Civil Liberty and Self-Government,* which first appeared in 1853, maintained that the great strength of the American system came from the fact that its "popular will" was not an expression of the numerical power of the masses or the majority, but a group consensus, shaped by a complex network of private and public institutions. Lieber defined this Anglo-American political principle as "institutional liberty," a doctrine vastly superior to the "democratic absolutism" or strict majoritarianism recommended by continental theorists. As an interpreter of American democracy, therefore, Lieber stood at the opposite pole from Walt Whitman. The American political and legal structure, with its common law, written constitution, semiautonomous state and local governments, and independent religious bodies, was to be praised precisely because it did not permit the simple and direct popular rule which had been advocated by some Jacksonian theorists. Despite its generally complacent tone, however, *On Civil Liberty* is not without its notes of Whiggish anxiety about the course of events in the United States. At one point, Lieber admitted to a fear that the principle of "democratic absolutism" was gaining influence in America, and he pointed to the dangers of universal suffrage, especially in the large cities. He also chided Americans for too much devotion to the theoretical as opposed to the practical and historical view of liberty. Reflected in all his thinking was his rejection of the natural rights philosophy of the eighteenth century—the doctrine that was still regarded by many as the American creed.[2]

Since Lieber was, after all, defending a liberal and republican system of government, his hymn of praise to inherited political institutions did not seem particularly reactionary. If this system, as it actually functioned, did not have the full respect of the more radical Northern thinkers, it at least commanded the loyalty of politicians and statesmen. It was otherwise, however, with defense of religious institutions and promulgation of the theory that the church should be, not just one of America's private bodies, but the very cornerstone of the social order. The disestablishment of the state churches and the subsequent rise of revivalism and religious liberalism—alike in their emphasis on the faith of the isolated individual—had made an anachronism of the traditional concept of the church as a quasi-governing institution, benevolently overseeing all aspects of human activity. This situation was a source of endless frustration to those conservative clergymen who looked back with nostalgia on an age of established religion, a time in the recent past when the minister had been the acknowledged intellectual and spiritual leader of the community.

One clergyman who took a particularly dim view of what was happening to the institutional basis of Christianity was Horace Bushnell, Congregationalist minister of Hartford and the most notable American theologian of his time. What was most disturbing to Bushnell was the prominence given by current American religious ideals to the isolated individual, as opposed to man as a member of the family, the church, and the social order. His great treatise on *Christian Nurture,* published in 1846, condemned revivalism for its reliance on the instantaneous conversion of wayward individuals, and argued that the only enduring basis for piety was the kind of education and environmental influence which would make a child grow naturally to Christian manhood. A strong, religious family life and a strengthened ecclesiastical structure, rather than occasional, violent revivals, were the foundation of religion. To those who accused him of advocating new and radical ideas, Bushnell pointed out that he was only trying "to revive, in a modern shape, the lost orthodoxy of the church."[3]

He might have added that he was also seeking to restore the authority of the clergy as the voice of order, tradition, and community.

Besides objecting openly to individualism in religion, Bushnell nourished a quiet distaste for the atomistic and libertarian political ideas which had come down from the revolutionary era. He would have argued for the strengthening of government in the political as well as familial and ecclesiastical spheres but was held back by the popular injunction against clerical discussion of politics. His foray into public controversy before the election of 1844 brought such a flood of criticism that he sulked in silence until the Civil War. Yet he did drop hints from time to time about his theory of the state. In an 1851 talk on "The Age of Homespun" in New England, he mentioned the modern "romantic visions" of the "reorganization of society," and to these he opposed his own ideal of "the Christian family state." Christian organicism was apparently Bushnell's answer to liberalism and reform.[4]

The clerical war against "romantic visions" was waged more openly by Henry W. Bellows, minister of the principal Unitarian church in New York City. Bellows, who was probably the single most influential Unitarian leader from the Civil War period until the 1880s, had little in common with radicals like Parker and Conway. Failing to respond to the transcendentalist impulse which had been given to Unitarianism by Emerson's "Divinity School Address" of 1838, Bellows emerged by the 1850s as the spokesman of the theologically conservative wing of the denomination. In July 1859, he gave his own Divinity School Address in Cambridge and presented a direct challenge to the transcendentalists. He argued that Protestantism had shown a regrettable tendency toward radical individualism. This development had reached an extreme in "the Emersonian and transcendental school" which was "Protestantism broken loose from general history, taken out of its place in the providential plan, and made the whole, instead of the part." What Protestantism required to get back into the mainstream of historical Christianity was an infusion of the Catholic emphasis on the church as an organization. Paying explicit homage to Orestes Brownson, the American Catholic publicist, and Cardinal Newman, Bellows argued for the "organic, instituted, ritualized . . . work of the Church" as the basis of Christianity.[5]

In the course of his assault on Emerson's idea of "churches of two, churches of one," Bellows struck briefly at the whole Emersonian anti-institutional philosophy. "Would that I could develop here," he said, "at a time so forgetful of the dependence of society on organization, *the doctrine of institutions,* the only instruments, except literature and the blood, by which the riches of ages, the experience and wisdom of humanity, are handed down . . . the only constant and adequate teachers of the masses. . . ."[6] This was a direct attack not only on Emerson but on reformers like Phillips who felt that the best "teachers of the masses" were men like themselves who stood outside of institutions.

Bellows seemed to many of his colleagues to be totally out of step with the age, and he admitted to a critic after the address that he had the feeling that he was "opening, in some respects, a new country" and that his views were perhaps "immature" and "crude" but that "the country is worth taking possession of. . . ." As it turned out, he was initiating a backward movement of Unitarianism from a radical disregard of forms toward a greater emphasis on organization and ritual. In the history of American Unitarianism, Bellows' Divinity School Address was almost as important as Emerson's.[7]

If Bellows' "doctrine of institutions" was "crude" and "immature," a suggestive insight rather than a fully developed theory, there was one Northern thinker of the 1840s and 1850s who carried this kind of "institutional" thinking to its furthest point of application and developed a thoroughly conservative and authoritarian view of society. This was Orestes Brownson, ex-Jacksonian and now one of the Catholic theorists whom Bellows had courageously invoked. During his stormy career, Brownson had gone from Presbyterianism to Universalism to Unitarianism, and finally in a dramatic reversal of what seemed to be an evolution toward extreme religious liberalism, he had passed over to Rome in 1844. Behind the changes in religious posture lay his political and social concerns. The most consistent motif of Brownson's career was his hatred of economic individualism and the new class of rich men it was raising up. At first, as a radical Jacksonian, he had pinned his faith on the popular majority to prevent capitalism from running wild. Profoundly disillusioned by the election of 1840, when the Whigs had seduced the majority by their log cabin and hard cider campaign, Brownson was converted to John C. Calhoun's view that the capitalistic Northern majority must be restrained by the agrarian South. Shortly thereafter, he found in the religious traditionalism of the Catholic Church a potential barrier to the materialism and greed of a liberal, entrepreneurial society.[8]

Brownson stated his fundamental views most strongly when dashing off polemics against the radicals and individualists. To give one example, *Brownson's Quarterly Review* for January 1851 featured a searching attack on the antislavery "higher law" doctrine which justified Northern disobedience to the Fugitive Slave Act of 1850. The idea of "higher law," Brownson wrote, "is wholly incompatible with the simplest conception of civil government. No civil government can exist, none is conceivable even, where every individual is free to disobey its orders when they do not happen to square with his private convictions of what is the law of God." This anarchistic philosophy, he argued, was the logical result of the "principle of private judgment, adopted by Protestants in religious matters." The safety of society lay in the reassertion of the traditional Christian doctrine that "government as civil authority is an ordinance of God," and "any course of action incompatible with the existence of government is necessarily forbidden by the law of God."[9]

The church-centered, organic view of society, with its stress on tradition and authority, was held by a small minority. It was clearly out of tune with the dominant trends of American thought. Even the clergy, with a few exceptions like Bellows and Bushnell, did not hold to such a doctrine; for such a backward-looking view was equally repugnant to pietistic evangelicals and liberal Unitarians. This ideal was especially unpalatable when linked in any way with Catholicism. Clericalism in America seemed to be a faith without hope. It would take an extraordinary set of circumstances to make it seem viable even for a moment.

II

If the clergyman was not in a position to call Americans back to a traditional sense of community, it was still possible to conceive of a secular priesthood, a conservative intellectual class based on learning and culture. Elitist visions of this kind came naturally in New England where for generations there had been a definable group which had attempted to combine intellectual achievement and social leadership. This was the aristocracy that Oliver Wendell Holmes called "the Brahmin caste of New England"—the descendants of historic families which had long cherished scholarship and erudition and at the same time provided leaders in law, politics, and commerce.

The Brahmin intellectuals of the 1850s, however, were in a poor position to be the defenders of conservativism. Not only had their social and political power recently declined as the result of new wealth and the demand for a more democratic style of leadership, but even on the level of abstract thought they had little to offer. They found it hard to take sides in the debate on institutions because their instinctive conservatism on pressing social issues was accompanied by a philosophical and religious liberalism—an inherited penchant for Enlightenment ideas which hindered their embracing social organicism as an alternative to American individualism. Despite the fact that they had no use for egalitarian reform, they went at least part of the way with Emerson and Parker in rejecting revealed Christianity and other dogmas which had buttressed a conservative social order. Some of the younger Brahmins of the 1850s actually became disciples of Emerson and the transcendentalists and were deflected from their normal course as responsible citizens. But their transcendentalism was of an extremely individualistic variety which did not lead them into reform; its major effect was to add to the difficulty of finding a gentleman's vocation in a democratic age.

One Brahmin transcendentalist was Charles Russell Lowell, the nephew of James Russell Lowell. As a Harvard undergraduate in the early 1850s, Lowell found himself unable to resist the mysteries of self-culture, and his valedictory oration of 1854 repeated the doctrine of Emerson's "American Scholar" that high thinking and idealism are more important than practical activity. Lowell, however, did not become a hermit after graduation. Although a believer in the priority of thought, he remembered that Emerson had defined the American scholar as a man of action as well as "man thinking." In letters of 1855 and 1856, he acknowledged that while "active life *alone* never made a man of anybody," he had always supposed that "action was necessary to complete my character." When he came to realize that he was not a literary genius or a seer, the types that Emerson called "divine men," he decided that he would have to be one of the "heroes of the world"—the other Emersonian type. He knew that "the 'divine men' " have "no need for work" but " 'Heroes' of the world have certainly needed work and had it and done it well, and it is Heroes that we must try to be."[10]

In his effort to live according to the somewhat self-contradictory ideals of Emerson, Lowell was confronting directly a form of the transcendentalist problem of "double consciousness" or duality. How was he both to develop an inner life and play an "heroic" role in the world? His problem was compounded by the fact that America seemed to deny its heroic roles to members of Lowell's social class. He tried working as a common workman in an iron mill, acting as a kind of missionary to the workers, while at the same time preparing himself for a role in industry; but his health failed before he went very far in this direction. Then like so many young gentlemen of the time, he traveled extensively in Europe to recover from his illness. While there, he thought of taking up farming but was afraid that for some transcendental reason, it was "not quite a 'life'." After his return from Europe in 1858, he went to Iowa as a railroad agent, but found that "The West may make a man strong, massy, rock-like— never large and generous and manly." By 1860, Lowell had still not found a vocation that combined self-culture with an active life. Part of his difficulty came from the lack of attractive positions for a young patrician in an egalitarian society, but equally important as a source of malaise was his Emersonian claim on the universe.[11]

The experience of Lowell's friend Henry Lee Higginson was

similar. Higginson was the son of a prosperous Boston merchant, but had no inclination for business himself. Like Lowell he was an Emersonian "radical," in a limited, philosophical sense, and he concluded that "Trade was not satisfying to the inner man for a life-occupation." He resolved instead to study music and spent four years in Europe learning harmony, but he could never take the extreme step, for a mid-nineteenth century American, of deciding on composition as a life's work. When he wrote to his father from Europe in 1859, Higginson admitted that "self-culture" was not enough. He was desperate for a profession. One of his friends, he noted, "sees nothing which a safe and honest man can begin with just now; he means of course a young man opening his course in life; but I must find something or I shall go into the Insane Asylum. I'd not live at home without employment for any possible reward. . . . Suggest something if you can."[12] Emerson's demand for a higher life had unfitted some young Brahmins for their "natural" social roles, but had opened no alternatives.

Other Brahmins avoided the pitfalls of Emersonian individualism and continued to see themselves as responsible members of an embattled patrician class. Men like Charles Eliot Norton, Oliver Wendell Holmes, Sr., and Francis Parkman devoted at least part of their energies to lashing out against the unwashed democracy that was stripping the old families of their political and social influence. Lacking orthodox religious faith, they recognized that it was neither possible nor desirable to rely on the clergy to restrain the masses, but hoped that Americans could yet learn to accept the leadership of a secular priesthood, composed of the well born and highly educated.

Charles Eliot Norton was the most forthright spokesman of this animus. Although he was the son of Andrews Norton, Unitarian "pope" of Massachusetts and main theological opponent of Emerson, young Norton had not followed a long line of ancestors into the ministry. After a brief attempt at a business career, he had turned to philanthropy and letters. In 1853, at the age of twenty-six, he published a little book which was the definitive statement of the elitism of "New England's Brahmin caste," looking back nostalgically to the days of Federalism. *Considerations on*

Some Recent Social Theories is an attack on the belief of European democrats like Kossuth, Mazzini, and Louis Blanc in the natural wisdom and virtue of the people. The fact that this work came in the wake of American enthusiasm for the revolution of 1848 and Kossuth's triumphant tour of the United States in 1851 and 1852 seems reason enough for its anonymous publication. The previous year, Francis Bowen, editor of the staid *North American Review,* had lost a pending appointment to a professorship at Harvard because he had expressed similar views.[13]

"The people," Norton boldly asserted, are not competent to work out their own destiny, for they "sit in the dark night of ignorance and know little of the light of love and faith." "It is not, then, to this people that we are to look for wisdom and intelligence . . . their progress must be stimulated by the few who have been blessed with the opportunities, and the rare genius fitting them to lead. Nor is their advance to depend on the discovery of any new remedies. There are now at work in the world, principles of virtue and strength enough for all the trials and exigencies of progress."[14] Norton believed, in other words, that the cultivated class must seize control of society and give it practical direction. This elitist doctrine, heretical as it seemed in the America of the 1850s, was firmly rooted in the New England tradition. Norton was seeking a return to the Federalist era, when "the intelligent and prosperous classes" had dominated New England society and molded its ideas. The problem posed by the 1850s for young men of Norton's background and prejudices was how to play the role of their ancestors in a time when patricians had been driven from power.

The leadership problem was particularly acute, Norton wrote, because the nation was in the grip of a debilitating prosperity which could destroy the national character. If the "intelligent and prosperous classes" did not exert moral leadership, America would be fatally corrupted by its "lavish abundance"; for plenty had always been the death of nations and civilizations. The widespread and undisciplined absorption in "the new fields of adventure, enterprise, and speculation" presented an overwhelming challenge to the ascetic ideals of a Puritan aristocracy.[15]

Some, who were more pessimistic than Norton, went so far as

to argue that the luxury and prosperity of the age had emasculated the patricians themselves and rendered them temporarily unfit for leadership. This was the view of Francis Parkman, the Brahmin historian, who believed that the American aristocracy had to redeem itself before it could redeem America. Parkman was perhaps the most determined patrician of the period—a man who defined the aristocratic virtues in the ancient sense of nobility won in tests of valor. It followed that as a young man in the Boston of the 1830s and 1840s he had been disgusted by the tender-minded and philanthropic Unitarianism of William Ellery Channing, the minister who had exerted such a great influence on Emerson and Parker. As he recalled in later life, he had detested Channing "for his meager proportions, sedentary habits, environment of close air and female parishioners, and his preachments of the superiority of mind over matter." He added that "it was a cardinal point with me that while the mind remains a habitant of earth, it cannot dispense with a sound material basis, and that to neglect and decry the corporeal part in the imagined interest of the spiritual is proof of a nature either emasculate or fanatical."[16]

When he went West to explore the Oregon Trail in 1846, Parkman sought not only to slake his thirst for the strenuous life, but to look for models of manliness among the Indians and frontiersmen to hold up as examples for the effete Bostonians he had left behind. The Indians disappointed him, for they were not the noble savages he had been led to expect from reading James Fenimore Cooper; but the character of his French-Canadian guide, Henry Chatillon, led him to announce that "the most highly educated classes among us are far from being the most efficient in thought or action. The vigorous life of the nation springs from the deep soil at the bottom of society."[17]

Such examples of plebeian vigor, however, did not turn Parkman into a democrat. He remained first and always a class-conscious patrician, filled with shame at the shortcomings of his peers. He came to believe that only struggle and hardship could strengthen the backbone of the American aristocracy. This view was shared by other Brahmins, notably Oliver Wendell Holmes, Sr. Holmes observed in 1857 that America's "chryso-aristocracy"

—its young men of wealth, culture, and family—was in sore need of an opportunity to develop physical courage. In other societies aristocrats were tested by military life. As a result, however, of the small American regard for the military profession and the "equal division of property" which "keeps the younger sons of rich people above the necessity of military service . . . the army loses an element of refinement, and the moneyed class forgets what it is to count heroism among its virtues." Holmes himself did "not believe in any aristocracy without pluck as its backbone."[18]

One of the forces which both Parkman and Holmes believed was undermining the manliness of the cultivated class was the humanitarian movement. Holmes was a constant critic of the abolitionists. Parkman went to great lengths to denounce the whole reform impulse. In *The Oregon Trail,* he wrote contemptuously that "soft-hearted philanthropists . . . may sigh for their peaceful millennium; for from minnows up to men, life is an incessant battle."[19] His experience in the wilderness and his sufferings from self-imposed hardship and chronic ill-health had confirmed his tough-minded view of life as a bitter struggle in which the most admirable qualities are endurance and martial valor. Of the soft-hearted philanthropists, it was the abolitionists who earned Parkman's particular disdain. As he wrote to Charles Eliot Norton in 1850, he deplored the "great row about the fugitive slave law" which the antislavery men were making in the North: "For my part, I would see every slave knocked on the head before I would see the Union go to pieces and would include in the sacrifice as many abolitionists as could be conveniently brought together."[20]

Parkman was not the only upper-class New Englander who had to go to the forest to prove his mettle in these years when the peaceful, reform-minded, and democratic society of the North provided little opportunity for the testing of "manhood." Theodore Winthrop, a young aristocrat from New Haven, directly descended from the colonial governors, also found his great moments in remote areas confronting savage nature. Winthrop revealed his philosophy of "adventure" in a lecture of 1856. "A man to be a complete man," he said, "must sometimes come into collision with the great facts of life."[21] For Winthrop, as for

Parkman, the only place for the aristocrat to be tested was outside society.

By retreating to the wilderness, Parkman and Winthrop, with all their social consciousness and belief in a class society with mutual duties and obligations, were actually putting themselves in the classic Emersonian posture of pursuing "self-culture," if only in a muscular way, and avoiding all responsibility for the conduct of society. The "strenuous life," as pursued in this period, was a conservative cul-de-sac, a last haven for the frustrated aristocrat. There seemed little immediate prospect that the patrician class as a whole would develop the rugged, masculine qualities required for leadership. There was no assurance that the democratic masses would acknowledge such leadership if available. What was obviously needed was a unifying national crisis in which the aristocrats would have to play a prominent role— some challenge which would call forth their best qualities, earning them self-respect and the confidence of society. Perhaps a crisis of this kind would also benefit the Christian conservatives by giving new urgency to their demands for an organic sense of community. In any case, however, there was no clear sense in the 1850s of how to accentuate the imperatives of national character and cohesion. There was indeed a crisis at this time—arising from the controversy over slavery in the territories—but it seemed a conflict which could only lead to further disunity and disintegration.

3

The Impending Crisis

THE PUBLIC EXCITEMENT OF THE MIDDLE AND LATE 1850S affected even the most cloistered intellectuals. As the nation faced the gravest crisis in its history, there was overwhelming pressure to interpret or modify social theories and styles of thought to make them relevant to the burgeoning national controversy.

The greatest challenge resulted from the growing willingness of Northerners to oppose slavery by force. The compromise of 1850, which had been designed to put an end to sectional strife, had actually opened a decade which saw angry controversy turning into violent skirmishes. Disorders in Boston and Syracuse over enforcement of the new Fugitive Slave Act were a prelude to guerrilla warfare in Kansas, which in turn set the stage for John Brown's incredible attempt to invade the South. As the battlelines were drawn, the sectional loyalties of Northern intellectuals were aroused. Some of the more radical became so deeply involved that they gave up their purely intellectual concerns to become exponents and exemplars of the new antislavery activism.

The foremost spokesman for the use of force in the righteous cause was Theodore Parker. Parker found it easy to be a rebel against authority because he was steeped in the traditions of the American Revolution. His grandfather had led the minutemen on

36

Lexington Green, and Parker never forgot this; he kept Captain Parker's musket hanging over his desk as a constant reminder. When efforts were made in the early 1850s to recapture fugitive slaves in Massachusetts under the new federal law, Parker came to the conclusion that the slave code had been brought to New England and that a revolutionary situation existed. Once again the time had come for citizen resistance to unjust laws. Parker became chairman of the Boston Vigilance Committee and directed the forcible attempts to rescue fugitive slaves from the authorities. His principal lieutenant was Thomas Wentworth Higginson, another Unitarian minister of transcendentalist background. It was Higginson, fresh from a meeting addressed by Parker, who led the antislavery mob which attempted to free Anthony Burns by assaulting the Boston Courthouse in 1854. As Henry Adams recalled of his youth in Boston of the 1850s: "One lived in the atmosphere of the Stamp Act, the Tea Tax, and the Boston Massacre."[1]

For Parker, the revolutionary creed of the Declaration of Independence had the dual sanction of tradition and conscience. The transcendentalist's intuitive sense of the moral law conveyed the same message that patriots of the eighteenth century had handed down to their descendants. Unlike Emerson, Parker had never spoken for a total disregard of the past. His great effort in political speculation, as in theology, was to take the great truths of intuition, and demonstrate by historical scholarship that these truths were also the lessons of human experience. It all came out so simple, so abstract, and so final. Slavery was wrong, and a form of tyranny: One had an historical justification, a natural right, and a moral duty to use any means to bring about its destruction.

Parker, however, was in middle age and failing health. There was little he could do except speak and arouse other men to action. It was his young disciple, Higginson, who became the first transcendentalist in arms when he went to Kansas in 1856 to fight for the free-state forces. Higginson's exuberance in the face of danger and death was extraordinary. For a clergyman of such natural energy and intense self-righteousness, nothing was more enjoyable than armed combat against the forces of evil.[2]

Higginson and Parker later emerged as leading figures in the

small group of Northern abolitionists who subsidized John
Brown's raid in 1859. Although these men had not known exactly
what Brown was up to, they had few misgivings about the bloody
results and insurrectionary implications. Parker heard the news
in Rome, where he had gone for his health and where he would
die the following year. He wrote to a friend that the slave had
"a natural right" and a "natural duty" to "kill" his oppressors,
and that the freeman has "a natural right" and a "natural duty" to
"aid them in killing all such as oppose their natural freedom."[3]
Here he took a more radical line than John Brown himself had
taken in his famous courtroom speech. Brown had pleaded innocent of the charge that he intended to cause bloodshed or start a
general insurrection and had claimed that he was attempting only
to gather a number of slaves and carry them to freedom. In his
defense of Brown as an out-and-out revolutionary, Parker proclaimed that "all the great charters of humanity have been written
in blood . . . it is plain, now, that our pilgrimage must lead
through a Red Sea, wherein many a Pharaoh will go under and
perish." Lest he appear too eager for violence, Parker hastened
to remind his correspondent that "you and I prefer the peaceful
method," but added that "I, at least, shall welcome the violent if
no other will accomplish the end. So will the great mass of
thoughtful and good men at the North; else why do we honor
the Heroes of the Revolution, and build them monuments all over
our blessed New England?"[4]

John Brown could look and act like an Old Testament prophet;
he could justify his action by the literal and unintelligent reading
of certain Biblical passages; but to Parker's mind he was still the
embodiment of the enlightened and progressive ideals of the
American Revolution. That the nation's foremost liberal clergyman could endorse the actions of a narrow-minded and possibly
insane religious fanatic suggested the degree to which intellectual
distinctions were being obliterated by a flood of emotion.

The crisis atmosphere of the 1850s created such a pressure for
commitment that not even Emerson could keep his eyes on a
personal lodestar. Emerson still refrained from joining any
abolitionist organizations or conspiracies and did not appear in
mob scenes, but he did on occasion come down from his Olympian

perch to take a place beside Parker as a spokesman for antislavery activism. His motives, however, differed from Parker's. Parker's anti-institutionalism, with all its radical reform overtones, had now boiled down to the uncompromising assault on a single institution—slavery. Emerson was less concerned with the destruction of slavery than with the ultimate value of the new methods of combating it. He realized that the widespread disobedience of the Fugitive Slave Act on the platform of "higher law" and the willingness to turn Kansas into a battleground of private armies implied a rejection of all authority that conflicted with the conscience of "the private man." The grounds for this new resistance to society as order and discipline might be narrower than Emerson would have liked, but rebellion against a proslavery government could be a first step in making radical individualism something more than just a literary fancy or a prerogative of isolated genius. Perhaps the time was approaching when every individual would realize that he had no further need of laws and governments. Following the lead of Thoreau, who had first made transcendentalism the basis for defying law in his doctrine of civil disobedience, Emerson passed from a theoretical anti-institutionalism to something approaching straight-out anarchism.

Emerson's new version of radical egoism came out most forcefully in his 1856 address to a Kansas relief meeting in Cambridge. After advocating direct aid from the Massachusetts state government to the embattled free-state settlers, Emerson went on to dismiss the argument that such aid would be illegal: "We stick at the technical difficulties. I think there never was a people so choked and stultified by forms. . . . I own I have little esteem for governments. I esteem them only good in the moment they are established. I set the private man first. He only who is able to stand alone is qualified to be a citizen." In reviewing the events in Kansas, Emerson welcomed the fact of anarchy as a confirmation of his belief that men could live without institutions. "I am glad," he said, "to see that the terror at disunion and anarchy is disappearing."[5]

John Brown's raid raised even more extravagant hopes for the triumph of transcendental anarchism. ". . . John Brown was an idealist. He believed in his ideas to that extent that he existed to put them all into action. . . ." said Emerson at a John Brown meeting, and he confided to his journal that courage like that of Brown "charms us, because it indicates that a man loves an idea better than all things in the world, that he is thinking neither of his bed, nor his dinner, nor his money, but will venture all to put in act the invisible thought of his mind." The example of Brown was just what the country needed: "what a contagion belongs to it. It finds its own with magic affinity all over the land. . . . Everything feels the new breath, excepting the dead old doting politicians, whom the trumpet of resurrection cannot waken."[6] Thoreau's sentiments were almost identical. For him, the greatness of Brown came from the fact that he was "a transcendentalist, above all, a man of ideas and principles," and a man who "did not value his bodily life in comparison with ideal things." Like Emerson he saw a revitalization of America. ". . . This man's acts and words," he wrote, are "the best news America has ever had." They have done more to quicken "the public pulse of the North" and pump "blood into her veins and heart than any number of years of what is called commercial and political prosperity could."[7]

Emersonian transcendentalism had thus changed from a contemplative philosophy into an activist creed. The "American Scholar" was no longer a withdrawn and harmless figure, reading the eternal truths of "Nature." He was John Brown, an idealist whose inner voice commanded him to shed blood. Emerson had always hoped that he would one day see "the transformation of genius into practical power," but had previously counseled "patience and patience" to those who would wait for this consummation.[8] If one could assume that John Brown was a "transcendentalist" filled with the truths of the spirit, who had dared to act in the visible world without compromising his vision, a strange kind of solution was provided for the transcendentalist dilemma of "duality" or "double consciousness." Action could be as sublime as thought. The "Oversoul" and the phenomenal sphere of human activity had apparently merged at Harpers Ferry.

The transcendentalists may have adjusted to the new situation with relative ease, but Bleeding Kansas and Harpers Ferry placed the Garrisonian abolitionists in a quandary. As pacifists, non-resistants, or believers in "moral suasion" as the best policy, they found it difficult to justify the use of force, even "defensively" against the aggressions of "the slave power." During the Kansas conflict, Garrison remained true to his principles by having no truck with those who were enlisting in the free-state forces or sending arms to help them. Yet a curious note crept into his 1856 criticisms of the Kansas effort. If someone had to be armed, he protested, it should be the slaves in the South rather than the Northern whites in the territories. If the resort to force had to be made, he seemed to be saying, it should be on such a scale as to bring down the whole slaveholding structure.[9]

Wendell Phillips compromised himself more directly by donating money to a Kansas rifle fund in 1855. He pointed out, however, that when it came to a struggle with rifles and Bowie knives, the slaveholders had an inherent advantage and would undoubtedly win; it was still better policy to take the high ground of moral suasion.[10] But the nonviolent ranks were thinning. Leading nonresistants like Gerrit Smith and Charles Stearns now reversed themselves completely and came out strongly for the armed defense of free Kansas, revealing that much antislavery pacifism had been the temporary result of opposition to the Mexican War as a proslavery adventure.[11] By 1858, Garrison was bemoaning the fact that abolitionists were "growing more and more warlike, and more disposed to repudiate the principles of peace, more and more disposed to talk about 'finding a joint in the neck of the tyrant,' and breaking that neck, 'cleaving tyrants down from the crown to the groin,' with the sword which is carnal, and so inflaming one another with the spirit of violence and for a bloody work." He feared that this thirst for violence would destroy "the moral power" of the abolitionists.[12]

The supreme test of Garrison's "peace" principles came the following year in the form of John Brown. Garrison's first reaction was to deplore the raid as a "misguided, wild, and apparently insane, though disinterested and well-intended effort." After the execution, however, he shifted his ground. At a meeting for the observance of Brown's martyrdom, Garrison endorsed

Brown in a way that seemed amazingly inconsistent: ". . . as a
peace man—an 'ultra' peace man—I am prepared to say: 'Success
to every slave insurrection at the South'. . . ." He went on to
affirm the spirit of "Bunker Hill, and Lexington, and Concord":
"Rather than see men wearing their chains in a cowardly and
servile spirit, I would, as an advocate of peace, rather see them
breaking the head of the tyrant with their chains."[13] This bold
statement constituted a repudiation of much that Garrison had
come to represent. It was an admission that moral suasion had
in fact failed to destroy slavery and that the methods of Parker,
Higginson, and John Brown were now generally condoned by the
abolitionists. Yet nonresistance was still the law of Christ. To
retain a shred of consistency, Garrison simply postponed the
millennium. Man was not capable of reaching "the sublime platform of non-resistance," in one easy step, as he had previously
supposed. He would have to go through a painful period of
preparation. The use of force by the oppressed as well as the
oppressor was actually "an indication of progress, and a positive
sign of moral growth." God, it seems, had decided that slavery
must come to a violent end. A slave rebellion was not something
Garrison was advocating, it was simply "God's method of dealing
retribution upon the head of the tyrant." The implication was that
even though John Brown had violated holy commandments, he
was nevertheless an instrument of divine judgment—like fire or
pestilence. No responsibility rested with the abolitionists; it was
the slaveholders themselves who had invited the wrath of God
by refusing to heed the moral appeals of thirty years of antislavery
agitation.[14]

Wendell Phillips also saw John Brown as an embodiment of
divine will. As he so graphically put it, Brown was "an imper-
sonation of God's order and God's law" and "a Lord High Admiral of the Almighty, with his commission to sink every pirate
he meets on God's ocean of the nineteenth century."[15] Yet Phillips
was not ready to admit that Brown's method was the necessary
or proper way to bring down slavery. "The age of bullets is over.
The age of ideas is come," he argued in his first speech on
Harpers Ferry; and at Brown's funeral, he tacked to the end of
his eulogy this strong reaffirmation of moral suasion: "I do not

believe that slavery will go down in blood. Ours is the age of thought. Hearts are stronger than swords."[16] Phillips would not give up his hope that slavery would fall from the weight of public opinion. John Brown was valuable to him, not as an antislavery tactician, but as a man whose eloquence and dignity in the face of execution had won public sympathy for the antislavery cause. "His words," Phillips proclaimed, ". . . are stronger even than his rifles"; they "have changed the thought of millions, and will yet crush slavery."[17] As a molder of public opinion, Phillips also rejoiced in the panic and consternation of Virginia when confronted with this single man of conscience. The Virginia reaction, he felt, had brought out most effectively the guilt-ridden anxiety of the slaveholders. What Phillips did not explain was exactly how an exacerbation of feelings on both sides of the Mason-Dixon line would lead to the peaceful demise of slavery. What he undoubtedly had in mind, however, was the old Garrisonian disunionist hypothesis. If a crisis could be reached which would cause the peaceful division of the Union, the South would be isolated. All support given to slavery by the federal government would be withdrawn and moral condemnation would be directed at the South from the rest of the world, eventually convincing even the die-hard slaveholders that they were in the wrong. In his own mind then, Phillips had not given up moral suasion by praising John Brown. Never having been a doctrinaire nonresistant, he could make an isolated outbreak of violence serve the essentially nonviolent cause of moral reform. Few noticed, however, that Phillips had not really come down on the side of force. Phillips made his greatest impression when he followed Garrison's path and showed how easy it was to justify Brown by the slogans of the American Revolution.

It was the circumstances of Brown's death, as dramatized by orators like Phillips and Emerson, which swept even the most peaceable of abolitionists along with the tide. To give one striking example: Moncure Conway, whose Southern background made him aware that the South's firm commitment to slavery could well lead to fratricidal war if the abolitionists took direct action, joined, after much agonizing, in the praise of Brown as a martyr.[18] One martyr was likely to beget others. Phillips to the contrary notwithstanding, it seemed more likely to be an "age of bullets" than an "age of ideas."

II

If strict logic had existed anywhere in this time of high feeling, the defenders of institutions would have come forward to denounce in no uncertain terms the civil disobedience and holy disorder that were being fomented by the radicals. What actually happened, however, was that the growing sectional controversy caused many conservatives to turn their wrath on the South and appear in the guise of reluctant supporters of the antislavery movement. The climate of opinion thus served to blur intellectual distinctions within the North and prevent one possible application of "the doctrine of institutions." This did not mean, however, that the conservatives entirely lost their sense of direction. The developing Northern consensus in which they shared came, not from humanitarian radicalism, but from fears of Southern expansion raised by the Kansas-Nebraska Act of 1854 and the Dred Scott decision of 1857. Men with a respect for the past and for the traditional balance of power within the Union were driven back to a defense of the Missouri Compromise, a "conservative" solution, which the "Slave Power" seemed to have overturned in a mad quest for national power. In the face of the apparent Southern threat, organic nationalism became sectional patriotism, and the "free-soil" doctrine served as a vehicle for conservative fears of Southern "barbarism" and a cloak for racist objections to the introduction of the Negro into Northern territories.

The path of Orestes Brownson was typical. As an uncompromising opponent of abolitionism and its anti-institutional social philosophy, Brownson more than anyone might have been expected to stand up against the spread of radical ideas in the North in the 1850s; for even on the subject of slavery itself he was ultraconservative. In 1851, he had asserted without hesitation that bondage was "the best practical condition of the negro race."[19] Yet for all his convictions, Brownson was steadily disarmed by events. In company with a vast number of moderate and conservative Northerners, he saw the Kansas-Nebraska Act as an attempt of the South to destroy the Missouri Compromise and upset the sectional balance. In January 1857, he announced to the readers of his review that although he had voted for Buchanan in the election of 1856, he opposed the Democratic administration's policy of making concessions to the South on the issue of slavery in the territories. He made it clear that his objection was not "on slavery or antislavery grounds," but solely out of concern for the "distribution of power." "The slave interest," he now believed, had become aggressive and was seeking political power beyond its real economic and social strength in the Union. It seemed that the South even more than the abolitionists was threatening the conservative ideal of government.[20] On immediate questions of policy, therefore, Brownson found himself heading in the same direction as the abolitionists, and his position as a critic of their "radical protestantism" was increasingly obscured.

Conservative clergymen also tended to shift their fire from Northern intellectual opponents to the agents of "the Slave Power." Since much of the Northern opposition to the expansion of slavery had a Christian basis, ministers could hardly ignore the religious enthusiasm to be tapped by agitating the territorial issue. The moral concern of community gave a new prominence to clergymen, and men like Henry Ward Beecher and George B. Cheever became famous for preaching against slavery. Conservatives like Horace Bushnell joined in the general chorus for reasons that had little to do with humanitarian revulsion from slaveholding.

Bushnell had actually spoken out on slavery long before the territorial crisis. In the 1830s, however, he had condemned slavery only on the narrow ground that it neglected the familial and religious life of the slave and had looked for reform from within the system. By the 1850s, he was taking a thoroughgoing anti-Southern stand and was supporting the most radical antislavery policies. He was careful to point out, however, that he was not, strictly speaking, an abolitionist. He believed that the Negroes were separately created as inferior beings and that immediate emancipation would lead to their competition with whites

and extinction as a race. It was not that he opposed such a "solution" to the race problem; he merely wished to postpone it. He
fully expected the Negro to disappear eventually as the result of
a swarming of Northern "free labor" into the South. Bushnell's
hostility to the South, therefore, was not rooted in a concern for
the slave. It was New England chauvinism which led him to
advocate forcible resistance to the Fugitive Slave Act and armed
conflict in the territories. For Bushnell, the capture of fugitives
in the North and the introduction of slavery in the territories
where New Englanders were going represented the direct assaults
of an alien Southern civilization on the New England way of life
and its destiny to spread over the entire continent. Although civil
disobedience was hardly compatible with his belief in order and
the sanctity of established institutions, his sense of a Southern
threat to the institutions and traditions of the North led him to
side, for all practical purposes, with the Parkers and the Higginsons.[21]

Some of the patrician intellectuals also became free-soilers for
nonhumanitarian reasons. Charles Eliot Norton was one example.
On a visit to the South in 1855, Norton commented on the demoralizing effects of slavery on the masters, although he clung
at this time to a conservative solution, feeling that the only hope
for the Negro was "the gradual and slow progress of the true
spirit of Christianity . . . a work of ages." He had no confidence "that any immediate, compulsory measures would improve
the condition of either master or slaves."[22] By 1857, the Kansas
troubles had aroused Norton's New England loyalties and made
him less charitable toward the South. Characteristically, however,
he did not follow Emerson in seeing the conflict as a healthy
example of anarchy. In the manner of Bushnell, he saw the apparent free-state triumph not as a victory for individualism but
for "organized emigration." The North would win out in the
territories because it could set up "centres of free population . . .
which will be kept together by having a church, a sawmill, and
a schoolhouse."[23] It was on such a platform of New England
"civilization" with its capacity for community life, as opposed to
Southern "barbarism" and lawlessness, that more conservative

New Englanders could support the antislavery side. This was the period when Frederick Law Olmsted was traveling in the South and sending back reports of social disorganization and chaos which would not have been tolerated in the North.

Just before the outbreak of the war, Norton adopted what amounted to an anti-Negro, antiegalitarian "free-soil" doctrine. Expansion of slavery must be resisted, he argued, because it constituted spreading the influence of an inferior race and enlarging the "transatlantic Africa" which the South had become. Wherever the Negro was brought, he would multiply faster than the whites and overwhelm them, bringing a return to barbarism. The South was already doomed; the question now was whether the rest of the country "shall be occupied a century hence by a civilized or by a barbarous race." The Negro must be confined at all cost within the South.[24]

Norton's ability to see the conservative uses of the most radical action was demonstrated in his response to John Brown's raid. Although he did not approve of Brown's methods, he found much to admire. "The magnanimity of the man," he wrote in a letter, "will do something to raise the tone of national character and feeling,—and to set in their just position the claims and pretensions of the mass of our political leaders. John Brown has set a standard by which to measure the principles of public men."[25] Norton sounded almost like Emerson and Thoreau in offering this example of self-sacrifice to a nation bedeviled by shabby politics and debilitating prosperity. It was not Brown the transcendentalist who appealed to Norton, however, but Brown the Puritan martyr. In an 1860 review of a book on Brown, he quoted the Scottish Covenanter who proclaimed before his execution that "suffering is a gift not given to everyone. . . ."[26] Norton had become convinced that the discipline of suffering was the only thing that would save America from its prosperity. John Brown had provided a powerful example of how to face suffering and death with Puritan dignity.

Francis Lieber, like Norton, joined the growing antislavery consensus of the 1850s and reacted favorably to John Brown's raid. Despite his twenty years in South Carolina and his well-

known belief in government by law, Lieber, now a professor at
Columbia University, was impressed by the fact that Brown
"died like a man," while "Virginia fretted like a woman."[27] He
also shared Norton's belief that the nation needed the discipline
of suffering. In the summer of 1860, he wrote in private like a
prophet of the apocalypse and came close to raining down curses
on the country that he had once praised so highly. "What we
Americans stand in need of," he wrote, "is a daily whipping like
a naughty boy. It were very wicked to pray to God for a chastising
calamity to befall our whole nation, as it fell on Prussia in 1806,
and led to regeneration; but as a historian I have a right to say
that when nations go on recklessly as we do—dancing, drinking,
laughing, defying right, morality and justice, money-making and
murdering—God in his mercy has sometimes condescended to
smite them, and to smite them hard, in order to bring them to
their senses, and make them recover themselves. . . ."[28] By
autumn, he was even more desperate: ". . . nothing can save
us but God and adversity," he wrote.[29]

III

The apocalyptic visions of Norton and Lieber reveal that even
the most cautious and conservative intellectuals were ready by
1860 to welcome a great national catastrophe. As the nation stood
on the verge of civil war there were a remarkable number of
"American Scholars" who desired just such a "chastising calamity." If the transcendentalists sought an outlet for a pent-up
"idealism," the conservatives wished to see the nation punished
for its sins against traditional values. Neither group was primarily
concerned with the possibility of war as a means of bringing
freedom to the Negro. The recklessness and extremism of the
intellectuals reached its culmination at the very moment when the
sectional crisis was coming to a head. Almost none were ready
to speak for compromise. Samuel Gridley Howe, the reformer and
philanthropist, spoke for the vast majority when he wrote in
January 1860: ". . . there is the prospect that with so many
sparks flying about in the powder magazine there may be a blow
up. Well—the Lord will save the pieces, and we'll have a North-

ern Union worth saving."[30] Thus with few backward glances the intelligentsia hurried the country along toward civil war.

The election of 1860 found almost all of the Northern intellectuals who have been discussed in the camp of the Republican Party—the first willfully sectional party in American history. Even the most otherworldly of all transcendentalists, Bronson Alcott, cast his first ballot in a presidential election, voting of course for Lincoln, like his friend Emerson. Younger men were able to quench their thirst for commitment by becoming active workers for the Republican cause—members of a party which for the moment seemed more than another political organization. George William Curtis gave an impassioned speech at the Republican convention for restoration of a plank endorsing the Declaration of Independence; William Dean Howells found his role by writing a campaign biography of Lincoln; and James Russell Lowell became a great exponent of the party and its principles in the pages of the *Atlantic Monthly*—to give three examples of young men of letters who found not only a cause but a place.

The philosophy of these young men, who were antislavery but not abolitionists of the most extreme stamp, was set forth by Lowell in the October *Atlantic:* "It is the tendency of all creeds, opinions, and political dogmas that have once defined themselves in institutions to become inoperative." The Republican Party for the moment was animated by the "vital and formative principle"; it would be the duty of the young intellectuals in the party to keep it from going the usual way of institutions; they must fight its tendency to "mere political argument, for the matter then becomes one of expediency," attention must remain focused on "the radical question of right and wrong."[31]

Only some of the most radical abolitionists, men like Phillips and Garrison, were lukewarm in their support of Republicanism during the campaign. Given their anti-institutional philosophy, they were justified in fearing the consignment of the sacred antislavery cause to a large and heterogeneous political party. It was up to the antislavery radicals within the Republican Party to deal if they could with the apparently impossible problem of fulfilling a transcendental impulse through a political organization. Here again, American idealism was facing the tragic duality which had plagued the transcendentalists. How could the pure idea become a practical force, when practicality meant politics, and politics was impure by definition?

If the abolitionists and humanitarians were worried about the effects of power or responsibility, the more conservative "free-soilers" welcomed it. They sought to discipline and control American society—through war if necessary. Although the intellectuals converged in their opposition to the South on the eve of the war, it was certain that once the war had begun they would fight not only against the South but among themselves for possession of the ideological meaning of the conflict and, more than this, to determine the meaning of America and the dominant style of American thought.

PART II

The War as Idea and Experience, 1860–1865

4

Secession, Rebellion, and Ideology

LINCOLN'S ELECTION GAVE THE SOUTHERN SECESSIONISTS THE opening for which they had been waiting, and by February 1, 1861, seven states of the lower South had voted to leave the Union. The fabric of American nationality seemed about to be rent. For the intellectuals, as for the rest of the North, secession posed basic ideological questions as well as problems of policy. What did secession mean, and what should be done about it? The policy alternatives at least were clear: peaceful separation into two nations or "coercion" to force the lower South back into the Union. For a time, the North was genuinely divided on what course of action to follow. The Republican newspapers, the journals most likely to be read with approval by the intellectuals, provided no sure guidance; they came out on opposite sides or vacillated hopelessly.[1] The North faced a real choice, and it was clear to everyone that the decision would determine the future of the country.

Underlying this obvious question was another query, which for some was the root of the matter. It concerned the effect of a breakup of the Union on the social cohesion of the North. There was a feeling that Southern secession, if not resisted, would set off a chain reaction of secessions and rebellions which would disrupt the social order in places like New York and Massachusetts. Emerson for one thought that it would, but professed no more fear of anarchy in this instance than when faced by Bleeding Kansas. In early April, he lectured on the national situation and described the division of the Union as an example of "the facility with which a great political fabric can be broken, the want of tension in all ties which had been supposed adamantine." Far from a cause of despair, this "new page in civil history" indicated "that the hour is struck, so long predicted by philosophy, when the civil machinery that has been the religion of the world decomposes to dust and smoke before the new adult individualism; and the private man feels that he is the State." The time had come to abandon "much of the machinery of government" and leave "to every man all his rights and powers, checked by no law but his love or fear of the rights and powers of his neighbor."[2] Here, as in the case of John Brown, history seemed to be moving in the direction "so long predicted by philosophy"—the philosophy of Emerson and the transcendentalists. Disunion was hailed as foreshadowing the triumph of radical individualism.

Initially, Henry W. Bellows also saw a breakdown of Northern institutional life as the probable result of Southern secession, but, unlike Emerson, he regarded this contingency with horror. When secession seemed imminent, in December 1860, he wrote to a friend that he was "not without serious apprehension that the loosening of the staple at Washington . . . might precipitate the whole chain of order into confusion and righteous chaos." On the same day, he wrote to his sister about "the possible insecurity of life and property, if secession and revolution should occur, driving our populace into panic for bread and violence toward capital and order. . . ."[3] The conservative defender of institutions was naturally enough frightened by the very circumstances that Emerson found salutary.

By February 1861, however, Bellows had regained his equilibrium. He now found that there were compensating factors in the situation. In a sermon on "The Evils of Serious Times," he argued that the crisis facing the country could result in strengthening civil ties rather than destroying them. ". . . when threatening and anxious times come upon us," he said, "then all great realities begin to shine out. Citizenship and nationality, . . . obedience to law and order, . . . oaths of office, and solemn compacts with man and God, that have been, perhaps, lightly and half-consciously taken . . ." all take on renewed meaning and become genuine obligations. "The loose and thoughtless tackle of things is quickly tightened up. . . ."[4] What encouraged Bellows most was the growing Northern desire to deal firmly with the South and assert the supremacy of the national government. A nationalistic response to secession might be just what was needed to dampen the spirit of individualism in all its aspects. He now anticipated "some very heavy drain on our property . . . some powerful necessity for learning that our private interests are subordinate to the public welfare" which would bring businessmen and others under the control of spiritual leaders like himself. It was even possible that the pressure of events would teach a sense of responsibility to the abolitionists and transcendentalists.

Relishing this chance to lecture the Garrisonians as well as the Southerners, Bellows blamed much of the nation's trouble on a lack of respect for "oaths, vows, promises, compacts" and "insulting, inflammatory, censorious and unscrupulous eloquence on platforms, [and] in pulpits." In conclusion, he registered his hope that the situation would lead to a new and deeper discussion of such matters as "the connection between politics and religion, the relative value of philanthropy and piety, the relations of the church and the world." For the moment, however, his native caution, his sense of the mixed feelings of his congregation, kept him from giving full vent to his own views on these questions.[5]

Bellows was but one of several Republican intellectuals who were early advocates of "coercion" even if it resulted in civil war. Another was Charles Eliot Norton, who was certain in December "that we shall come at length to the rifle and the sword as the arbitrators of the great quarrel," but had "no fear of the result."[6] George Templeton Strong, a New York lawyer and one of the great diarists of the period, gave some of the reasons why conservative men were not afraid of war. In late November, as South Carolina was preparing to secede, Strong wrote in his diary that universal suffrage was "at the root of our troubles," but took comfort in the belief that secession would bring demands for "a strong government." As a result, "democracy and equality and various other phantasms will be dispersed and dissipated and will disappear forever when two hostile families of states stand side by side, and a great civil war becomes inevitable."[7] Strong thus gave voice to what Bellows had only implied, to the hope that the crisis at hand would serve to discipline America and weaken the democratic and humanitarian impulses which had seemed so powerful before 1860.

Horace Binney, octogenarian jurist of Philadelphia and one of the few remaining ex-Federalists, held a similar view, but was less optimistic than Strong. In a letter of March 1, 1861, Binney announced that he expected from the secession crisis nothing less than "a universal demoralization, such as we witnessed in the French Revolution." There was still hope, however, if only the government would decide "firmly and calmly to deny and resist [secession]; to assert the obligation of the supreme law, and to enforce it, by every means at command which can reasonably promise success."[8]

The views of Bellows, Strong, and Binney suggest that those intellectual figures within the Republican camp who had least sympathy with the party's strain of humanitarian idealism had no doubts whatever about the policy to be followed. They favored coercion for reasons that contradicted clearly and directly the professed ideals of the antislavery radicals. They saw in secession a threat to conservative interests and to the stability and order of society and looked forward to a war which would re-establish the rights of authority.

The abolitionist response was somewhat more complicated. At first, the entire spectrum of antislavery leadership seemed to favor peaceful separation. Besides Garrison and Phillips, who had always favored disunion, men of less extreme views like Henry Ward Beecher, Samuel Gridley Howe, John Greenleaf Whittier, James Freeman Clarke, Gerrit Smith, Charles Sumner, and Joshua Giddings all came out at one time or another in favor of letting the South go in peace.[9]

The reasons for this unwillingness to use force to save the Union are not hard to find. As we have seen, many of the abolitionists had also been enthusiastic supporters of "the American peace crusade." Moderate peace men had limited themselves to objecting to offensive wars, but "nonresistants" like Garrison and Henry Clarke Wright had gone to the point of declaring the absolute inviolability of human life. John Brown's raid had revealed that these views could, in certain circumstances, be put aside; but Southern secession did not initially seem like such an occasion. Those advocating coercion seemed to have little concern with slavery, and abolitionists had no desire to sacrifice their peace principles on the altar of a mundane nationalism. Moncure Conway spoke for many when he asked, in a sermon of December 1860, "What are nationalities to the hearts of men and women?" and replied that "nationalities are stains upon the globe when they purchase their soulless corporation life with the human happiness they should foster." Describing the "groans and cries" that "conflicts of national selfishness" have "wrung from innocent hearts and homes," Conway took the extreme pacifist view that not "even the holy crusades nor the wars for freedom" are " 'good fights' much less the wars for an abstract nationality."[10] As a native Virginian, Conway knew that the South could be subjugated only by a long and desperate war. As a resident of Ohio, he suspected that the North, in fighting such a war, would have no higher motive than "national selfishness."

A second factor setting some leading abolitionists against the use of force to preserve the Union was the fact that "coercion" was inconsistent with their theory of "moral reform." Although their position had been compromised by the way they reacted to Bleeding Kansas and John Brown's raid, they still held to moral suasion in principle, except presumably in cases involving "self-defense" against "the slave power" or slave insurrections started by someone else.

Wendell Phillips made the most forceful statement of this view in his Boston Music Hall address of January 20, 1861. Feeling at the time was running high against the abolitionists—they were blamed by many for the national crisis—and the hall was surrounded by an unfriendly mob as the meeting opened. At the conclusion of his speech, Phillips described *his* idea of *"coercion."* It was "Northern pulpits cannonading the Southern conscience; Northern competition emptying its pockets; educated slaves awakening its fears; civilization and Christianity beckoning the South into their sisterhood." Soon, he indicated, the North would hear "the music of repentance," and South Carolina would "carve on her Palmetto, 'We hold this truth to be self-evident,—that all men are created equal'."[11] The key word was "repentance"; for abolition could only be successful if it changed the hearts of the slaveholders. Men like Phillips were not simply working to get rid of slavery; they sought the universal reign of Christian charity.

Phillips' statement also suggests a third factor contributing to the disunionist point of view—the fact that many of the abolitionists were fundamentalists of the Declaration of Independence, men who believed in an unqualified right to "government by consent." Despite the fact that the South on the whole justified its actions in terms of the legal right to secession rather than the supralegal "right of revolution," many abolitionists believed that the South could legitimately withdraw from the Union on the basis of the social contract theory which had sanctioned the American Revolution.

James Freeman Clarke, one of the best-known antislavery ministers, stated categorically in early 1861 that "according to the fundamental principles of our government, the secessionists are right in their main principle." Peaceful withdrawal from the Union was in accordance with "the principles of self-government, which are asserted in the Declaration of Independence" and several state constitutions, on the right of the people to alter or abolish the government to secure their own happiness.[12] Horace Greeley, the most celebrated antislavery defender of the South's right of revolution, maintained in December 1860 that the South was merely applying the "great principle" of the Declaration that "governments derive their *just* powers from the *consent of the governed:* and that whenever any form of government becomes distructive [*sic*] of these ends, it is the *right of the people to alter or abolish it. . . .*" If this doctrine "justified the secession from the British Empire of Three Millions of colonists in 1776," Greeley could "not see why it would not justify the secession of Five Millions of Southrons from the Federal Union in 1861."[13]

The belief that the South had the same right as the American colonies of 1776 was widespread in the North, and other Republican newspapers besides Greeley's *Tribune* adopted this line of reasoning at one time or another.[14] If a majority of the South really wanted to withdraw, "our philosophy of government" recognized their right, not under the Constitution, but under the Declaration of Independence, to live under a government of their own choosing. As *Harper's Monthly* complained in March, the Southern secessionists and the Northern abolitionists were two comparable groups of "doctrinaires" who "persist in treating us as if we were got up by some chemical formula, and could be made and unmade at pleasure, instead of being a living body, with living antecedents."[15] But the Northern version of the "chemical formula," the belief that all government was based on a contract which could be broken at any time by the popular will of a substantial geographical unit, was not limited to abolitionists. It was even conceded by Lincoln in his Inaugural Address, although his ability to refute the Southern legal argument allowed him to evade the issue of whether the "revolutionary right to dismember and overthrow [the government]" could be legitimately invoked by the South.[16]

Greeley, Clarke, and other defenders of the South's "right" to set up its own government put forth various procedural conditions that the South would have to fulfill before its secession would be acceptable. This was not simply an escape hatch. The talk of conventions, popular votes, and formal negotiations was in part an attempt to formalize the doctrines of the Declaration by establishing regular procedures for separation. What these men failed to understand was that a revolutionary situation can never be governed by formal rules and that government by its very nature cannot admit a legal "right of revolution." They were captives of the same naive hope as some of the transcendentalists—the faith that the great abstract ideals of human liberty could be completely embodied in practical instruments.

Although most of the leaders of the movement favored peaceful separation, there were abolitionists who opposed disunion in early 1861. The most prominent antislavery intellectual who advocated coercion was James Russell Lowell. In the February *Atlantic,* Lowell argued that the time had come to put nationality over philanthropy as a basis of action. "Slavery is no longer the issue of debate," he wrote, "and we must beware of being led off upon that side-issue. The matter at hand is the reëstablishment of order, the reaffirmation of national unity, and the settling once for all whether there can be such a thing as a government without the right to use its power in self-defense." Lowell, who only a few months before had claimed that forms and institutions deserved little respect because they could not embody for long any "vital and formative principle," had now decided that "this government, like all others, rests upon the everlasting foundations of just Authority," and that coercion could be justified by "an appeal to that authority which is of divine right, inasmuch as its office is to maintain that order which is the single attribute of the Infinite Reason that we can clearly apprehend and of which we have hourly example."[17]

It would appear that Lowell had been suddenly converted from the party of transcendental liberty to the party of transcendent order. In reality, however, his anti-institutionalism of the previous fall had been conventional and superficial. He had written in the spirit of the time, but it was a spirit with which his deeper consciousness had little real sympathy. Lowell's real resignation from "the party of hope" to join "the party of memory"—to use Emerson's labels for the reformers and the conservatives—had come ten years earlier when he had traveled in Europe and been awakened to the value of tradition and social organicism. After this time, Lowell's commitment to antislavery radicalism had been nominal.[18] If the excitement of the election of 1860 had temporarily revived his utopian idealism, secession had brought back his strong conservative instincts. Events were to show that Lowell was not the only antislavery militant of 1860 whose commitment to radicalism was skin deep, but certainly he was one of the first to see where his real concerns lay.

As "the great secession winter" wore on, others showed signs of wavering. Gerrit Smith, the famous upstate New York philanthropist and abolitionist, came out for coercion on February 6. On February 23, Greeley's *Tribune* began to call for action to punish the South for its assaults on government property and its insults to the American flag.[19] But to all appearances, most of the leading abolitionists stood by their principles and opposed the use of force right up to the firing on Fort Sumter and the beginning of the war.

Psychologically speaking, however, the antislavery disunionists were fully prepared by April 1861 to consent to an armed crusade against the South. For several years their professed pacifism had barely held sway over deeper impulses which needed only the right occasion to come to the surface. The praise for John Brown had revealed a growing impatience and frustration. After secession, it had become obvious that moral reform, instead of converting the nation to antislavery purity, had only confirmed the South in its proslavery views. Driven by a growing hatred of the recalcitrant slaveholders, which for some had become a more powerful motive than compassion for the slave, the abolitionists stood ready for Armageddon. Then came the bombardment of April 12 and Lincoln's call for troops. The desire to pass from agitation to force came at last into the open, and the abolitionists, almost to a man, rallied to the support of the war for the Union.

All that was required to make the transition easy was an invocation of Divine Providence, which relieved the abolitionists of all responsibility for the turn of events. The most dramatic claim of a providential release from principle came from Garrison. The former disunionist, in announcing his support of Lincoln's war policy, did not actually suggest that nonresistants take an active part in the fighting, but he did allow them, in all good conscience, to "stand still and see the salvation of God." Lincoln and his party, who had not impressed Garrison during the campaign of 1860, had suddenly become "instruments in the hands of God" to bring about emancipation. John Greenleaf Whittier, "the gentle Quaker," also accepted the war as "the chastisement which Divine Providence is inflicting on the nation" for the sin of slaveholding. Even Conway went along with the idea that this was a "holy war," willed by God to end slavery. Behind this hard decision taken against his instincts was the conviction that no other kind of war could possibly be justified.[20]

Characteristically, Wendell Phillips adapted even more easily to the situation than his doctrinaire colleagues and was less concerned with divine sanctions than with the chances that were offered to strike a blow against slavery. In his first speech after Fort Sumter, Phillips described the war as a repetition of the American Revolution. It was an uprising of the plain people of the North, "the cordwainers of Lynn, the farmers of Worcester, the dwellers of the prairie" against the "rebellious aristocracy" of the South. The Declaration of Independence, he thought, was "the war-cry of the North," and the result of this national rediscovery of its revolutionary heritage would be the final triumph of brotherhood and racial equality.[21]

The revolutionary ideology, however, was a double-edged sword. If the American Revolution could be invoked by Phillips when he called the Northern war effort a popular uprising against a Southern oligarchy, it could also be used to justify the South, since a majority of the Southerners seemed to favor resistance to Northern power. Was it really possible to put down a popular uprising and remain loyal to the doctrine of "government by consent"?

The fact that a few Southern orators invoked the right of revolution was not particularly disturbing. The South's sincerity in employing this portion of the Declaration, after having repudiated the section which contended that "all men are created equal," could well be questioned. What was galling to the Northern radicals was the general feeling in Great Britain that the rebellion was a legitimate fight for independence not unlike the American Revolution (a parallel which the English took delight in drawing). A strict adherence to the idea of government by consent seemed to dictate that the Southerners, like the Poles, the Hungarians, and the Italians, with whom liberal British opinion had sympathized, should be allowed to set up their own government. Before the Emancipation Proclamation, at any rate, there was considerable doubt in Britain as to whether the North had a right to fight a war for "union"—revolutions might not always be in the right, but efforts to put them down by force were almost invariably wrong.[22]

A few antislavery men who were particularly doctrinaire in their concept of government by consent actually came out against the war. One was George W. Bassett of Illinois, a veteran of twenty years in the abolitionist movement, who announced in a speech of August 1861: "The same principle that has always made me an uncompromising abolitionist, now makes me an uncompromising secessionist. It is the great natural and sacred right of self-government." Bassett had supported John Brown and would have welcomed a slave uprising in the South, but he disapproved of the motives of the North in using force against the Confederacy. "Passions, which for malignity and intenseness are not surpassed by ancient barbarism" were rife in the North, he complained. The North was not fighting for the Negro, but was "contending for the identical object of Lord North in his war on the American colonies." Its aim was "not the freedom of the black man, but the enthrallment of the white man," and, as if this were not enough, the government seemed determined to use the occasion to destroy popular liberty in the loyal states by the ruthless suppression of free speech. No one, Bassett argued, could deny the South its revolutionary right by questioning its motives; for the great right was based solely on the desire of a people to change their government, on "laws of nature and of nature's God; and not on the sandy and mutable foundation of human motives." Bassett was an old-line Jeffersonian radical. Through his eyes the cause of the North looked like the cause of centralized power against all the traditional ideals of American democracy.[23]

If one grants Bassett's interpretation of the Declaration and recalls that in 1861 the Lincoln government had given no sign of moving against slavery, his views can be seen as more than a weird aberration. They suggest that the Unionist position in the Civil War could be justified only by reinterpreting or revising the democratic creed.

Most of the abolitionists who supported the government swept into some corner of their minds the ideological problems raised by the use of force to put down a popular uprising. Those who thought at all about the consistency of their position were placed on the defensive. Obliged to repudiate the disunionist line they had taken before Sumter, they tried to reconcile suppression of the rebellion with the ideology of the Declaration of Independence. As the reasoning of Wendell Phillips suggests, they could do this only by denying that the South was legitimately exercising its natural right. In his speech at the beginning of the war, Phillips admitted that "the right of a state to secede, as a revolutionary right, is undeniable," and that "you cannot maintain a war in the United States of America against a constitutional or a revolutionary right," but went on to argue that the Confederacy had not gone through the proper procedures. The South, he contended, had returned by secession to a state of nature, and this meant that the Negro was entitled to his inalienable rights and had to be consulted on the choice of governments. If a referendum on secession showed that five million whites wanted to leave the Union and that four million Negroes were opposed then Phillips would accept the decision of the majority and "acknowledge the Declaration of Independence is complied with, that the PEOPLE south of Mason's and Dixon's line have remodelled their government to suit themselves; and our function is only to recognize it."[24] If this argument was meant to be taken seriously it put Phillips in a strange position; for if such rigid majoritarian standards had been applied to the American Revolution, the great touchstone of Phillips and his followers, that rebellion would not have qualified either. Not only had the slaves not been consulted in 1776 but no popular referendum of any kind had been taken on the question of independence.

What the abolitionists were really saying—and Garrison's war statements bear this out—was that there are two kinds of revolutions: good revolutions and bad revolutions. This kind of reasoning would have been defensible if clear and reasonable criteria had been established, but the distinction of the abolitionists rested finally on purely subjective grounds.[25]

Ideological confusion among the abolitionists was nothing new. They had previously attempted to yoke the revolutionary tradition of Lexington and Concord to a pietistic theory of moral reform that abjured the use of force. But now there was a new ambiguity. At the moment when the revolutionary theories of the Enlightenment had apparently triumphed for good, the situation had made their application unclear. As Bassett pointed out, the North of 1861 was obviously not engaged in a crusade for Negro freedom. The radicals could still support the war in the hope that it could be turned into a "revolution" against slavery, but it was also possible that they would be trapped into supporting a nationalistic policy which contradicted all their prewar ideas. Paradoxically, the opening of a war, which had been to a great extent caused by agitation over slavery, found the abolitionists as far as ever from positions of leadership and, in a way, more vulnerable than ever.

5

The Spirit of '61

THE SOUTH'S ATTACK ON FORT SUMTER, WROTE THE *New York Times* three days after the event, has made the North "a unit"; for "one intense, inspiring sentiment of patriotism has fused all other passions in its fiery heat." Two weeks later, another paper described the "wonderful transformation which has taken place in the public mind since the fall of Fort Sumter," and called the enthusiastic response to the President's call for volunteers "the most remarkable event of this and probably of any age."[1] As a group, the intellectuals participated fully in the public enthusiasm. Unlike more unreflective patriots, however, they sought to explain and justify their passion, and, as might be expected, the explanations and justifications were various and contradictory.

Emerson, who only a few days earlier had been willing to see the Union go to pieces in the hope that "adult individualism" could now replace formal institutions of government, rejoiced in the post-Sumter "whirlwind of patriotism" which was "magnetizing all discordant masses under its terrific unity." What impressed him most about the public reaction was its spontaneity. "It is an affair of instincts," he told his lecture audience; "we did not know we had them; we valued ourselves as cool calculators; we were very fine with our learning and culture, with our science that was of no country, and our religion of peace;—and now a sentiment mightier than logic, wide as light, strong as gravity, reaches into the college, the bank, the farm-house, and the church. It is the day of the populace; they are wiser than their teachers. . . . I will never again speak lightly of a crowd."[2] Emerson, who had always been an admirer of "noble passions" but had heretofore considered them the prerogative of isolated genius, had now lost his contempt for the masses and for crowds of all kinds and seemed willing to accept collective feeling as the equivalent of individual intuition. The war spirit was inspiring because there seemed to be nothing formal or institutional about it; it was "a sentiment mightier than logic" which was reaching into dead institutions and bringing forth live men.

If the opening of the war had apparently converted Emerson to the Whitmanic faith that divine human nature could be expressed by mass democracy, it had made Whitman himself more optimistic than ever about the capabilities of the people en masse. Up to this time, Whitman had never really found an answer to the question of what would hold together the unorganized populace, if one dispensed, as he desired, with all institutions; but the spirit of 1861 suggested that the ideological fervor of a people at war for the democratic idea could be the cohesive force; and Whitman celebrated this fervor in his early war poems.

From the beginning Whitman, like President Lincoln, regarded the slavery question as secondary. "The negro was not the chief thing," he recalled in later years; "the chief thing was to stick together."[3] Yet, even though he was not an abolitionist, his Unionism (again like Lincoln's) derived in no essential way from the rights-of-authority school. It was based squarely on the idea of an American mission—the belief that the advance of democracy in the world depended on the preservation of the American nation. Whitman and Lincoln were almost alone among the philosophers of Unionism in giving a strong democratic meaning to the conflict.[4]

One way in which the war would realize the promise of American democracy, according to Whitman, was by raising men's sights from material interests. Whitman, who before the war had described his disgust with American materialism, as reflected in "the shallowness and miserable selfism of these crowds of men, with all their minds so blank of high humanity and aspiration," had come to recognize that the great danger of democracy was the opening it gave for the wrong kind of individualism—the pursuit of personal advantage.[5] As a result, he was quick to hail the new patriotic spirit as an antidote to materialism.

Long, too long, O land,
Traveling roads all even and peaceful, you learn'd from joys and
    prosperity only;
But now, ah now, to learn from crisis of anguish—advancing, grappling
    with direst fate, and recoiling not;
And now to conceive and show to the world, what your children
    en-masse really are;
(For who except myself has yet conceived what your children en-masse
    really are?)[6]

In addition to being tested by adversity, Americans were also being saved from an excessive attachment to institutions. In "Beat! Beat! Drums!" Whitman rejoiced in the manner of Emerson at the way the war spirit would go "Into the solemn church and scatter the congregation" and "Into the school where the scholar was studying." It would not even leave "the bridegroom quiet with his bride." In another poem, he expressed genuine pleasure at the disruption of ordinary institutional life that preceded the creation of a mass army. Describing the "torrents of men" going to war as representing "DEMOCRACY" breaking forth with thunder and lightning, Whitman indicated that his hunger for "primal energies," for "Nature's dauntlessness" was finally satisfied. "I am glutted," he wrote;

I have witness'd the true lightning—I have witness'd my cities electric;
I have lived to behold man burst forth, and warlike America rise.[7]

Since Whitman's "DEMOCRACY" was an irrational, quasi-natural force, or a collective emotion, he could easily lead himself to think that all war patriotism was enthusiasm for liberty, equality, and fraternity. For him, as for Emerson, all large passions seemed to come from the cosmic spirit.

Other believers in a cosmic spirit, however, were not satisfied with patriotic or even ideological enthusiasm as the expression of the divine energy. They hoped that the spirit of 1861 could be deepened and transformed into an explicitly religious feeling, a burning millennial faith.

One such millennialist was Henry James, Sr., a Swedenborgian philosopher, who had often sounded like Emerson. In a lecture of 1849, James had proclaimed that "society affords no succor to the divine life in man,"—"there exists no tie either natural or social, as society is now constituted, which does not tend to slavery, which does not cheat man's soul of its fair proportions." But he had rejected Emersonian individualism as an end in itself. Existing society, he felt, should be replaced by a communal order based on love—what he called the reign of "divine-natural humanity."[8] In this aspiration, James was in complete agreement with "fraternity" transcendentalists like Parker and Conway. In the Fourth of July oration he gave in Newport in 1861, James described the war as a great step in the progress of mankind toward "divine-natural humanity." The American idea of liberty, for which he believed the North was fighting, was not simply liberty under a constitution, it was that transcendental liberty "which is identical with the God-made constitution of the human mind itself, and which consists in the inalienable rights of every man to believe according to the unbridled inspiration of his own heart, and to act according to the unperverted dictates of his own understanding."[9]

Unlike Whitman, and more emphatically than Emerson, however, James made his national fulfillment dependent upon a conscious repudiation of slavery. Without this change of heart, there was no value in patriotic or Unionist fervor. He spoke for the abolitionists in considering it essential that the war be turned into an antislavery crusade, that it be fought for universal and religious rather than national and political concerns. With such a righteous aim, American society would, in James' Swedenborgian terms, pass "from appearance to reality, from passing shadow to deathless substance." For it was "the hour of our endless rise into all beautiful human proportions, into all celestial vigor and beatitude, or [in the unlikely event that slavery was not abolished and as a result of the war] of our endless decline into all infernality and uncleanness."[10] The Jamesian vocabulary was unique, but his millennial expectation, his belief that an affectionate society of free individuals would somehow emerge out of the bloodshed and hatred of war, was characteristic of the thinking of many abolitionists in 1861.

There were others who thought, in the late spring and early summer of 1861, that the war, rather than encouraging anti-institutional or transcendental ideas, would have the opposite tendency. Charles Eliot Norton, for example, interpreted the unity of the North as being the product of no "contagion of a short-lived popular excitement," but a result of the people's "conservative love of order, government, and law."[11]

Norton apparently felt that these conservative instincts needed some encouragement, for he quickly turned to the writing of patriotic tracts. His first effort, *The Soldier of the Good Cause,* was directed at the man in the field. In it, Norton tried to impress on the new recruits the value of discipline. "Enthusiasm will not supply the place of discipline," he wrote, "and there is need of more than a good cause when it comes to the push." One thing that was needed was the professional military attitude—the conviction that "the first duty of a soldier is obedience." The volunteer should also understand that motives such as "enthusiasm for the flag, devotion to the Union, indignation against traitors, patriotic pride, an honest love of liberty, and hate of slavery . . . are of too external a character to form a safe and sufficient reliance in this great contest." Norton then described in a vague way "motives of deeper and more spiritual origin." Since the war was "a religious war . . . a man must carry with him the assurance that he is acting in the immediate presence and as the commissioned soldier of God."[12]

Norton did not explain further what he meant by the "religious" motive, but the fact that it could be separated from hatred of slavery showed that he was not speaking the language of the abolitionists. Whatever he meant, his use of Cromwellian rhetoric gave him the momentary sense that he was playing the role of his

Puritan clerical ancestors, that people were listening to him as the preacher of a stern faith. It is curious to see emancipated Unitarians, of rationalistic, almost positivistic beliefs, like Norton and the elder Oliver Wendell Holmes, writing in 1861 like seventeenth century Puritans. Holmes, whose urbane and amusing "One Horse Shay" had put forth the claim that Calvinism was dead, was now writing poems like the "Army Hymn," a fervent appeal to the Puritan God of battles.

It was left to Henry W. Bellows to work out with clarity and consistency the meaning of the "religious" impulse in the war. Preaching as the news of Fort Sumter was still coming in, Bellows told his congregation that he wished "to know nothing of that kind of religion which will not defend the sacred interests of society, with all the power, physical and moral, which God and nature have supplied."[13] A week later, he further developed his analysis of the close connection of religion and defense of the Union. Deploring "the unhappy alienation of church and state" in America, he argued that the state should be "the body of the church . . . as essentially and vitally connected with the prosperity and life of the church as the health of our bodies with the welfare of our spirits." He then went on to define "the state" in a way that put to good use his "doctrine of institutions" of 1859. It was nothing less than "the great common life of a nation, organized in laws, customs, institutions; its total social being incarnate in a political unit, having common organs and functions; a living body, with a head and a heart . . . with a common consciousness. . . . The state is indeed divine, as being the great incarnation of a nation's rights, privileges, honor and life. . . ."[14] Here was one of the ablest statements of the organic social theory to come out of nineteenth century America. Because he could argue that the war was being fought for the maintenance of order and in defense of an inherited way of life, Bellows had a strong position from which to attack all varieties of anti-institutionalism.

He even found the courage to hint at the supreme heresy—the idea that all recognized nationalities and established governments rest on the same solid religious basis as that of the United States. He spoke of nationalism as "sublimely . . . exhibiting itself" in Czarist Russia. He praised Napoleon III, although "a despot,"

as being "true to [France's] national instincts and aspirations. . . ."[15] Whether Bellows realized it or not, this kind of
reasoning could lead to a repudiation of the doctrines of the
Declaration of Independence.

Orestes Brownson in the July issue of his review echoed Bellows in giving a conservative meaning to the struggle. Incredibly
exuberant about the war for a man who a few years previously had
espoused the theories of Calhoun, Brownson called the conflict
"the thunderstorm that purifies the moral and political atmosphere." Like almost everyone else, he foresaw salvation of the
national character from materialism—its principal vice. A people
which had "seemed to be wholly engrossed in trade and speculation, selfish, and incapable of any disinterested, heroic or patriotic
effort" had responded magnificently to the call for self-sacrifice.
War thus seemed an excellent means of bridling the economic
individualism which had always been Brownson's major complaint about American life. In addition, the war might teach another lesson. "In asserting popular sovereignty, in appealing to
the people, and exaggerating both their wisdom and their virtue,"
Brownson complained, "we have overlooked the necessity and
authority of government. . . ." He implied, however, that the
war would reveal to all the limitations of the democratic philosophy and wean the American people from their absurd political
notions.[16]

With such varying views as those of James and Brownson being
enunciated in July 1861, it would appear that the first three
months of the war had brought no consensus on the meaning of
the conflict. The most diverse conclusions had been drawn as to
what was signified by the fact that the American people had
divided into two warring nations. There was agreement only on
the fact that the conflict would have a salutary effect on the country, and that pecuniary selfishness, for one thing, would be cured
by the stern purgative of battle. Beyond that, intellectuals looked
either for a closer approximation of the utopia which they saw
foreshadowed in the national creed, or for a society which would
reject the more "dangerous" aspects of that creed and return to
the "sound" principles of conservative government. Both parties
could not be satisfied.

II

For young men of military age, sharing in the patriotic outburst meant volunteering to fight, rather than speculating on the meaning of the new Unionist spirit. Personal commitments, however, could speak louder and more eloquently of the concerns of the upper-class intellectuals of the North than all the sermons, articles, and pamphlets. Many of the younger generation of New England Brahmins, for example, rallied to the colors with an enthusiasm which revealed not only a desire to regenerate the nation but also a hope for personal salvation. Like Charles Eliot Norton, these grandsons of the old Federalist elite had been seeking something worth doing, and the opportunity for a commission in the army seemed an answer to their prayers.

The Brahmin response to the call for volunteers was seen by Oliver Wendell Holmes, Sr., as the answer to his plea for a military experience to stiffen the backbone of America's "chryso-aristocracy." Noting happily that "the war fever" which had seized the North had infected "our poor 'Brahmins'," and brought many of them into the army, he suggested that the time had come at last for the testing of the American aristocrat.[17]

Some young patricians were especially eager to get into the fray. Scarcely a week after the firing on Fort Sumter, Charles Russell Lowell, aroused because the first contingent of Massachusetts volunteers had been attacked by a mob while passing through Baltimore, set off for Washington to join up. Since rail transportation to the capital was cut off, he had to travel on foot. The young Emersonian, who had spent so many years in search of a profession which would satisfy his ideal aspirations, had at last found a vocation. He wrote to his mother from Washington, after gaining a commission in the regular army, that ". . . the Army is to assume a new position among us—it will again become a profession."[18] Fighting in such a glorious war seemed the way to combine the highest idealism with practical activity. Lowell's friend Henry Lee Higginson was another who found going to war a release from the anxiety of being unable to enter any of the acceptable professions. Higginson was mustered in as a second lieutenant on May 11, 1861. As he observed later, "I always did long for some such war, and it came in the nick of time for me."[19]

Another well-born wanderer who found a home in one of the first regiments was Theodore Winthrop. This young novelist, who, like Parkman, had found his only prewar fulfillment in the thrill of remote travels and explorations, thought he had now discovered a more fruitful way to spend his time. After enlisting in the first regiment raised in New York, he wrote to a friend that he had undertaken a life's task. Since he believed that the South would have to be occupied after the war, that the North "must hold the South as the Metropolitan police holds New York," he wished to enroll himself "in the *Police of the Nation.* And for life, if the Nation will take me. I do not see that I can put myself,—experience and character—to any more useful use."[20] Winthrop's lifetime service was tragically short. He was killed in June—one of the first "martyrs" of the war.

III

The death of Theodore Winthrop and a few others may have given the North some preview of what was to come; but it was the unexpected defeat of the Union forces at the First Battle of Bull Run on July 21 which gave both soldiers and civilians their first real sense of what the war would be like. Strangely enough, this disaster was greeted by some of the intellectuals with even greater joy than they had shown after Sumter. Moncure Conway reported after a visit to Concord that Thoreau was "in a state of exultation about the moral regeneration of the nation." Wendell Phillips, according to the recollections of one observer, described the defeat as exactly what was needed and the best thing that could have happened to the North. Henry W. Bellows agreed; he wrote to the *Christian Inquirer* on the "moral necessity of the late defeat," claiming that "nothing but the disaster could thoroughly arouse the country to the efforts, the reforms, and the spirit essential to the proper and vigorous conduct of this war." For Thomas Wentworth Higginson, the defeat was valuable for a more specific reason; it forced Congress to pass a stern confiscation law which, on paper at least, freed those slaves directly employed in the rebellion. In this action, Higginson saw the first signs of "a war of emancipation." Since all these men hoped for a long war which would give free rein to the favorable impulses they observed, Bull Run was welcome proof that peace would not come too soon.[21] A review of the fuller comments on the new picture of the war suggests, however, that the greatest encouragement was given to those who sought a reversal of the democratic and humanitarian tendencies of American thought.

Charles Eliot Norton, to take one exuberant conservative, waxed lyrical over "the advantages of defeat" in the September *Atlantic*. Norton, who had long feared that prosperity would lead to national decadence, could now exult in the fact that "we are not to expect or hope for a speedy return of what is called prosperity." How fortunate it was that "we, who have so long been eager in the pursuit and accumulation of riches, are now to show more generous energies in the free spending of our means to gain the valuable object for which we have gone to war." But Norton hoped for more than just the expenditure of wealth by a people grown too fond of luxury. Striking at the humanitarian reformers, especially the nonresistants who had believed in the inviolability of human life, Norton argued boldly that human life had been overvalued in America: "We have thought it braver to save it than to spend it; and a questionable humanity has undoubtedly led us sometimes into feeble sentimentalities, and false estimates of its value." Now, however, "the first sacrifice for which war calls is life; and we must revise our estimates of its value, if we would conduct our war to a happy end." There should be no flinching at "the prospect of the death of our soldiers," not even at the prospect "that a million men should die on the battlefield."[22]

In his assault on the "feeble sentimentalities" of an age which had devoted itself to alleviating suffering rather than justifying it, Norton not only spoke to the necessities of the hour, but marshaled a powerful new argument which was destined to become a formidable weapon against philanthropy and reform. Norton had been much impressed with Darwin's *Origin of Species* when it appeared in 1859, and he now presented his tough-minded view of war as a new and profound application of

Darwin's theories. "Nature is careless of the single life," he wrote. "Her processes seem wasteful, but out of seeming waste, she produces her great and durable results. Everywhere in her works are the signs of life cut short for the sake of some effect more permanent. . . ."[23] In what may have been the first use of Darwinism to justify war, Norton argued from the premise that human progress, like that of the animal kingdom, was built on pain and loss of life. Invoking such a concept of evolution was one way to give meaning to the suffering of the Civil War.

Francis Parkman, in a long letter to the *Boston Advertiser* which appeared about the same time as Norton's article, also described the post-Bull Run situation as favorable to national progress. Parkman, however, had a clearer idea of what form the regeneration of America would take. "Our position," he wrote, "is a solemn, a critical, but not a melancholy one." If American society had heretofore been "cramped and vitiated" by a "too exclusive pursuit of material success," there were signs of a change. If, "in the absence of an exigency to urge or any great reward to tempt it, the best character and culture of the nation has remained for the most part in privacy, while a scum of reckless politicians has choked all the avenues of power," it was evident already that, "like a keen fresh breeze, the war has stirred our clogged and humid atmosphere." "The time may come," he concluded, "when, upheaved from its depths, fermenting and purging itself, the nation will stand at length clarified and pure in a renewed and strengthened life."[24] Parkman, the most pessimistic of the deprived aristocrats of the ante-bellum period, was thus awakening to the prospect that "the best character and culture" had a new chance to regain national leadership. In a desperate situation, the nation might scorn the "scum of reckless politicians" and turn to its "natural leaders"—the heirs of the old Federalist elite. Parkman's optimism was undoubtedly buttressed by the fact that Lowells and Higginsons had found in the army the positions of prestige and authority that peacetime society had denied them.

Horace Bushnell, in a sermon delivered on the Sunday after the Bull Run disaster, went even further than Parkman in heralding the return to an earlier social ideal. Bushnell, who up to now had lacked an occasion to express his profound hatred of the enlightenment basis of American politics, seized on Bull Run as evidence that the nation was being punished for the heinous sin of disregarding God's own idea of human government. For Bushnell, the origin of the national troubles lay in the faulty philosophy of the Declaration of Independence. The American government, he asserted, had been founded "without moral and religious ideas; in one view merely a man-made compact. . . ." The dangerous, atheistic doctrines of natural rights and government by consent had been a poison in the national life: ". . . we have been gradually wearing our nature down to the level of our doctrines; breeding out, so to speak, the sentiments in it that took hold of authority, till at last, we have brought ourselves down as closely as may be, to the dissolution of all nationality and all ties of order. Hence the war."[25]

Bushnell could not completely repudiate the American Revolution, so he alleged that there was also present in the beginning of the nation an "historic element," opposed to the visionary speculations of men like Jefferson and based on those inherited political ideas of New England which had been "shaped by religion." The New England way, which specified that government, rather than being based on consent of the governed, was an ordinance of God, had been overwhelmed by the democratic impulse set in motion by the Jeffersonian heresies. To Bushnell's Old Testament way of thinking, the secular eighteenth century ideology had thereafter functioned as an American golden calf which had smiled down on the most licentious behavior. Now, however, the wrath of God could be seen in a disaster like Bull Run, punishing the people for their idolatry and sinfulness and recalling them to proper respect for traditional authority. "Peace will do for angels," he proclaimed fiercely, "but war is God's ordinance for sinners, and they want the schooling of it often. In a time of war, what a sense of discipline is forced. Here, at least, there must and will be obedience; and the people, outside, get the sense of it about as truly as the army itself. . . ."[26]

Sermons like those of Bushnell signified a revival of the spirit of New England Federalism, with its abhorrence of the religious and political views of Jefferson and its passion for order and popular "obedience" to ministers and others in authority. It was at this time that the *Anarchiad,* an almost forgotten collection of virulent attacks on democratic ideas by Federalist poets of the eighteenth century, was republished, to the great joy of the conservative *North American Review.* "The publication is well timed," announced the journal, "at an epoch when we are again threatened with disintegration and anarchy."[27]

By December 1861, Wendell Phillips thought he observed some signs of this recrudescent Federalism in the policy of the government, particularly in its suspension of the writ of habeas corpus. Phillips himself had fully repudiated his Federalist ancestors. In his "Disunion" lecture of the previous January, he had noted with pleasure that Federalism seemed safely dead. "Our theological aristocracy," he claimed, "went down before the stalwart blows of Baptist, Unitarian and Freethinker," and "theoretical democracy" had "conquered the Federal Government, and emancipated the working-classes of New England. Bitter was the cup to honest Federalism and the Essex Junto." Phillips even saw the abolition movement as the culmination of the "Democratic principle," which, "crumbling classes into men," had "reached the negro at last."[28] But now, eleven months later, he was afraid that the "democratic principle" was, for the moment at least, in some danger.

He pointed to the fact that the government was following a dangerous course in regard to civil liberties, that each of the three essential rights—"*habeas corpus,* the right of free meeting, and a free press—is annihilated in every square mile of the Republic." He concluded that "we are tending toward that strong government which frightened Jefferson; toward that unlimited debt, that endless army. We have already those alien and sedition laws which, in 1798, wrecked the Federal Party, and summoned the Democratic into existence."[29] Phillips did not realize it, but even as he spoke, Horace Binney, one of the last of the Federalists, was completing a pamphlet which would provide an elaborate legal defense for the government's suspension of habeas corpus. For Binney, as for Phillips, the time of the Alien and Sedition Acts had returned, but for Binney it was an occasion for rejoicing.[30]

Despite all his misgivings, however, Phillips was not giving up his hope that the war would contribute to national salvation.

". . . I do not complain of this state of things; but it is momentous" was the conclusion of his catalogue of evils.[31] The moral was that the people should make certain that the price in bad precedents was worth paying by insisting that the conflict be transformed from a war for the Union into a crusade against slavery.

The abolitionists were beginning to realize in late 1861 that the war was a complex affair. It was not a short and easy road to emancipation. It had released forces which threatened the kind of America that the abolitionists hoped to bring into being. It had provided an occasion for the open expression of a form of conservative thinking that had been underground since the victory of Jefferson in 1800. It had led to thoughts of a revival of the elitism of the Federalist era in the minds of those who had quietly cherished the Federalist tradition. The situation was truly "momentous."

6

"This Cruel War":
The Individual Response to Suffering

THE FIRST BATTLE OF BULL RUN HAD DEMONSTRATED THAT THE war would be a hard and pitiless affair; but it was not until the period from April to November 1862, with its series of extremely bloody engagements—Shiloh, the Seven Days, Second Bull Run, Antietam, and Fredericksburg—that the full horror of the struggle was brought home to the people of the North. Shiloh came as the first great shock, and its incredible carnage, accurately portrayed in Northern newspapers by the artist Henry Lovie, did much to destroy the 1861 image of the war as an heroic picnic.[1] Then there was Second Bull Run, where thousands of maimed and dying men were left unattended on the battlefield for several days, showing the frightful inadequacy of the provisions for the wounded.[2] The aftermath of Antietam was equally grim. It was described by the elder Oliver Wendell Holmes, who was searching for his wounded son. The crowd of dead and wounded, Holmes wrote, was "a pitiable sight, truly pitiable, yet so vast, so far beyond possibility of relief, that many single sorrows of small dimension have wrought upon my feelings more than the sight of this caravan of maimed pilgrims."[3] Antietam, however, had at least been a partial victory, halting the Confederate advance into Maryland. Fredericksburg, a few weeks later, in November 1862, was a disastrous defeat, and the morale of the North sagged to an all-time low, as the public contemplated the immense sacrifice which seemed to have accomplished nothing.

Such large-scale suffering was a new experience for Americans, and the intellectuals who favored a fierce war were faced with the seemingly difficult task of justifying and explaining this colossal bloodletting. Many, however, had no doubts or hesitations. Charles Eliot Norton, for example, made no retreat from his tough-minded view that the greatest suffering and loss of life would be good for the country. As he wrote to a friend in the very wake of casualty reports from Shiloh: "I can hardly help wishing that the war might go on and on till it has brought suffering and sorrow enough to quicken our consciences and cleanse our hearts."[4] Orestes Brownson agreed with Norton on the need for a tough-minded attitude toward suffering. He wrote in January that the nation must forget the "charming sentimentalities of well meaning philanthropists," and recognize that "it is real blood, not red paint that flows, and real life-warm blood must still flow and flow in torrents. We must not have only the courage to be killed, but we must have . . . the harder courage to kill. . . ."[5] He thus anticipated the events of 1862, and he showed no signs of flinching when his predictions came true, and blood did "flow in torrents."

Of those who prescribed pain as a cure for the nation's ills, no one felt more sure of his ground than Horace Bushnell. As he had maintained in his Bull Run sermon of the previous year: "Adversity kills only where there is weakness to be killed. Real vigor is at once tested and fed by it." It "requires adversity," he explained, for the newly awakened spirit of submission and obedience to be "made a fixed sentiment." Foreseeing that suffering would make people turn to religion to ease their burdens, he argued that "there must be tears in the houses as well as blood in the fields"; for then "religion must send up her cry out of houses, temples, closets, where faith groans heavily before God."[6] The battles of 1862 seemed to fulfill Bushnell's prophecies as anxious or sorrowing wives and parents turned to the church for consolation.

Emerson, for reasons that are not so clear and straightforward, also came to accept and almost welcome a tremendous loss of life.

In June 1863, while the North was still smarting from its defeats and losses of the previous year, and before Vicksburg and Gettysburg had raised hopes for a quick Northern victory, Emerson wrote to the parents of a colonel who had been killed that "there are crises which demand nations, as well as those which claim the sacrifice of single lives. Ours perhaps is one,—and that one whole generation might well consent to perish, if by their fall, political liberty & clean & just life could be made sure to the generations that follow."[7]

In the case of the abolitionists, justifying the suffering of war was not always so easy. Insofar as they remained humanitarians, they were bound to be impressed by the inhumanity of war. It was difficult to forget how the antislavery movement had focused on the suffering of the slave, how abolitionist writings like *American Slavery As It Is* by Theodore Weld and *Uncle Tom's Cabin* by Harriet Beecher Stowe had presupposed a Northern revulsion from cruelty and pain. Mrs. Stowe in particular had appealed to the antislavery sensibility by effectively combining the sentimental tradition in literature—which had taught readers to weep over the lot of abandoned wives, orphans, and dying maidens—with the timeliness and seriousness of such intelligent exposés of inhumanity as the reports of Dorothea Dix about cruelty to the insane and the writing of Richard Henry Dana about the mistreatment of merchant seamen. People who had wept and raged over the fate of Uncle Tom might be expected to quail before the horrors and cruelties of the battlefield. To a surprising degree, however, the abolitionists, many of whom had been pacifists because the barbaric cruelty of warfare seemed to contradict all their humanitarian ideals, reconciled themselves to the war even after it became clear how brutal it was going to be.

This willingness to live resignedly in a sea of blood and tears was based first of all on the conviction that the present agony was willed by God, whereas the suffering of the slave had been a result of the sins of the slaveholder. This line of argument shows the confusion of an age which believed in both the free-will theology of Charles Grandison Finney and Nathaniel Taylor and the deterministic concept of Divine Providence. Inexplicably, Providence could be invoked to explain and justify some evils, while others were deemed to be the product of human agency and could therefore be eliminated. The abolitionists could consent to the evils of war by arguing that suffering and death in this situation were divine chastisements, for which they and others who supported the Northern war effort had no personal responsibility, except insofar as they had supported or tolerated slavery before the war.

A second way in which humanitarians put their doubts to rest was by foreseeing such glorious results from the conflict that the price would be clearly worth paying. In September 1862, after the terrible battles of the spring and summer, William Henry Furness, abolitionist and Unitarian minister of Philadelphia, preached a sermon entitled "A Word of Consolation for the Kindred of Those Who Have Fallen in Battle." "It baffles the imagination," he told his congregation, "to depict the glories of the age which, amidst the bloody confusion of this hour, is opening upon us, the new world, which is coming into existence arrayed in a millennial splendor. . . ." This vision of an impending millennium, "wherein the distinctions of race . . . shall be obliterated, and men shall live together in the relations of a Christian brotherhood," could reconcile the most tenderhearted abolitionists to the sorrows of war.[8] The patriotic abolitionist, who was also a genuine humanitarian, could not doubt that war would lead to national perfection and perpetual peace, for his feelings would admit no lesser result from such a struggle.

The most important basis for the abolitionist acceptance of the inhumanity of war, however, was a more complex attitude which had deep emotional roots in the movement. Despite the appeal to tenderness, there had always been an ambiguity in the antislavery view of suffering. While seeking to relieve the suffering of the slave, the abolitionist, as a man with a "martyr complex," had welcomed it for himself.[9] Those who were particularly impressed by the claim that the North was fighting a "holy" or "religious" war found little difficulty in calling for the millions of the North to welcome martyrdom as they themselves had done.

The Reverend Octavius B. Frothingham of Boston was one of the many antislavery men who saw the suffering of the war in terms of martyrology. In a sermon preached in New York in

November 1861, Frothingham employed the analogy of plant reproduction, in which "the living germs . . . are dropped or thrown out by the breaking of the shell" to take new root. When the martyr or hero dies for a cause, Frothingham insisted, he too becomes a regenerating force; Christ was "a regenerating principle . . . embodied in the form of a young Galilean," and the "deaths of noble young men in battle . . . are the snapping open of so many brave caskets, and the dropping into the fruitful soil of humanity of the quick seeds of a new national and human life."[10] By focusing on individual "martyrs" like Theodore Winthrop, Frothingham was able to make the suffering comprehensible to an audience which had seen great value in the death of Lovejoy, the first victim of a proslavery mob, and in the execution of John Brown. The ante-bellum American sensibility had demanded a meaning in the death of the individual. In both the abolitionist martyrology and the conventions of sentimental literature, the moment of death had been seen as the revelation of perfection. By dying in a beautiful and heroic way, Brown, Lovejoy, or, for that matter, Little Eva, or Uncle Tom, had continued to "live" as good influences. The battles of 1862 raised the question of whether the thousands of soldiers who were being killed in the war could serve the same function. Did they, in other words, possess a noble spirit of self-sacrifice which would make their deaths beautiful and instructive, or were they, as might easily seem to be the case, like so many cattle being herded to the slaughter?

To make sure that the right spirit was present, some antislavery writers began to call for an heroic mood of self-abnegation on the part of all Northerners, and a strident, almost inhuman propaganda resulted. Gail Hamilton, a former writer for the antislavery *National Era* and a close friend of Whittier, wrote in this fashion in an early 1863 *Atlantic* piece entitled "A Call to My Country-Women." "Take not acquiescently, but joyfully, the spoiling of your goods," she commanded. "Not only look poverty in the face with high disdain, embrace it with gladness and welcome. The loss is but for a moment; the gain is for all time. Go farther than this. Consecrate to a holy cause not only the incidentals of life, but life itself. Father, husband, child,—I do not say give them up to toil, exposure, suffering, death, without a murmur—that implies reluctance. I rather say, Urge them to the offering; fill them with sacred fury. . . . Be large and lofty. Count it all joy that you are reckoned worthy to suffer in a grand and glorious cause."[11]

If the abolitionists in general were losing their humanitarian revulsion from pain and suffering, one can at least point to some cases of ambivalence which suggest that the spirit of compassion was not entirely dead. To give one example: Lydia Maria Child, the abolitionist author, wrote after First Bull Run that although she had "said all along that we needed defeats and reverses to make us come up manfully to the work of freedom," she had to admit that "these last battles, with all their terrible incidents, have made me almost down sick. Night and day I am thinking of those poor soldiers, stabbed after they were wounded, shot after they dropped down from fatigue. My heart bleeds for the mothers of those sons."[12] This same ambivalence can be seen in two entries in the 1862 diary of Josephine Shaw, nineteen-year-old daughter of the antislavery philanthropist Francis George Shaw. On June 6 she described the "sense of admiration and delight" which filled her soul when she thought "of the noble fellows advancing, retreating, charging and dying, just how, when, and where they are ordered." She went on to explain that "one loses sight of the wounds and suffering, both of the enemies and one's own forces, in thinking of the sublime whole, the grand forward movement of thousands of men marching 'into the jaws of death', calmly and coolly." Less than a month later, however, after being reminded that 50,000 had been killed on both sides, she took less pleasure in "the thought of those poor suffering boys and men." She now imagined "the cold young faces turned up to the beautiful stars." "Every new battle," she wrote, "makes one feel how wicked, wicked it is, the desolate homes and empty hearts, created by men's evil deeds."[13]

John Greenleaf Whittier felt the same tension between the sense of "the sublime whole" and the contemplation of particular sufferings. In 1861 Whittier had been full of the sacred fury which flinches before no possible sacrifice, and had been responsible for such rousing Cromwellian verses as those of his new version of "Ein' Feste Burg Ist Unser Gott." By early 1863, however, he was greatly chastened.

Though faith and trust are stronger than our fears,
And the signs promise peace with liberty,
[We do not] trifle with our country's tears
And sweat of agony. The future's gain
Is certain as God's truth; but meanwhile, pain
Is bitter and tears are salt. Our voices take
A sober tone; our very household songs
Are heavy with a nation's griefs and wrongs;
And Innocent mirth is chastened for the sake
Of the brave hearts that nevermore shall beat,
The eyes that smile no more, the unreturning feet.[14]

It was impossible after the carnage of 1862 to sustain the joyous spirit of the opening months of the war. The thought of "the sublime whole," at least in Whittier's case, had become a last refuge and consolation, like the vision of heaven which carried the medieval Christian through the misery of his earthly pilgrimage.

II

More personal and vivid than the reactions of people who viewed the war from a safe distance were those of intellectuals who actually served as soldiers and nurses. They knew the suffering, pain, and death at first hand and sometimes found it hard to think of "the sublime whole" when confronted with the horrors of the moment.

A soldier, of course, cannot afford to dwell on the death of comrades or the suffering of the wounded, lest his mind be distracted from the principal business of killing the enemy. But there were some, like Colonel Robert G. Ingersoll, whose reactions had been so conditioned by humanitarianism and middle-class sentimentality that they found such detachment impossible. Ingersoll, who led a regiment of Illinois volunteers in the battle of Shiloh, was an unusual commanding officer. He confessed that he "never saw his men in the fighting line without thinking of the widows and orphans they would make, and half hoping they would miss their aim." The chaplain of his regiment later recalled Ingersoll's constant attendance on the sick and wounded and his self-sacrifice on the field at Shiloh when he gave his own blankets to the wounded and slept on the bare ground in a cold, pouring rain.[15]

Ingersoll summed up his view of war in 1862 in a letter from the front. "War is horrid beyond the conception of man," he wrote. "It is enough to break the heart to go through the hospitals. Old gray-haired veterans with lips whitening under the kiss of death—hundreds of mere boys with thoughts of home—of sister and brother meeting the dark angel alone, nothing but pain, misery, neglect, and death around you, everywhere nothing but death—to think of the ones far away expecting the dead to return —hoping for one more embrace—listening for footsteps that never will be heard on earth—for voices that have grown still and forever—it makes one tired—tired—of war."[16] This was the kind of sensibility that had read *Uncle Tom's Cabin* and had both relished the sweet death of Little Eva and raged at the cruelty of Simon Legree and the slavery system. Genuine compassion was mixed with the inclination of a sentimental age to dwell excessively on scenes of sorrow. The war proved too much for the sensitive Ingersoll, and he resigned his commission as soon as he could honorably do so, to take up, in the years that followed, his vocation of polemicist against revealed religion.[17]

Of sterner stuff were New England aristocrats like John W. De Forest and Oliver Wendell Holmes, Jr., both of whom regarded pity as a plebeian and unmanly emotion. As Holmes wrote to his mother in late 1862: ". . . it's odd how indifferent one gets to the sight of death—perhaps, because one gets aristocratic and don't value a common life—Then they are apt to be so dirty it seems natural—'Dust to Dust'—I would do anything that lay in my power but it doesn't much affect my feelings—" Before convicting Holmes of wanton callousness, however, it should be noted that he had seen some of the worst fighting of 1861 and 1862 and had been seriously wounded twice. Numbness was a natural result. What sets him off is his candor in expressing such feelings without shame or hesitation.[18]

Captain John W. De Forest, novelist and scion of a prominent Connecticut family, had a similar attitude. De Forest had found nothing worth doing in prewar America, at least until he had embarked on a literary career—which up to the beginning of his war service had not been noticeably successful. His military experience resulted in a series of sketches, some of which were published in magazines during the conflict.[19] These pieces are distinguished by a hard-bitten stoicism. In addition to realistic, completely unsentimental descriptions of carnage and the sufferings of the wounded, De Forest portrayed in great detail the more ordinary, day-to-day hardships of men at war—hunger, fatigue, discomfort from cold and rain. As he indicated in an 1863 letter to his brother, however, he had no sympathy with those who complained about such conditions. "We waste unnecessary sympathy on poor people," he wrote. "A man is not necessarily wretched because he is cold & hungry & unsheltered; provided those circumstances usually attend him, he gets along very well with them; they are annoyances, but not torments. . . ."[20]

The hardships of war, one must conclude, could contribute to a very tough or "aristocratic" attitude toward the ordinary sufferings of humanity, at least in the case of New England gentlemen who prided themselves on their ability to bear up under severe stress. It is noteworthy that De Forest and Holmes, the pioneers of "realism" in their respective fields, literature and the law, should have demonstrated in their attitudes toward the suffering of war an early form of their contempt for the "soft" and "sentimental" way of reacting to what they considered unavoidable conditions.

The nurses saw the war in a different perspective from the soldiers. They were forced, whether they liked it or not, to concentrate on scenes of agony and death. Also, being women, they were not so likely to feel the need for a "manly" suppression of feelings. Yet the demands of their work often made it necessary to control emotions which they would otherwise have felt free to express.

Louisa May Alcott was a budding writer of sentimental fiction when she went to Washington in December 1862 to work in the hospital, then overflowing with wounded men from the recent Fredericksburg disaster. Her responses are significant because she was deeply imbued with ante-bellum conventions of sensibility, and believed that the sight of human suffering should bring a strong and open personal reaction. On her first day, as she reported in her *Hospital Sketches:* "The sight of several stretchers, each with its legless, armless or desperately wounded occupant, entering my ward, admonished me that I was there to work, not to wonder or weep; so I corked up my feelings, and returned to the path of duty, which was rather 'a hard road to travel' just then." On another occasion, after hearing from a doctor that one of her favorite patients was going to die, she could have sat down for a moment and cried, but she had "learned the wisdom of bottling up one's tears for leisure."[21] Clearly she could not behave like the impressionable heroine of a romance; she had to learn a kind of internal discipline which did not come easily.

If her own opportunities for tears were limited, however, those of her readers were not. In putting her hospital experiences in literary form, she followed the conventions of sentimental fiction. Instead of the horror and anonymity of the general spectacle, the nub of her narrative was the case of a single soldier. She described in great detail the death of "John," whose end was rendered poignant and touching in a way which suggests the standard deathbed scene of the sentimental novel. The suffering and death of war could be made palatable to middle-class readers, if seen in terms of those individuals who were lovingly attended and whose noble qualities were duly recorded.

Miss Alcott, however, did touch at one point on the disturbing problem of the anonymity and randomness of the average death in the hospital. Recalling the sudden and unattended death of a man with whom she had not yet become acquainted, she admitted having felt for a time, "bitterly indignant at this seeming carelessness of the value of life." But she consoled herself eventually with a version of "the sublime whole,"—"with the thought that, when the great muster roll was called, these nameless men might be promoted above many whose tall monuments recall the barren honors they have won."[22] It was only by falling back on some such hope that she could accept the lonely death of unknown soldiers, an end which was far more common in the Civil War than the demise of perfect souls in the presence of loving friends.

Louisa May Alcott did not remain a nurse very long. A month after her arrival, she contracted typhoid and was forced to return home. Perhaps her sensibilities as well as her health were not equal to the strain. A woman of similar background and attitudes who stood up better under pressure was Clara Barton. Like Louisa May Alcott, Clara Barton was a New England spinster who had been a schoolteacher. Her war service has become legendary, both because it was the first relief work for the woman who later founded the American Red Cross, and because, unlike most nurses, she worked on the battlefield, often under fire, rather than behind the lines. To give one example of her ability to go where she was needed: she managed to arrive at Antietam before the first gun was fired.[23]

Clara Barton immersed herself in this work of mercy despite the fact that she was acutely sensitive to the pain and agony of the battlefield. She even developed the disconcerting habit of imagining that the young soldiers, lying dead or wounded before her, were the pupils she had taught in her classroom years before and was horrified at the thought of "the same fair heads . . . that I have smoothed and patted in fond approval of some good or well-learned task, so soon to lie low in the Southern sands, blood-matted and tangled, trampled under foot of man and horse, buried in a common trench 'unwept, uncoffined, and unknown'."[24] As with Louisa May Alcott, it was the anonymity of death in war that was horrible to contemplate.

For Clara Barton, such grim thoughts only led to a fierce determination to do as much as she could to relieve the suffering and loneliness of the grownup schoolboys who were being maimed and killed. Despite the fact that she was a free lance, working on her own rather than for the Sanitary Commission, the great central relief organization, or for the Army Nurse Corps, she did effective work in battlefield relief and nursing, although, as she admitted on one occasion, she could devote more time to a single particularly pathetic case than was consistent with the greatest good for the greatest number. Through it all, she refused to see the soldiers en masse; they were always individuals who required personal and affectionate care. Somehow, she managed to combine compassion and efficiency in a way that few others had the moral strength to imitate.[25]

Quite different and probably more characteristic was the manner in which a woman like Katherine Prescott Wormeley came to terms with her emotions. Miss Wormeley, the daughter of an American-born admiral in the British Navy, was living at the beginning of the war in the fashionable society of Newport. A highly cultivated woman with an advanced taste in literature—she would be notable in the postwar period as a translator of nineteenth century French classics—she served during the war as a nurse on a hospital ship of the United States Sanitary Commission, which operated during the Peninsula Campaign of 1862. Here, as in all Sanitary Commission work, the goal was cool, impersonal efficiency. As Miss Wormeley wrote in one of her letters: ". . . we are here with health, strength, and *head*. To think or speak of the things we see would be fatal. No one must come here who cannot put away all feelings. Do all you can and be a machine—that's the way to act; the only way."[26] Clara Barton would have found it neither possible nor desirable to act like a machine; but under the usual confused and bloody circumstances, it was easy to find a pragmatic justification for coolness of heart and head.

One wonders, however, about the effect of such self-control on the conventions of sensibility. The war taught De Forest to have less sympathy with the poor; it gave Holmes a contempt for the common life; it taught Katherine Wormeley to act and think like a machine. These attitudes seemed more useful in most war situations than the somewhat sentimental humanitarianism of Ingersoll or Louisa May Alcott. A process of natural selection was occurring which was giving more relevance to impersonal efficiency than to pity or compassion. At the same time, since there were clear limitations to what could actually be accomplished for the relief of the wounded and dying, a stoical and fatalistic sense of the inevitability of large-scale suffering was also being inculcated. Implicit in both developments was a challenge to those antebellum humanitarians who believed that sympathy was the noblest of emotions and that all suffering for which human beings could be held responsible was unacceptable and called for immediate relief.

III

The most celebrated encounter with the suffering of the war was that of Walt Whitman. Like Clara Barton, Whitman was a believer in the practical power of compassion; but his case was more complex. With the role of compassionate friend of the wounded and dying, he tried to combine the role of a flaming patriot. The difficulties—both personal and aesthetic—which he encountered provide the most dramatic illustration of how the ante-bellum sensibility confronted the horrors of the Civil War.

During the first year and one-half of the war, Whitman remained in Brooklyn, following his usual occupations as poet, journalist, and *flâneur* of the New York streets, although his routine now included an occasional visit to one of the local hospitals which were filling up with sick and wounded soldiers. But in December 1862, after being notified that his brother George had been wounded in the battle of Fredericksburg, Whitman headed for the front lines. Arriving in the vicinity of Falmouth, Virginia, the author of "Beat! Beat! Drums!" first encountered the reality of war in the form of an immense heap of amputated arms and legs. Although George's wound turned out to be so slight that he was already back on active duty, Walt hung around for eight or nine days, both fascinated and appalled by the sights and sounds of an army in the field. He spent most of his time touring the field hospitals and talking to the wounded, and when he left Falmouth for Washington on December 28, 1862, he was placed in charge of a trainload of wounded men. In Washington, he managed to get a part-time job in the office of the Army paymaster, but his real reason for remaining in the capital was to follow his new vocation of sympathetic visitor to the sick and wounded.[27]

During the next three years, Whitman, according to his own accounting, made six hundred visits to the hospitals, comforting between eighty and one hundred thousand dying or convalescing soldiers. Besides cheering talk, he provided cool drinks, fruit, preserves, tobacco, articles of clothing, small sums of money, and wrote letters for the patients. Whitman's benevolent activities are usually explained either as a manifestation of saintliness or as an outlet for homosexuality.[28] Both of these explanations lose sight of the fact that Whitman was, before everything else, a poet. Moreover, he was the kind of poet who has to "live" his poetry before he can write it. He was capable, therefore, of adopting a way of living to test a voice or personality he hoped to express in verse. Earlier in his career, he had suddenly doffed his middle-class apparel and appeared as a New York rowdy, because this was his way of accepting the fierce beauty that lay behind the ugliness of the New York streets. Now he sought a *persona* which would give him access to the deepest emotions of the war.

As a role player, Whitman was acutely conscious of his appearance when he entered the hospitals. "I fancy the reason I am able to do some good in the hospitals, . . ." he wrote in a letter of 1863, "is that I am so large and well—indeed like a great wild buffalo, with much hair—many of the soldiers are from the west, and far north—and they take to a man that has not the bleached shiny & shaved cut of the cities and the east."[29] As a living symbol, therefore, he could represent to the boys the America that was temporarily in hiding, the buoyant and healthy place of *Leaves of Grass*. His chief literary motive in entering the hospitals, however, was not to embody the poetry he had already written, but to lay a groundwork for poetry that was to come. By being "the wound dresser," he could represent the humanity and comradeship which he hoped the war would inspire.

Being a wound dresser also put him in a position to be a witness to the most intense drama the war had to offer. He made this clear in March 1863, when he wrote candidly to two friends about why he spent so much time with the wounded: "these thousands, and tens and twenties of thousands of American young men, badly wounded, all sorts of wounds, operated on, pallid with diarrhea, languishing, dying with fever, pneumonia, &c open a new world somehow to me, giving closer insights, new things, exploring deeper mines than any yet, showing our humanity, (I sometimes put myself in fancy in the cot, with typhoid, or under the knife), tried by terrible fearfulest tests, probed deepest, the living soul's, the body's tragedies, bursting the petty bonds of art. To these, what are your dramas and poems, even the oldest and tearfulest?"[30] Other comments reveal the same enjoyment of an elemental experience. As a poet thirsting for authentic tragedy, Whitman was admittedly "fascinated" by the suffering in the hospitals and proud that he was able "to feel the reality" of the war "more than some" because he was "in the midst of its saddest results so much." As he summed it up after the war: "Those three years I consider the greatest privilege and satisfaction"; for despite the agony, they had "brought out . . . undream'd of depths of emotion," and given him his "most fervent views of the true *ensemble* and extent of the States."[31]

As he systematically probed the symbolic possibilities of the hospital experience, Whitman concluded that the hospital was an adequate symbol of the war itself and thus the best vantage point from which to capture the essence of the war. As he wrote to his brother in February 1863: "America seems to me now, though only in her youth, but brought *already here,* feeble, bandaged and bloody *in hospital."* When in November he proposed a war book to publisher James Redpath, he was conscious of exploiting his experiences. "It should be got out *immediately,"* he wrote, ". . . an edition, elegantly bound, might be pushed off for books for presents &c for the holidays. . . . It would be very appropriate. I think it a book that would please women. I should expect it to be very popular with the trade." One almost has the impression of Whitman proposing a sentimental gift book on the prewar model to be fabricated somehow out of gangrene and diarrhea, although of course he made it clear that his work would contain a strong democratic message.[32]

With all his ambitions, however, Whitman was unable, then or later, to make significant literary use of his experiences with the wounded. It is true that some of his journal entries of the time, probably only slightly altered, with a few additional paragraphs on the war, were to find their way into *Specimen Days,* published in 1882 and 1883; but, as he confessed in that work, "The real war will never get in the books."[33] His proposed book of prose exclusively about the war was never written, and his poetry deals only in a marginal way with his hospital experiences. Yet his very failure to represent in his art what he considered the most profound experience of his life may provide the key to his importance as a witness of the Civil War.

As for "the real war," it was a horrible thing, and Whitman knew it. He remembered it as "the seething hell and the black infernal background of countless minor scenes and interiors."[34] These minor scenes of hell often caused his ebullient optimism to fail. As he wrote his mother on one occasion in 1863: "One's heart grows sick of war after all, when you see what it really is— every once in a while I feel so horrified & disgusted—it seems to me like a great slaughter-house & the men mutually butchering each other . . ."; and again the following year: "I sometimes think over the sights I myself have seen, the arrival of the wounded after a battle, & scenes on the field too, & I can hardly believe my own recollection—what an awful thing war is— Mother, it seems not men but a lot of devils & butchers butchering each other." In his journal for May 12, 1863, Whitman described the field after Chancellorsville as "butchers' shambles" and re-corded "the groans and screams—the odor of blood" in what he termed "that slaughterhouse." It was well, he continued, that mothers and sisters "cannot conceive, and never conceiv'd these things." The sickening scenes of pain and mutilation which were then described presumably would not have been included in the book he was planning for the feminine market.[35]

However intense these periodic expressions of the horror of the war may have been, they did not shape Whitman's view of the war in general, for they alternate in his letters and memorandums with expressions of a strident patriotism which flinches before no sacrifice for the national honor. One letter of 1863, for example, conveyed his fear that if the South were successful, the United States would become a third-rate power at the mercy of England and France; and Whitman would see the nation "spend her last drop of blood, and last dollar, rather than submit to such humilia-tion."[36] These contradictory reactions can be seen as the conflict between the democratic imperialist, who identifies the future of the world with American nationalism, and the democratic humani-tarian, who feels acutely the suffering and death of ordinary men and finds it hard to consent to organized "butchery."

In the war poetry, Whitman played up his exuberant demo-cratic nationalism, deliberately suppressing the other side—his real sense of the war as meaningless suffering, a nightmare of pain and terror. The manuscript version of the poem which was to appear in *Drum Taps* as "The Veteran's Vision" and in later editions of *Leaves of Grass* as "The Artilleryman's Vision" con-tains vivid descriptions of the carnage: "Some of the dead, how soon they turn black in the face and swollen"—"there is no hell

more damned than this hell of war." The published version, however, leaves out everything of this nature, conveying the excitement and enthusiasm of battle without its attendant horrors.[37] In
only one poem, "The Wound Dresser," does Whitman dwell on
physical suffering and mutilation, but this poem is largely de-
scriptive, giving no hint of emotions other than gentle compassion; there is none of the shock and disgust that he revealed
privately.

Why did Whitman distort his own sense of the war? Why did
he fail to convey adequately in his published works "the real war"
that he knew well? It is possible that raw descriptions of the
hospital life and battlefield carnage were too jarring and sensational to be suitable material for poetry. Yet Whitman could have
expressed his sense of meaningless butchery in some more subtle
way had he chosen to do so. (One thinks of Stephen Crane's
bitterly ironic war poems, which in form owed a great deal to
Whitman.) His decision to suppress and censor some of his
reactions may have been based in part on his understanding of
what the sensibilities of the time would stand. He could write
poignantly of the death of individual soldiers in poems like
"Come Up From the Fields Father" and "Vigil Strange I Kept on
the Field One Night," because here he did not have to depart
excessively from the conventional idea of death as expressed in
the "graveyard poetry" or sentimental fiction of the period. In
these cases there was someone to mourn, and the loving memory
of the living made death more palatable. Yet Whitman was not
a hack writer who toadied to the conventions of his time—his
understanding of sexuality had led to frank and vivid poems that
shocked his contemporaries—and he knew in a profound way that
individual soldiers were not usually mourned on the spot, as in
"Vigil Strange." He could give no formal expression to his sense
of the war as an anonymous "slaughterhouse," not only because
his readers could not assimilate such an insight, but because,
ultimately, he could not accept it himself. As a believer in progress, the natural goodness of man in a democratic society, and the
beneficence of the universe, Whitman had no place in his world-
view for organized "butchery."

Living day after day with so much death, Whitman soon found

it difficult to react properly and even began to fear that he was growing callous. After "so much horrors . . . such suffering and mutilations," the death of individuals seemed to have little effect on him. His apparent callousness, he managed to explain, was most likely a product of his sensitivity to suffering, because death was often "so welcome & such a relief."[38]

It was this sense of death as a merciful release that led to the final resolution of Whitman's conflict. By the end of the war, he had, by a pantheistic glorification of death, persuaded himself that the horrors were unreal, that there was a substantial beauty and peace beneath the appearance of ugliness and butchery. In his late war poems, he emphasized increasingly that death was a return to the Oversoul, and mass death, the entrance to collective immortality.[39] As he turned away from the particulars of death to the general and abstract, he crippled his ability to express immediate impressions of the war, but his struggle led him to an intensity of expression culminating in "When Lilacs Last in the Dooryard Bloomed," a work which gains much of its power from its hard-won vision of the reconciliation of man and nature through death.

Philosophically, however, simple pantheism was not sufficient to satisfy Whitman. The war experience transformed and complicated his theory of the universe. The author of "Song of Myself" (1855) might have been described either as a pantheist or as an idealist of the traditional kind, believing that matter was the expression or incarnation of an unchanging spiritual reality, but the author of "Chanting the Square Deific" (1865) wrote in Hegelian terms of a "general soul" which reveals itself through the struggle of opposites. Severe judgments on humanity, symbolized by the God of wrath, and evil itself, represented by Satan, are as much a part of the progressive divine plan as the compassionate Christ figure. "Chanting the Square Deific" is Whitman's final word on the Civil War; all the contradictions which the war had laid bare—the love and the hate, the butchery and the heroism, the cruelty and compassion—could be understood as part of a spiritual dialectic.[40]

Whitman's spiritual struggle reveals in a unique and personal way the challenge that was presented by the suffering of the war to the American mind and sensibility. His solution took an unusual form; but his Hegelianism, in the final analysis, represented one avenue of consent to the pain and death of the moment on the theory that it contributed to a cosmic whole—another was the more conventional Divine Providence of the abolitionists. Whitman, one can even say, was indirectly sanctioning the tough-mindedness of patrician officers like Holmes and De Forest, who as good soldiers had played their role in the cosmic drama. But the great readiness of some to consent to the horrors of war would have been distasteful to the compassionate Whitman. In his case, acquiescence had been purchased at a cost which a Norton, a Holmes, or a De Forest would never have understood.

7

The Sanitary Elite:
The Organized Response to Suffering

FOR A LARGE NUMBER OF PEOPLE, THE GORY BATTLE ACCOUNTS and long casualty lists of 1862 led to no profound speculation on the meaning of suffering but simply to a strong desire to bring relief and comfort to the wounded. Already at hand as an apparent outlet for this flood of sympathy was the United States Sanitary Commission, the largest, most powerful, and most highly organized philanthropic activity that had ever been seen in America.

The commission had come into being in the early months of the conflict as an outgrowth of the Women's Central Association of Relief for the Sick and Wounded of the Army, founded in New York City in April 1861. Not knowing exactly how to proceed, the women of the Central Association had turned for advice to a group of prominent men, who in turn had decided that nothing could be accomplished without official approval and a satisfactory working relationship with the military authorities. In May, a delegation was sent to Washington to request recognition not only for a semiofficial relief organization but for a voluntary group with much more comprehensive functions—a "Commission of Inquiry and Advice in respect of the Sanitary Interests of the United States Forces." A month later, President Lincoln approved the scheme, and the commission undertook a variety of activities which, in addition to coordination of relief, included sanitary inspection of camps; provision for nurses, hospitals, and ambulance service—to supplement the Regular Army effort along these lines; and the gathering of vital statistics and other scientific data. Before the spring of 1862, however, the commission was hampered in its operations by the resistance of the Army Medical Bureau, which distrusted interlopers in its domain. In order to gain what it considered its proper authority, the commission was forced to go into politics. In April, it pushed through Congress a reorganization of the Medical Bureau and wrested from the War Department the appointment of a man favorable to the commission as Surgeon General of the Army.[1]

From this time to the end of the war, the commission's position was secure, and it won increasing public favor. Eventually its work became part of the Northern Civil War legend—a particularly valuable part because it seemed to show that amidst all the brutality of war the North had exhibited a humane and philanthropic spirit.

Basing their accounts on the undeniable fact that the commission did some excellent work, historians have contributed to this legend by describing the whole Sanitary effort as a kindly beacon, standing out against the dark background of war. An inquiry into the philosophy and attitudes of the Sanitary leadership, however, suggests that this view will have to be modified. The commission did provide an outlet for Northern benevolence—especially the longing of Northern women to relieve the suffering of the soldiers; but the motives of the elite that ruled the organization were more complicated than those of women who rolled bandages and packaged medicine.

It is significant, first of all, that the commission on the whole was staffed not by a cross section of the American public but by members of the highest social class. As a volume on the philanthropy of the war noted in 1864: ". . . men brought up in luxury, with all the advantages of high and generous culture and foreign travel, but who, ennuyed by life without an object, had been almost ready to regard existence as a burden, have found in the work of alleviating the sufferings of the soldier their true vocation, and have given it their best energies. . . ."[2] An account of the hospital transport service run by the commission during the Peninsula Campaign of 1862 revealed that "among those who served as administrative officers, matrons and nurses, the most honored historical families of New England, New York, New Jersey, and Pennsylvania were represented."[3] It would appear that even on a rank-and-file level, the Sanitary Commission was a predominantly upper-class organization, representing those patrician elements which had been vainly seeking a function in American society.

Patricians, however, have been known to act as disinterested custodians of the public interest. What really distinguished the men in important positions in the commission was not a matter of birth but of social philosophy. The organization was ruled in a supremely authoritarian manner by a small number of men— designated as the commissioners. While this body included scientists and experts on military and public health, it was dominated by intellectuals with more general interests—men who took time from their Sanitary duties to write and speak on the broadest political and social questions. At least two were leading representatives of the small but increasingly confident coterie who favored a much more conservative idea of government and society than the prevailing prewar ethos had been willing to allow. Other commissioners were in full sympathy with these views.

President and mainspring of the organization was Henry W. Bellows. In September 1861, while the Sanitary Commission was being organized, Bellows made a forthright statement of his opposition to the perfectionist and millennialist strains in American reform. He denounced the public tendency to see a philanthropic meaning in the war and attacked those "ideal or abstract aspirations, which clothed, now in the garb of religion, and now of philanthropy, are nevertheless revolutionary and anarchical."[4] With all his contempt for abstract philanthropy, Bellows nevertheless emerged as the philanthropic leader of the war. According to the official history of the Sanitary Commission, this was precisely because he was cut from a different cloth from the clergymen who had been militant reformers: "He had the credit of not being what so many of his profession are, an *ideologue;* he had the clearest perception of what could and could not be done. . . ."[5]

Even more fiercely conservative than Bellows was George Templeton Strong, treasurer of the commission. This New York lawyer reached a height of aristocratic rage when he considered the results of the election of 1862, which had gone against the Republicans in New York. As he wrote in his diary: "Neither the blind masses, the swinish multitudes, that rule us under our accursed system of universal suffrage, nor the case of typhoid can be expected to exercise self-control. . . ."[6]

Although he had less clearly defined conservative ideas, Frederick Law Olmsted, the executive secretary of the commission until 1863, was no more a humanitarian on the ante-bellum model than Bellows or Strong. His famous travel writings about the South had little in common with abolitionist attempts to portray the sufferings of the slave. The hardheaded Olmsted had concerned himself less with the inhumanity of slavery than with its apparent unprofitability. His principal career was landscape architecture, and, at the opening of the war, he was director of New York's Central Park project. To the commission, according to the official historian, he brought "the rarest administrative ability"; for his "studies and experience had thoroughly trained him in a science little understood in this country,—that of administration."[7]

Next in importance to Bellows as a social philosopher on the commission was Charles Janeway Stillé, a member of the executive committee who was to become the historian of the movement. Stillé was a Philadelphian of prominent family who had been admitted to the bar in 1842 but had quickly given up active practice for literature and travel. In 1863, he gave a notable address on "The Historical Development of American Civilization" which revealed a Burkean view of society, hopelessly at odds with the natural rights tradition of American political thought.[8] For Stillé, no expression was more distasteful than "humanitarian." Five years after the war, when he delivered a eulogy on the occasion of the death of another leading Philadelphia member of the Sanitary Commission, Horace Binney, Jr. (son of the old Federalist), Stillé could find no higher praise for Binney than to say that "he was no humanitarian." "He was guided by a sentiment far deeper and more enduring than a vague sentiment of philanthropy, and that was, obedience to duty divinely commanded."[9] Stillé and Binney, like Bellows and Strong, apparently found something in their Sanitary work which could not be mistaken for "a vague sentiment of philanthropy."

The only notable reformer who was a member of the commission was Samuel Gridley Howe, who in the past had taken time off from his famous work with the blind and deaf and dumb to support many other humanitarian crusades; and Howe rapidly lost interest in the commission once it was set up. Like many of the New England philanthropists who had been active in the antislavery movement, he found work involving the Negro "contrabands" or freedmen more rewarding than service with the Sanitary Commission.[10]

If the commission was directed by a conservative elite, the question remains as to what these men hoped to gain from the creation of a gigantic philanthropic organization. It would of course be cynical to ignore Christian charity and *noblesse oblige* as motives of action. Yet there is evidence that the commission's work was regarded not only as a duty, but as a heaven-sent opportunity for educating the nation. In a book published in 1863 as a semiofficial statement of goals and purposes, Katherine Prescott Wormeley described the commission as more than an instrument for doing a necessary job; it was "a great teacher . . . guiding the national instincts; showing the value of order, and the dignity of work. . . . It has within it the means for a national education of ideas as well as of instincts."[11] Statements of this kind suggest that the work of the commission was as much an attempt to revise the American system of values as to relieve the suffering of the wounded.

An examination of commission literature reveals that it was made clear from the outset that the organization was not concerned with the relief of suffering as an end in itself. As one report put it: "Its ultimate end is neither humanity nor charity. It is to economize for the National service the life and strength of the National soldier."[12] Brutally stated, this meant that the commission saved the soldier in the hospital so that he could die a useful death on the battlefield. This much might have been expected. What is surprising is that some of the commissioners not only accepted the necessary agonies of war but welcomed them as good in themselves. Although formally engaged in a work of mercy, they could be as tough-minded and insensitive as Norton, Brownson, or Bushnell. Bellows is a good case in point. On the day that Fort Sumter was fired upon, but before the news was out, he wrote to a friend that he had "a longing for a time of personal sacrifices to begin." After the Bull Run disaster, he blandly told the same correspondent: "Our people . . . are not really suffering *anything* as other peoples know suffering. That they may be gradually schooled to endure hardship like soldiers is my most solicitous and constant prayer."[13] It was a few months later, when he visited the Bull Run battlefield, that Bellows revealed the depths of his insensitivity to the tragedies of war. As he described it himself, he casually picked up "a very nice *bone*, the hip bone of a loyal hero," took it home to show his friends, and was surprised that this bone and a skull he had also picked up "wounded some people's sensibilities." These reactions, however, did not stop him from giving a lecture on his tour of the battlefield which, he admitted, "offended some people by the lack of a more serious tone in speaking of battlefields and slaughter and suffering."[14] This callousness would not be so striking had Bellows not been the head of an organization thought to represent the humane feelings of the American people.

Bellows' right arm, commission treasurer George Templeton Strong, was also a believer in suffering as a valuable experience for the American people. In November 1862, after a series of terrible battles, Strong confided to his diary that "the logic of history requires that we suffer for our sins far more than we yet have suffered. 'Without the shedding of blood there is no remission of sins'."[15]

The nature of Sanitary propaganda shows that the attitude of Bellows and Strong was characteristic of the commission as a whole. Not only did the commission reject humanitarianism as a primary motive, it even refrained, as one report indicated, from making a public appeal to "humanity and sympathy." The commission, it was stated, "declines to stimulate those feelings, as it might, most effectively, by dwelling on the pathetic and touching incidents of its work. . . ." Its appeal was "not to the sentiment but to the practical good sense of the community," and it chose to emphasize the fact that the saving of life would reduce the monetary cost of the war for the taxpayer and preserve the soldier as a worker or "producer" when he "returned to the industrial pursuits of civil life." For the benefit of taxpayers and property holders, the report pointed out that each soldier's life was worth to the community "no less than one thousand dollars."[16] This tough-minded dollars-and-cents approach was a far cry from the emotionalism of most ante-bellum movements for relief of the unfortunate.

The commission's ultimate interest, however, cannot be described in terms of money and property. It was, as Katherine Wormeley suggested, a matter of teaching order and discipline, and in its operation the commission showed an almost obsessive concern for the preservation of discipline in all its forms. Frederick Law Olmsted's sanitary report on the First Battle of Bull Run, for example, laid greater emphasis on purely disciplinary problems than on the questions clearly involving sanitation and care of the wounded.[17] There is, of course, an obvious relationship between military health and discipline; but, at times, the interest in teaching military subordination to the unruly volunteer army carried the commission into areas that were none of its business. The commissioners protested continually against President Lincoln's merciful policy of pardoning many of the deserters condemned to death by military tribunals. The commission even passed a resolution early in the war upholding General McClellan against the President in his endeavors to apply "the utmost rigor of military law" to all cases of desertion or insubordination.[18]

In its own domain, the commission showed its Spartan concept of discipline in its peculiarly rigid set of rules governing the distribution of medical supplies in the hospitals. A full explanation was required from the surgeon in charge as to why an item was needed and why he did not have it in stock. This was a good way to improve the efficiency of the medical service, but it often meant that a lifesaving drug in the satchel of the Sanitary agent was withheld from a dying man because the proper procedures had not been followed.[19] Stillé in his history justified this and other examples of Sanitary red tape as necessary for military discipline. The commission, he wrote, "subordinated all its plans, even for the relief of suffering, to the maintenance of that discipline in its strictest form." "It never forgot that the great purpose of any Army organization was to train men to fight and conquer. To effect this object perfect subordination and accountability were essential; and just as it was impossible that an Army which had gained a victory should be delayed in the pursuit of a retreating army in order to look after its wounded, so it determined that if the relief of suffering required a violation of those rules of military discipline . . . the sacrifice should be made for the general good."[20]

Perhaps from a medical point of view, the Sanitary regulations did more good than harm. What is interesting in terms of underlying attitudes, however, is the satisfaction some of the commissioners appeared to derive from such hard policies. Men like Bellows, Strong, and Stillé welcomed the sufferings and sacrifices of the hour because they served the cause of discipline in a broader sense than demanded by purely military requirements. An unruly society, devoted to individual freedom, might be in the process of learning that discipline and subordination were good in themselves, and the commissioners wanted to play their role in teaching this lesson. As a result, they were willing, one might almost say happy, to sacrifice men in the hospital as well as men in the field.

The full scope of the commissioners' definition of the disciplined society came out in their attitude toward the benevolent public. They regarded the spontaneous benevolence of the American people, not as something embodied and expressed in their own work, but as a great danger to the discipline of the army which it was their business to limit and control. Bellows made this point forcefully in a *North American Review* article of January 1864. In discussing the *raison d'être* of the commission, he pointed out that under ideal conditions the government would have performed all the functions of the commission. However, "in a national life like our own,—a democracy, where the people universally take part in political affairs,—the government has no option in the case. The popular affections and sympathies will force themselves into the administration of the army and other affairs. . . ."[21] The problem was "how shall this rising tide of popular sympathy, expressed in the form of sanitary supplies, and offers of personal service and advice, be rendered least hurtful to the army system . . . ?" This was where the Sanitary Commission came in. It conceived of itself less as a benevolent enterprise than as a barrier between the irresponsible benevolence of the people and the army. The greatest danger came not from the possibility that the soldiers would suffer from lack of care and supplies, but, as Bellows put it on another occasion, from the probable "rush of philanthropic men and women to the hospitals and to the field."[22] The desire of people at home to bring comfort and relief to the soldiers was regarded by the conservatives on the commission in much the way they had regarded the reform impulse before the war. If not limited and controlled, it would be a danger to established institutions. In this case, the institution to be protected was the army, and behind it, the state which it was defending.

Bellows went on to justify the commission's rule that all supplies, not only medicines, had to be distributed by medical personnel, that no "outside parties" were to be allowed to give direct comfort to the soldiers. "The discipline of the hospitals, with the authority of the officers, medical and otherwise, was to be carefully upheld."[23] According to the doctrines of the commission, allowing "good Samaritans" the freedom of the hospitals would undermine military rule. If the commission had had its way, Walt Whitman would never have been allowed among the wounded.

In its effort to discourage "good Samaritanism" in all its forms, the commission adopted the much criticized policy of using paid agents rather than volunteers for its relief work. This decision was based on a conviction that the work was "altogether too full of toil, drudgery, and repulsive reality, to be upheld by any mere sentimental pity or sympathy for the poor soldier."[24] The idea that compassion could accomplish nothing was a profound challenge to prevailing beliefs. Walt Whitman, a volunteer who believed intensely in the power of love and pity, expressed a fairly common opinion when he railed at the Sanitary agents as "hirelings." "As to the Sanitary Commissions & the like," Whitman wrote to his mother in June 1863, "I am sick of them all & would not accept any of their berths—you ought to see the way the men as they lie helpless in bed turn away their faces from the sight of the Agents, Chaplains &c (*hirelings* as Elias Hicks would call them—they seem to me always a set of foxes & wolves)—they get well paid & are always incompetent & disagreeable—"[25] Whitman, as a thoroughgoing anti-institutionalist, believed that the spontaneous spirit of benevolence could not survive formal organization and the professionalization of service. To him the most important role to be performed by hospital visitors was to convey "the fullest spirit of human sympathy and boundless love"—"the magnetic flood of sympathy and friendship, that does, in its way, more good than all the medicine in the world."[26] This could not be accomplished by a large, impersonal organization staffed by professional workers.

The Sanitary view of volunteerism not only raised the hackles of solitary Samaritans like Walt Whitman, it also led to a bitter controversy with the Christian Commission, another organization which, in addition to performing its primary task of distributing religious tracts, engaged in a limited way in military relief. The Christian Commission, with its evangelical religious basis, placed a premium on the devotion, piety, and zeal of its volunteer workers. Their system, "the Christians" proudly proclaimed, was not one which depended on paid agents, but the "system adopted eighteen hundred years ago by our Lord." Since their delegates were "at work in the apostolic spirit, for the apostolic pay," they shared Whitman's contempt for the Sanitary "hirelings" and made much of the fact that their delegates gave supplies, whenever possible, directly to the men in the hospitals and not, like the Sanitary, only to the doctors to distribute as they saw fit. They were also like Whitman in thinking of their role as primarily a spiritual one which demanded personal contact. They sought to "enhance the value of both gifts and services by kind words to the soldier as *a man,* not a machine."[27] The Sanitary Commissioners were contemptuous of the Christians because of their "sentimentality" and amateurish lack of emphasis on rules, systems, or organization. Stillé spoke for all of them when he charged that the Christians went about their work with absolutely no regard for "ideas of fitness, practical usefulness, efficiency, or of anything else essential to the success of the object in view."[28]

What the Sanitary Commission had demonstrated in employing paid agents was that it put greater trust in the professional than in the zealous volunteer. The same point was made by Olmsted when he argued that the commissioners had a right to dictate to the local branches because of their expert knowledge of army regulations and sanitary science, and by Bellows when he contended that only a few men could understand the commission's "scientific basis" and its "profound regard for politico-economic principles . . . on which a humane work must proceed."[29] This belief in the need for an expert to act as intermediary between irrational popular benevolence and the suffering to be relieved was the great contribution of the Sanitary Commission to American philanthropic ideas. But their work was important in a broader sense; for they were contributing to a general assault on the long-standing American belief in volunteerism. Sanitary professionalism paralleled the gradual application of Regular Army methods of discipline to the volunteer regiments—a reform for which the commissioners themselves actively lobbied.[30]

At times, the commissioners were not content with their role as expert administrators of a philanthropic empire, but saw themselves as bidding for even greater power and responsibility. In September 1861, Bellows described the role of the commission in a revealing letter. The commissioners, he wrote, have "acted not merely as a Board of military health, but as a kind of Cabinet & Council of War—boldly seizing anomalous power, advising the Government, & seeking to influence the men, military and otherwise who command the position."[31] This comment explains the interest of the commission in general questions of military organization and suggests ambitions far beyond their authorized responsibilities.

When he was particularly upset by the conduct of the war, Bellows even thought in terms of a nonpolitical group, very much like the commission, seizing national power from the politicians. In a letter to Charles Eliot Norton, written in the dark days after Bull Run, he described the "melancholy decay of leadership— the lack of competent statesmen and officers—the paucity of administrative ability." He would not be surprised, he went on, if the country were "driven to the necessity of a provisional government." His own proposal was to compel the President "to call about him men of middle age with the business confidence, the moral approval, the patriotic reliance of the nation. He must throw overboard all mere politicians. . . ." As an immediate step, Bellows was thinking of "inviting together two or three hundred men of standing, moral weight and courage, to form a sort of volunteer congress & debate, consider and agree upon some wise course for the preservation of the country—to shape a policy for the government."[32] What Bellows was really proposing was the establishment of a kind of enlarged Sanitary Commission which would prepare itself for taking power from the incompetent and corrupt politicians. In these proposals he clearly revealed his basic distrust of democracy and his hope of restoring a dispossessed upper class to national leadership. Norton, long an advocate of elitism and a leader of the Boston branch of the commission, responded enthusiastically to these suggestions.[33] There were practical difficulties in the way, however, and the proposal came to nothing; in part probably because of the growing conviction of men like Bellows and Norton that Lincoln, although a plebeian, was giving the country the strong conservative leadership that it needed. There can be little doubt, however, that some of the Sanitary leaders had found a model for American society in the new institution, with its elitist direction by members of "the prosperous and cultivated classes," which had arisen out of the necessities of war.

With all their ulterior motives, however, the commissioners undeniably performed a valuable work. If it was justifiable for the North to subordinate all considerations to the winning of the war, the methods of the commission were, on the whole, appropriate to the occasion. A nation engaged in total war cannot afford the luxury of too much democracy or humanitarianism; military efficiency must be the paramount consideration. To see how the conservative, basically nonhumanitarian philosophy of the commission was suitable to this special situation, one has only to compare their work with similar activities of Dorothea Dix, the finest representative of ante-bellum humanitarianism, who tempo-

rarily gave up her work for the care of the insane to be superintendent of army nurses.

Miss Dix was as sensitive to the suffering of soldiers as she had
been to the agonies of the insane. She never left a hospital without
praying "God give us peace," and she wrote to a friend, in the
midst of the conflict, that "this war in my own country is breaking
my heart."[34] Unfortunately, her sensitivity could be a serious
handicap in the hospitals. As one of her biographers has noted,
she often "became overwrought and lost the requisite self-control.
That pathetic sympathy with human suffering which had been the
mainspring of her long and wonderful philanthropic career, now,
when she was brought face to face with such massive suffering she
could not relieve, served only to unnerve her." She engaged in
sharp quarrels with doctors whom she felt to be incompetent or
failing to do their utmost, and, "tried to stand over the sick and
wounded soldiers as the avenging angel of their wrongs."[35] The
Sanitary Commission remained on reasonably good terms with the
medical service by refusing to be concerned with individual cases
and generally avoiding any interference with the doctors, no
matter how incompetent.

Miss Dix also quarreled with the commissioners themselves.
They tended to regard her as an irresponsible do-gooder, and she
thought of them as too hardhearted when it came to individual
cases. The commission's view was suggested by Strong when he
wrote of Miss Dix in his diary: "She is disgusted with us, because
we do not leave everything else and rush off the instant she tells us
of something that needs attention. The last time we were in Washington, she came upon us in breathless excitement to say that a
cow in the Smithsonian grounds was dying of sunstroke, and she
took it very ill that we did not adjourn instantly to look after the
case."[37]

Dorothea Dix eventually came to the painful realization that her
war career was a failure. "This is not the work I would have my
life judged by," she once exclaimed.[38] She had failed because of
the very qualities which had produced her prewar triumphs. A
"pathetic sympathy with suffering" was seemingly out of place in
time of war, and it was this knowledge that made the Sanitary
Commission effective. Nowhere does the departure of the com-

mission from the spirit and methods of prewar philanthropy and reform come out more clearly than in comparison with the work of Miss Dix.

A basis for assessing the final importance of the Sanitary Commission in the history of American social attitudes has been suggested by Allan Nevins in his *War for the Union*. Nevins argues that some of the most important results of the war came from the way it "transformed an inchoate nation, individualistic in temper and wedded to improvisation, into a shaped and disciplined nation, increasingly aware of the importance of plan and control."[39] One prime example of this new capacity for organization was the Sanitary Commission. Its success and the public acceptance of its policies, its victories over the voluntarists and the individualists, symbolized this new willingness of Americans to work in large, impersonal organizations. It is appropriate that Bellows, who had defended "the doctrine of institutions" against the individualists and the millennialists in his prewar speculations, should have headed an organization which did much to teach Americans the practical value of institutions as opposed to spontaneous action. As Bellows himself expressed it, the war was "God's method of bringing order out of chaos," and he might have added that the commission had been one of God's instruments.[40]

It was in the field of philanthropy, however, that the commission had its most clearly definable effect. Much prewar philanthropy had been inspired by utopian ideals of social reform. At the same time, however, there had been a conservative philanthropy, concerned primarily with social control. This upper-class benevolence had often taken the form of charitable work to teach social responsibility to the potentially dangerous urban masses.[41] While the Sanitary Commission had followed the conservative tradition in its essential spirit, it had suggested important changes of method. Before the war, upper-class philanthropy had been an individualistic proposition; the whims of the giver were law. The characteristic view had been stated by the Boston philanthropist William Appleton when he said: "I part with money in various ways of charity but much like to do it in my own way and not to be dictated to or even asked but in a general way, to give with others."[42] The Sanitary Commission had instituted a board of experts between the giver and the recipient which would decide on a "scientific" basis how the money could best be spent or the goods distributed. The freedom and independence of the donor were taken away by the policy of refusing gifts earmarked for specific regiments or even armies. The highly organized and "scientific" benevolence of the commission set an important precedent for the operation of postwar philanthropy.

A less tangible influence of the Sanitary philosophy came from its encouragement of a new attitude toward suffering. The commission's concept of "scientific" philanthropy with its tough-minded "realism" and its emphasis on discipline and efficiency could lead to a genuinely hardhearted approach to the problems of the unfortunate—an approach which could readily be justified in terms of "scientific" social theories. It was conceivable that when former Sanitarians faced the ordinary suffering of the civilian population in time of peace, they would remember the greater suffering that had been tolerated during the war and, like John W. De Forest, use it as a standard by which to determine how much "discomfort" unfortunate people could be expected to endure.

A final effect of the Sanitary experience was to give the conservative activists of the upper class, who had been outside most of the prewar reform movements, a stronger sense that philanthropy and reform could be carried on for practical, nonutopian, even profoundly conservative purposes. They were encouraged to greater social activity and given an expectation that principles of order and stability, a greater reverence for the institutions which they favored, could be instilled in the popular mind by an aristocratic elite operating in a private or semiofficial capacity. They began to believe that the kind of democratic politics they detested was not the only path to power and influence.

8

The Meaning of Emancipation

FOR A LARGE NUMBER OF NORTHERNERS, THE SUFFERINGS OF war took on new meaning after the announcement of the government's emancipation policy. This was evident on New Year's Day, 1863, when most of the New England men of letters gathered in the Boston Music Hall to celebrate the signing of the Emancipation Proclamation. Among those who joined in the festivities were Emerson, Parkman, Norton, Whittier, Longfellow, Edward Everett Hale, and Harriet Beecher Stowe. The formal part of the program featured Emerson's reading of his "Boston Hymn," written for the occasion, and a stirring choral rendition of Holmes' "Army Hymn." The great moment of the afternoon came, however, when official word was received that the proclamation had been signed as scheduled. The audience burst into tremendous applause, sending up three cheers for President Lincoln, followed by three cheers for William Lloyd Garrison, who was present in the house. Everyone, it appeared, had become an abolitionist.[1]

If the intellectual community of New England was united in hailing emancipation, intellectuals from other parts of the North were only slightly less enthusiastic. Even those who had been most apposed to abolitionism and its radical social philosophy found cause for satisfaction. A few, like Charles J. Stillé, continued well into 1863 to regard freeing the slaves as incompatible with conservative Unionism,[2] but others of similar orientation had come to favor emancipation as a positive good even before Lincoln's preliminary proclamation of September 1862. The die-hard Federalist Horace Binney, for example, had written in August that he was not going to "become an abolitionist," but if freedom for the Negroes resulted from the government's policy, he would "not complain of it. The Negroes are part of the enemy. . . . We shall be whipped as sure as fate, if we fight with one of our hands tied behind our backs. . . ."[3] The belief that emancipation was "a military necessity" gained force with every Northern reverse, and when Lincoln's proclamation finally came, it was apparently based solely on such considerations of policy. Freeing the slaves for reasons of state was a conservative act which made sense to conservative men.

One of the most fervent believers in the expediency of emancipation was Orestes Brownson. As early as October 1861, Brownson had offended some of the conservative Catholic readers of *Brownson's Review* by calling for an antislavery policy. His argument proceeded not only from the usual diplomatic and military considerations, but rested on a psychological premise, which suggests the cynical modern concept of propaganda as an instrument of the state. Brownson felt that Americans had "so long been accustomed to sympathize with rebels, to aid and encourage revolutionists abroad, and to visit with their severest denunciations the acts of legitimate government to suppress insurrection . . . that they cannot be rallied with much enthusiasm under the simple banner of Law and Order. . . ." It was necessary, therefore, to "give them another battle-cry"—to encourage the idea that the North was fighting for liberty—as a way of mobilizing a people so prone to radical and revolutionary thinking that they would fight for conservative principles of government and authority only if under the illusion that they were engaged in a libertarian or humanitarian crusade.[4] Brownson continued writing in this Machiavellian vein throughout most of the war, supporting the policies of Northern radicals for the most conservative reasons. As might be expected, he got himself into difficulty. Overplaying his role as a radical, he joined with men like Wendell Phillips in supporting Frémont

against Lincoln in 1864; but just before the election he seemed
to wake up to the dangerous implications of the Radical Republican philosophy. Creeping back into his writings were the old fears
of a "democratic or Jacobinical centralism, threatening to change
our federal republic into a huge democracy."[5]

Brownson's deviousness was unusual, but in one important
respect his thinking was characteristic of the times. His 1861 defense of abolition on military, diplomatic, and psychological
grounds had included, for the benefit of Northern racists, a prediction that emancipation would not bring social equality for the
Negro, even in the South. He will remain, Brownson wrote, "an
inferior element," a permanent "laboring population . . . with
which the white race will not mingle."[6] There were others in the
North who cared little about the dangers of "mongrelization" in
the South but wanted to make sure that there would be no race-
mixing on their own side of the Mason-Dixon line. An October
1862 *Atlantic* article maintained reassuringly that the Negro was
adapted by nature to the Southern climate, and, if freed, would
remain where he was, rather than go into Northern states which
were "desirous to perpetuate in its purity, the Anglo-Saxon
blood."[7] By January 1, 1863, the Northern conservatives who
favored emancipation but denied that the Negro had a right to
social and political equality were in step with majority opinion.

Some conservatives, however, eventually came to advocate a
greater measure of equality for the Negro, including the right to
vote. They were driven, like many radicals, by a vindictive desire
to punish the South, but also, in some instances, by other motives.
After an Irish mob had resisted the draft laws in New York in
the summer of 1863, it became fashionable to defend the rights
of the Negroes, as a way of showing one's contempt for the Irish
immigrants. Strong's diary of that period begins to praise the
Negroes for the first time, by comparing them with the despised
Irish, and an *Atlantic* review of 1864 recommended Negro suffrage by arguing: "The emancipated negro is at least as industrious and thrifty as the Celt, takes more pride in self-support, is
far more eager for education, and has fewer vices. It is impossible
to name any standard of requisites for the full rights of citizenship which will give a vote to the Celt and exclude the negro."[8]

Thus the loyal Northern conservative might well support emancipation by 1863, but for reasons which involved little, if any, genuine sympathy for the Negro.

II

The abolitionists, instead of viewing emancipation as a necessary act of war, considered the war solely as a means for the abolition of slavery. Having advocated immediate emancipation since the beginning of the conflict, they had been quick to hail Generals Frémont and Hunter when they freed the slaves under their military jurisdiction, only to be bitterly disappointed by the President's decision in both cases to overrule his precipitate antislavery commanders. The abolitionist view of Lincoln's cautious policy before September 1862 was well conveyed in the theory of men like Phillips and Conway that Lincoln was too much the Kentuckian to be an adequate leader of the North.[9]

The mixture of optimism and anxiety which characterized the antislavery mood before emancipation was well conveyed in Moncure Conway's thin volume, *The Rejected Stone,* which was published in late 1861 and reprinted the following year. This work, called by Lydia Child "the most powerful utterance the crisis had called forth," became a wartime antislavery bible; at least one copy went into battle in the breast pocket of a New England soldier and saved the man's life by deflecting a bullet.[10] Conway, once such an unqualified opponent of civil war, now acknowledged that the conflict was a good thing, because it was "hastening the day of freedom," and he took a strong stand against those who called for peace at any price. "No war, however bloody or interminable," he wrote, "can be so horrible as that peace offered us by traitors in our midst." Invoking simultaneously the providential justification and the millennial hope, he called the conflict "a revolution," by which "God fulfills the oath he has sworn, that every wrong shall be overthrown, and the kingdoms of this world shall become the Kingdom of Christ forever." The administration's policy, however, led him to protest that the nation was increasing its own suffering by not adopting an out-and-out emancipation policy; for only a war fought vigorously and with a "freedom frenzy" could be shortly ended. The work concluded with a note of fear and uncertainty. If slavery were not abolished early in the war as a humanitarian measure, Conway warned, it would have to be done later as "a fierce and fearful war measure almost as painful to the party forced to use it as to those at whom it will be aimed." Thus Conway suggested that the nation must act quickly; if it did not, it might lose its chance of redemption, whatever its final decision on slavery.[11]

A few New Englanders of antislavery background, however, had no such fears and were willing even before emancipation to condone the methods of the slow-moving Kentuckian in the White House. James Russell Lowell, who had parted company with most of the leaders of the abolition movement on the secession issue, now became the outright opponent of those who demanded immediate emancipation. His second series of *Bigelow Papers*, which began to appear in the *Atlantic* in late 1861, were as expressive of a moderate, gradualist view of the slavery question as the first series of the 1840s had been of the radical approach. In one humorous poem, which appeared in the April 1862 *Atlantic*, he compared the abolitionists to a group of frogs who had decided to turn the pollywogs of their pond into full-grown frogs by cutting off their tails. As might be expected, the results were disastrous; nature should have been allowed to take its course. Commenting on the poem in the character of Parson Wilbur, the educated voice who introduces and frames the dialect passages in *The Bigelow Papers*, Lowell announced that he was not prepared to "jog the elbow of providence" on the slavery issue. "No desperate measures for me til we are sure that all others are hopeless."[12] This paper was immediately denounced by the radical abolitionists, who viewed Lowell as an apostate. To Conway, Lowell's definition of emancipation as "a desperate measure" demonstrated "the almost hopeless condition of the public mind."[13]

Another member of the prewar antislavery group who saw no need for immediate abolition in the spring of 1862 was the Boston minister and man of letters Edward Everett Hale. Hale's sermon of April 13 on "The Future Civilization of the South" expressed the shallow optimism and smug provincial pride that reached such proportions in New England during the Civil War. Hale believed that a formal act of emancipation was unnecessary because a Northern victory would bring the colonization of the South by Yankee veterans and the automatic spread of New England "civilization" with its inevitable "church and schoolhouse . . . forge and factory." In such an environment, slavery would die of its own accord. He rejoiced that "six hundred thousand men have armed that they might carry good manners, honorable behavior, and a Christian civilization, to the South."[14] Hale spoke for the growing number of antislavery men who saw the future of the South in terms of what amounted to imperialistic exploitation under the guise of Yankee benevolence.

When Lincoln finally announced his emancipation policy, most antislavery spokesmen responded with enthusiasm. Many agreed with the Reverend William Henry Furness, the veteran Unitarian abolitionist and transcendentalist, when he announced after the September proclamation that the President's action was opening a "new world"—a world which was "coming into existence arrayed in millennial splendor, wherein the distinctions of race, which have always been such active causes of contempt and hatred and war shall be obliterated, and men shall live together in the relations of a Christian brotherhood." To Furness, as to many others, the only obstacle to America's fulfilling its God-given mission as model and forerunner of the world's millennial future had been the institution of slavery. Now that slavery was being abolished, all the hopes of prewar reformers were to be fulfilled. Instead of a mere political union, based on institutions of government, Furness' America would become "a living, moral Union" which is "not the result of any human devices, any political arrangements, but a product of the generous forces of Nature, a divine creation, like the air and the light, whose hidden fountains are in God. . . ." To Furness, the old friend of Emerson, the wildest dreams of the transcendentalists were about to come true. In terms of Conway's prewar expectations, "World Soul" would soon "harmonize with Oversoul."[15]

The millennial enthusiasm of the hopeful reached a peak immediately after the final Emancipation Proclamation had been issued in January. Another Unitarian radical, the Reverend David

A. Wasson (described by Emerson as "the first choice of the 'Fraternity people' after Parker"),[16] proclaimed in the February *Atlantic* that once the slaves have been freed, "our shame, our misery, our deadly sickness will be taken away; no more that poison in our politics, no more that degradation in our commercial relations. . . ." According to Wasson, the promise of the Declaration of Independence, the uniquely American vision of a nation devoted to the universal concerns of humanity, was about to be realized. When the nation "has got out of its blood the venom of this great injustice, it will, it must, arise beautiful in its young strength, noble in its new-consecrated faith and stride away with a generous and achieving pace upon the great highways of historical progress."[17] The rhetoric of men like Wasson and Furness may have been completely out of harmony with the grudging tone of Lincoln's proclamations and with the very practical and pragmatic basis of the government's policy, but this did not bother the more ecstatic members of "the party of hope."

There were others, however, who were keenly disappointed by the motivation of the Emancipation Proclamation and the fact that it applied only to those areas still under Confederate control and hence freed no slaves that were actually under federal jurisdiction. As Lydia Child wrote to a friend in 1863: "However we may inflate the emancipation balloon, it will never ascend among the constellations. The ugly fact cannot be concealed that it was done reluctantly and stintedly, and that even the degree that was accomplished was done selfishly; was merely a war measure, to which we were forced by our own perils and necessities; and that no recognition of principles of justice or· humanity surrounded the political act with a halo of moral glory."[18] Robert Ingersoll also found little value in the proclamation. ". . . it certainly will never amount to anything in practice . . ." was his conclusion.[19] The gulf that separated such doubters from the optimists who had convinced themselves that they were on the threshold of the millennium laid the basis for a deep split in the antislavery movement. The question of the hour was whether the government should be supported for its limited and hesitating steps in the right direction, or whether abolitionists should take their traditional high ground and demand all or nothing.

There were some, however, who avoided both horns of this dilemma by fully accepting the proclamation in the spirit in which it was presented, indicating their complete conversion from the celestial politics of moral reform to the earthly politics of President Lincoln. One who took this path was Emerson, who up to September 1862 had joined the critics of the government in attacking the cautious Unionist policy.[20] In November, Emerson wrote a piece for the *Atlantic* in which he hailed Lincoln as a great and virtuous sovereign who had been chosen by Divine Providence as "an instrument of benefit so vast." He praised the President's prudence and moderation, admitting that what he had taken for evasions and unnecessary delays had really been reflections of "endurance, wisdom, magnanimity."[21] Emerson, always on the lookout for "representative men," had once given extravagant praise to the revolutionary fanatic, as personified by John Brown. Now he was equally entranced by Brown's opposite, the practical statesman.

Lowell, even more than Emerson, found the virtues of the proclamation and the whole Lincoln policy in the same pragmatic quality that offended Lydia Child. On the eve of the final proclamation, he discussed the Northern cause in one of his *Bigelow Papers* and made it clear in the face of all the talk about emancipation that he "would not have our thought and purpose diverted from their true object,—the maintenance of the idea of Government. We are not merely suppressing an enormous riot, but contending for the possibility of permanent order coexisting with democratical fickleness. . . ."[22] Lowell, who considered himself a spokesman for the Lincoln government, actually wrote in more conservative tones than Lincoln himself would have used. Far from wanting a strong government to keep "democratical fickleness" under control, Lincoln identified the cause of union with a positive and optimistic evaluation of democracy and with the encouragement of the democratic principle both in America and abroad.

Lowell's full evaluation of Lincoln and his emancipation policy did not come until January 1864, when he published his eloquent defense of "The President's Policy" in the *North American Review*. In this article Lowell's basic conservatism came strongly to the fore, and his former allies, the radical abolitionists, were implicitly taken to task. What Lincoln had done, Lowell pointed out, was to make "a somewhat impracticable moral sentiment" into "the unconscious instrument of a practical moral end." The President's greatest problem, he argued, had come from the fact that the Republican Party had won in 1860 on the basis of arguments drawn "not so much from experience as from general principles of right and wrong." As a result, the moral feeling of the people had been dangerously aroused on the slavery question. Lincoln's greatness had been revealed in the way he had held off as long as possible the emotional and idealistic advocates of immediate emancipation. "It is always demoralizing," Lowell concluded, "to extend the domain of sentiment over questions where it has no legitimate jurisdiction; and perhaps the severest strain on Mr. Lincoln was in resisting a tendency of his own supporters which chimed with his private desires, while wholly opposed to his convictions of what would be wise policy."[23]

This certainly was not the same Lowell who had warned before the election of 1860 that the Republican Party must keep alive its idealism, its concern with "the radical question of right and wrong," and never give way to "expediency" in any form. Lowell, once a young Quixote who hoped to nurture a transcendental fire in a political party coming to power, now praised Lincoln as a Sancho Panza, noting that "while Don Quixote was incomparable in the theoretic and ideal statesmanship, Sancho with his stock of proverbs, the ready money of human experience, made the best practical governor."[24] Prewar idealists like Emerson and Lowell were being taught a welcome lesson in practical politics. The pressures of war were laying bare the conservative instincts of some of the radicals of 1860.

III

For men of letters like Emerson and Lowell, the crusade against slavery had been but one of many absorbing interests. Accepting the Lincoln policy was a more difficult and momentous step for those who had devoted their lives to the antislavery movement and were deeply imbued with its perfectionist view of politics.

The way a dyed-in-the-wool abolitionist responded to the Emancipation Proclamation could determine his future as a reformer. If the abolitionists accepted the government's way of doing things, they made themselves and their philosophy of reform irrelevant, but if they did not, they might be obstructing the achievement of Negro freedom as a practical objective.

After emancipation, William Lloyd Garrison, for one, was quite willing to declare himself unnecessary and close up shop. Although he had been a critic of Lincoln in the first eighteen months of the conflict, he now became a moderate who refused to rock the boat by raising objections to the conduct of the war. The same issue of the *Liberator* which carried the preliminary proclamation of emancipation announced that any government which formally abolished slavery *"can receive the sanction and support of every abolitionist, whether in a moral or a military point of view."*[25] Garrison was as good as his word, although his new patriotism led him far from his "no-government," nonresistance philosophy of a few years before. Without admitting it to himself, Garrison had denied a basic premise of the antislavery movement—the idea that emancipation must be accompanied by a national change of heart toward the Negro. Abolition from military necessity would not guarantee a national commitment to racial equality; it might signify no more than it did to those conservatives who viewed emancipation as a useful tactic in a war fought for conservative nationalism and the rights of authority.

Another notable abolitionist who steered a contradictory course was Gerrit Smith. In late 1862, Smith could still repeat the old antislavery cliché that America would be "regenerated" only when it had "penitently put away slavery."[26] But despite this acknowledgment that national salvation, like that of an individual, requires a change of heart, Smith had already become a firm supporter of the administration and of a policy which would abolish slavery without necessarily reflecting national repentance for the treatment of the Negro. In a speech of 1863, Smith went so far as to defend the Lincoln government for the very reason that it put other considerations ahead of the fate of slavery. Addressing himself to conservatives, he called it "an injustice and an insult" to the President to "charge him with turning the war into an abolition war." Lincoln deserved support precisely because "his sole end is to put down the Rebellion" and "whatever he does with slavery is done but incidentally." "Do you wonder," he asked his audience, "that I, so old and radical an abolitionist, have expressed no concern about slavery. I could not express what I did not feel. Since the bombardment of Sumter I have felt no concern about slavery." Slavery, he was certain, was doomed by circumstances, and he was perfectly willing to see it chipped away little by little as the by-product of a war fought for the Union rather than as a result of national repentance. He attacked those abolitionists who made their support of the war conditional on strong action to free the slaves, because they had "let the crime of slavery fill the whole field of their vision and blind them to the greater and more comprehensive crime of rebellion."[27] In 1864, Smith showed how far he had departed from his "old and radical" abolitionism when he opposed a constitutional amendment to abolish slavery, because it might stir up dissension and hinder the war effort.[28]

There were many abolitionists who followed the acquiescent path of Garrison and Smith. A few, however, tried to remain true to the old reform principles. In the case of Moncure Conway such inflexibility led to a profound sense of disillusionment which revealed much about the impact of the war on the humanitarian philosophy.

Conway's disenchantment with the Northern cause began in 1862, when his deep-seated hatred of war came again to the fore, overcoming his bellicosity of the previous year. In April, he wrote to Charles Sumner that he had discovered on his recent lecture tour "a growing misgiving that a true peace cannot be won by the sword in an issue of this nature."[29] His second book, *The Golden Hour*, which was published that same year, displayed an increasing concern with the evils of war. "The moralization of the soldier," Conway now wrote, "is the demoralization of the man. War is the apotheosis of brutality. . . . Should we continue this war long enough, we shall become the Vandals and Hessians the South says we are." Complaints about the low morale of the troops meant to him simply that the Northern soldier was still civilized and under the influence of Christian morality. The inescapable conclusion was that the longer the war continued, the more savage and brutalized the North would become. Here he generalized the insight at the end of *The Rejected Stone* that if emancipation did not come before it became a "fierce" necessity, it would reflect war passions rather than benevolence.[30]

Conway, however, was as yet unwilling to follow this insight to its logical conclusion and adopt a pacifist position. Although he felt that the North was far from adopting a meaningful emancipation policy—the only policy, as he saw it, which could bring a quick conclusion to the war—he refused to give up on the Northern effort. He fell back, as he had done before, on the providential theory. God would simply mete out more suffering to a sinful nation. "Bleed, poor country," he commanded; "let the pale horse trample loving hearts and fairest homes; if only thus thou canst learn that God also has his government."[31] The view that it was God's will that the people be punished until their hearts were changed was hard to reconcile with Conway's earlier argument that if the North did not seize "the Golden Hour" and come out for freedom soon, its collective heart would be hardened beyond help. But war to Conway in 1862 was both something the abolitionist could watch without qualms as a beneficent working of Divine Providence and a man-made evil which he must cry out against. He both affirmed and denied human responsibility. In the end the easiest way out was to place all the blame and responsibility on President Lincoln: "A million blood stains crimson your hands, Mr. President, damned spots, which not all the rivers and lakes in America can wash away; but in one globule of ink upon your table you may wash them away. . . ."[32]

After the President did take up his pen and sign the Emancipation Proclamation, Conway felt that it was too little and too late. In part this may have reflected his disappointment that the war continued as fiercely as ever; for he had refused as an optimistic humanitarian to believe that the eradication of one evil might require acceptance of another. It was essential to Conway's faith in the universe to believe that once the North was fighting for truth and right the rebellion would evaporate—the fault must be with Lincoln's manner of proceeding. Conway nevertheless had a partially defensible argument. A case can be made for the theory that Lincoln framed and enforced his edict in such a way that the fewest possible slaves would be freed—while at the same time taking the bite out of antislavery criticism of the administration. Conway particularly condemned the President for not putting antislavery generals in a position to carry out rapid emancipation in occupied areas of the South and for allowing whites in some of these areas to hold their former slaves to labor under temporary "apprenticeship" arrangements.[33]

By April 1863, when he sailed for England as an unofficial envoy of the American abolitionists, Conway was completely fed up with the bloody conflict which he saw as inflicting terrible damage on the South without adequate justification. He had concluded that Lincoln did not really intend to carry out emancipation and that, in any case, war was a worse evil than slavery. In terms of policy, he had become interested in the unpopular proposals of ex-Representative Martin F. Conway of Kansas, who had reverted to the prewar disunionist position by calling for the North to abolish slavery in its own territory and, at the same time, unilaterally give up the war.[34] Conway, therefore, was a poor choice to represent abolitionists in England because he was, without being fully aware of it, out of step with most of his colleagues.

Soon after arriving in England, Conway stirred up a hornet's nest by making a peace offer to James M. Mason, the Confederate envoy, which he innocently misrepresented as coming from the American abolitionists. Conway proposed to Mason that if the South would abolish slavery on its own, the antislavery men of the North would "immediately oppose the further prosecution of the war . . . and, since they hold the balance of power, will certainly cause the war to cease by the immediate withdrawal of every kind of support from it."[35] Mason seized on this letter as a chance to embarrass the Northern abolitionists and published it. The storm that broke over the head of poor Conway was something from which he never fully recovered. Almost to a man the abolitionists condemned and repudiated his offer. Wendell Phillips was kindest; although doubting Conway's wisdom, he paid tribute to his motives. Conway now understood, apparently for the first time, that many of the abolitionists were devoted to a war which would crush the South even if slavery were removed as an issue.[36]

He knew he had blundered, "but it never entered my mind," he wrote to his wife, "that any leading antislavery man wd question the principle involved—wd in any way support the war simply for Conquest or Union whether Liberty were or were not involved. The wholesale slaughter of men is vile enough anyway; but to slaughter them except for the holiest cause is *worse* than treason to any govt. that does it. I for one wash my hands of it forever!"[37]

At this point, Conway not only gave up his antislavery mission but seceded from both the Civil War and the United States. He became an expatriate man of letters and minister to an English Unitarian congregation—a kind of one-man lost generation of the Civil War. He would not return to the United States until 1875 and then only for a lecture tour.[38] Conway had started down the same road as the rest of the abolitionists in 1861, but was pulled back by humanitarian sensitivity to the horrors of war. His resistance to the Northern war spirit had been bolstered by a Southern background which made it impossible for him to turn hatred of slavery into hatred of Southerners; but as a "peace" man in 1864 he had nothing in common with Copperheads like John L. O'Sullivan, his fellow exile in England. He was in fact a more uncompromising abolitionist than ever, and that year published a book in defense of Negro equality which advocated miscegenation as a solution to the race problem.[39] Conway had simply reverted to the prewar Garrisonian position on the method of moral reform—it must be nonpolitical, free from compromise and involvement with power—and because others were not willing to follow him, he was washed high and dry out of the mainstream of American history.

Perhaps the most revealing commentary on what the war had done to Conway is found in his novel *Pine and Palm,* published in 1887.[40] An account of life in both the North and South before the Civil War, it centers on intersectional friendship and romance, involving a Virginia family and some New Englanders. Set against a grim background of abolitionist meetings, Bleeding Kansas, and John Brown's raid (one of the heroes is a Conway-like Southern abolitionist who is misunderstood when he arrives too late to stop John Brown in his plans), the action proceeds conventionally through a series of complications to a happy ending. The sectional differences are resolved after the North-South marriage by having most of the characters move to Washington, where they live as one happy family. But according to the chronology of the book, it is now 1860 or 1861 and the reader anxiously awaits the impact of secession and war on the characters. But nothing happens; no mention is made of the crisis. We are even led to believe that everyone will live happily ever after. The grim struggle which would probably have upset everything is simply not allowed to take place, as Conway suspends the course of history to reach his blissful consummation. He was kinder than God. After years of brooding on the nightmare quality of the Civil War, Conway was still unable to understand why the benevolent God of the ante-bellum humanitarians could not have behaved like the conventional romancer who sets limits on disaster and guarantees happy endings.

The abolitionist, it would now appear, could surrender to the pressures of the time in one of two ways. He could follow the example of Garrison and Smith and give up his uncompromising role as a reformer by turning the reins over to the politicians; or, like Conway, he could retain a sterile kind of purity by withdrawing all support from the war. A third road was taken by Wendell Phillips, who refused to surrender at all. He managed to combine a general acceptance of the struggle, a willingness to work in the war context, with his familiar role as an agitator for racial equality. While recognizing that the proclamation was a step forward, Phillips continued to be a vigorous critic of the Lincoln administration for its failure to give wholehearted support to the ideals of egalitarian democracy.

In an address of May 1863, Phillips made it clear why the President's action provided no basis for Garrison's belief that the work of the abolitionists was done. If the Emancipation Proclamation was to have any meaning, he argued, it would have to be transformed from a piece of paper into a living reality. The government, however, was hesitant and vacillating; it would lay solid foundations for racial democracy only if driven by an aroused public opinion demanding full equality for the Negro. The agitator or moral reformer was needed more than ever to goad and bedevil the politicians in the name of their masters, the people; ". . . our government is not at Washington, neither the brains nor the vigor of Washington guide the people. It only blocks the path of the real government,—the people,—the people whose substratum purpose, underlying all honest parties and cliques, is to save the Union by doing justice and securing liberty to all." Phillips' place was still with the populace, arousing a disorganized public to a demand for equality. He concluded his address by saying: "Never until we welcome the negro, the foreigner, all races as equals, and melted together in a common nationality, hurl them all at despotism, will the North deserve triumph or earn it at the hand of a just God."[41]

Phillips, therefore, almost alone of the leading abolitionists, continued hopefully in his prewar role. His quarrel with Garrison on the question of antislavery support for Lincoln split the New England Anti-Slavery Society at the seams in 1864. In that same year, however, Phillips fell into a trap almost as disastrous as the one into which Garrison had tumbled. He temporarily compromised his idea of the reformer as a moral agitator, standing outside of power politics, by becoming a leader of the ill-conceived and abortive effort of some Radical Republicans and other disgruntled individuals to run Frémont for president against Lincoln. The Frémont movement seems to have been based in part on a bold-faced desire to exploit the South. One of its planks was the confiscation of Southern plantations, to be divided, not among the slaves, but among Northern soldiers and settlers.[42] In this instance, Phillips' twin hatred of the Lincoln government and of the Southern rebels dimmed his vision and led him into a kind of caballing politics which had more to do with the vindictive passions of war than concern for the rights of the Negro.

In their various ways, then, all the abolitionists were demoralized or forced into denying their own philosophy of reform. The war situation had apparently made the moral reformer as much an anachronism as the tenderhearted humanitarian who had been superseded by the practical and "realistic" Sanitary Commissioner. It remained to be seen, however, whether the act of emancipation by itself could be an educating influence, which, despite the spirit and circumstances of the proclamation, could lead to a national conversion from racism to the egalitarian principles of the Declaration of Independence. The signs in 1863 and 1864 were not propitious. The American millennium seemed as remote as ever.

9

The Doctrine of Loyalty

SOME OF THE ABOLITIONISTS MAY HAVE BEEN OVERJOYED BY the Emancipation Proclamation, but for most Northerners the six months beginning on January 1, 1863, constituted the period of the war which brought the greatest despair and frustration. A lack of military success, an accumulation of suffering and hardship, doubts about the constitutionality of emancipation, the rigors of the first conscription policy in the nation's history, and the increasing number of arbitrary arrests of individuals suspected of sympathy for the rebels—all combined to increase dissatisfaction with the administration and the war. In these circumstances, the Peace Democrats, or "Copperheads," gained a hearing for their platform of peace at any price. In January, the Copperhead leader, Clement Vallandigham of Ohio, openly opposed continuation of the war on the floor of the House of Representatives, and the months that followed saw a dramatic increase in antiwar sentiment, especially in the Midwest. The state legislatures of Illinois and Indiana, captured by the Democrats in the elections of 1862, passed peace resolutions; mobs in several states resisted enforcement of the draft laws; and there were frightening rumors of secret organizations like the "Knights of the Golden Circle," which were allegedly launching vast pro-Southern conspiracies.[1]

The spirit of patriotism and dedication to the Union which had followed the attack on Fort Sumter appeared to be breaking under the strain. The North seemed in danger of losing the war because of the unwillingness of its own people to make the necessary sacrifices. In this situation, the federal government went to new lengths in forceful suppression of "disloyal" practices. In May, Vallandigham himself was arrested by military authorities for his increasingly effective antiwar speeches and banished to the Confederacy without the benefit of a civil trial.

A number of Northern intellectuals, in the course of observing the national scene in these months, became vitally concerned with the growing problem of "disloyalty." Seeking to do everything in their power to support the government, they endorsed its repressive policies, attempted to refute the arguments of the Copperheads, and in general used all the influence they could command to discourage "disloyal" ideas and practices. Their activities took the outward form of setting up "Loyal Publication Societies" to distribute Unionist literature and forming "Union League Clubs" with other patriotic members of "the intelligent and prosperous classes" to enforce "loyalty" by social pressures. Most significantly, the intellectuals contributed a flood of sermons, speeches, and articles meant to convey a sense of what the situation demanded from the citizen in terms of loyalty and obedience.

A high point of this effort was the establishment in New York on February 14, 1863, of the Loyal Publication Society, an organization with the announced purpose of countering "the efforts now being made by the enemies of the Government and the advocates of a disgraceful PEACE." Francis Lieber became the guiding spirit of this propaganda mill, which eventually distributed 900,000 copies of 90 different pamphlets.[2] In the same month, Henry W. Bellows penned a first draft of a constitution for the Union League Club of New York in which he indicated that "the condition of membership shall be absolute and unqualified loyalty to the Government of the United States and unswerving support of its efforts for the suppression of the rebellion. The primary object is to rebuke by moral and social influences all disloyalty. . . ."[3] Similar organizational efforts were soon made in New England. On March 10, the New England Loyal Publication Society came into being under the editorial direction of

Charles Eliot Norton. At about the same time, the New England men of letters began participating in the activities of the Union Club of Boston. Even Emerson, who had never been much of a joiner, became a wholehearted member.[4]

As they mobilized in defense of "unconditional loyalty" to the Union, some of the intellectuals were led into far-reaching speculations on the deeper meaning of such current bywords as loyalty, patriotism, and nationality. This re-evaluation of basic concepts led to a harvest of political thought which is among the most interesting intellectual products of the war.

The efforts to define "loyalty" and give it a firm philosophical foundation were conditioned by the polemic challenge offered by Copperhead spokesmen. Opponents of the war could raise troubling questions which had to be answered—such as those suggested by John L. O'Sullivan, one of the ablest and most widely noticed theoretical defenders of the peace position. O'Sullivan, who had been a leading Jacksonian, editor of the *Democratic Review* for many years, and a champion of "manifest destiny," turned out a pair of blistering pamphlets in 1862 and 1863 which took the North to task for its allegedly unjustifiable war against the South. Writing from the safety of England, O'Sullivan put his greatest stress on the argument that the South was being denied "the inherent right of any and every great mass of human population . . . to choose and change at will its form of government."[5] Northern war policy struck at the basis of "Americanism" by denying the principle "that the only just foundation of government is 'the consent of the governed'." Whether the South was right or wrong in the first place, O'Sullivan wrote in 1863, the fact that it was fighting single-mindedly for independence showed that there could never be " 'consent' on the part of Southern people to the government of the Union." The North's effort to put down the rebellion, therefore, acted only "to stultify our revolution; to blaspheme our very Declaration of Independence; to repudiate all our history . . . to sanction all . . . the alien dominations, of other ages and countries; to justify the tenure of writhing and bleeding Poland by Russia at this very moment."[6]

O'Sullivan was answered in one of the early pamphlets of the

Loyal Publication Society by Francis Lieber. Lieber's riposte was the natural upshot of his general views on the nature of government. As might be expected from his German background, Lieber had always been a strong proponent of nationalism. Like many nineteenth century European liberals, however, he saw no conflict between nationalism and constitutional liberty. As a young man, he had yearned for both a free *and* a united Germany, and the political theory he developed after coming to the United States identified legitimate nationalistic aspirations with the protection of individual rights. Having been a victim of despotism himself, he had welcomed the revolutions of 1830 and 1848 as efforts to establish the modern liberal state, thereby revealing that he had little in common with ultraconservatives like Brownson or Bushnell. During the Civil War, however, when the suspension of habeas corpus and other violations of rights forced him to choose between nationalism and constitutional liberty, he unhesitatingly chose the former.[7]

In his pamphlet, Lieber denounced O'Sullivan's concept of "Americanism." It amounted, he felt, to a defense of "separation without any reference to the reasons or objects . . . as though disintegration of itself were a valuable thing." The American Revolution (also presumably most of the nineteenth century European revolts) had been justified because it had come from a legitimate nationalistic impulse. The South, however, was clearly not in the position of the American colonies in 1776; it "formed no distant dependency of ours," rather it was "part and parcel of one great continuous country, marked as one by the dignified geography of our land . . . as well as by the history of the people and of their better institutions." Geography thus sets off one nation from another; but it is not the only factor in judging nationalisms. Moral judgments are also relevant; the colonists, according to Lieber, had fought for liberty, but "the South separates on the avowed ground of slavery." O'Sullivan's "Americanism" failed to recognize that "consent of the governed" applies "to the foundation of government and the permanent enacting of laws" and not "to each case in which the government acts." The criminal caught by the policeman "does not consent to be collared."[8]

In asserting the prerogatives of the state within a framework of ideas that was essentially liberal, Lieber was qualifying the right of revolution, but not rejecting it. Closer to moderate nineteenth century European liberalism than to the Enlightenment radicalism of the Declaration of Independence, he could with some consistency identify the cause of the North with that of Mazzini's Italy. "We live," he wrote in another of his war pamphlets, "in an age when the word is Nationalization, not Denationalization; when Fair Italy has risen, like a new-born goddess, out of the foaming waves of the Mediterranean."[9] In weighing the demands of a doctrinaire adherence to "government by consent" against the claims of "legitimate" nationalism, Lieber gave priority to the claims of nationality. Loyalty meant fidelity to one's homeland, as defined by geography, race, and cultural tradition.

As O'Sullivan's pamphlet and Lieber's reply would suggest, a major element in the Copperhead defense of "disloyalty" was the appeal to an unqualified right of revolution. Vallandigham even used this doctrine in appealing to Midwestern Democrats forcibly to resist the draft.[10] It was therefore vital for Northern philosophers of loyalty to redefine the right of revolution and the underlying theory of "government by consent" in such a way that they could not conceivably apply either to the South or to the Copperheads.

Lieber had made a start in this direction, but the most ambitious effort was that of Joseph Parrish Thompson in his 1864 address to the Union League Club of New York. Thompson, a Congregational minister who served as pastor of New York's Broadway Tabernacle from 1845 to 1871,[11] maintained that the understanding of the right of revolution which justified the South stemmed from "a fallacy of Mr. Jefferson"—his celebrated theory that "the earth belongs to the living," who may remodel society without regard for what previous generations have erected. The right of revolution, according to Thompson, is "at best a qualified and conditional right" and very much dependent on what a people has inherited from the past. Once a free popular government has been established, "the right of revolution ceases from that community, and an armed uprising . . . must be always and simply a crime." His historical view of democracy even denied that an overwhelming majority had a right to change their form of government by irregular means once it had been established. Rejecting the theory of "the infallibility of the people," he argued that reliance should be placed rather on "free institutions"—the church, the school, the press, local government—which supply "a regulative power against the misdirection of government, and against the abuse of popular sovereignty." He concluded with the ingenious argument that a victory for the North would encourage the right kind of European revolutions. The desires of Poland, Hungary, and Venice for a stable nationalist democracy would be discouraged by the failure of a republic like the United States to hold together.[12]

The thinking of men like Lieber and Thompson, with all its solicitude for European revolutions, reflected a waning of the evangelistic democratic spirit which had responded so warmly to popular uprisings before 1860. A cooling of the ideological temperature had probably already taken place before the Civil War, but the war gave direction to the necessary adjustments in political thought. If American "loyalty" meant anything to men like Lieber and Thompson, it meant that the American Revolution was over and that revolutionary ideology had no further application to American society. The loyal citizen must resist all attempts to defy the laws and change the established order. Even majorities lacked the right to interfere with the traditional workings of "free institutions." Thomas Jefferson, with his defense of Shays' Rebellion and his advocacy of a revolution every twenty years, was rejected as a philosopher of "Americanism."

II

If Lieber and Thompson had been careful to make it clear that absolute obedience to the state was appropriate only where free institutions had been established, there were other publicists who went further and affirmed, or came dangerously close to affirming, the heretical doctrine that *all* well-established governments are ordained by God and deserve the unconditional fealty of their subjects. This willingness to use the war situation to affirm a pre-Lockean view of the social order, a conservative doctrine that went beyond the needs of the hour, suggests the latent vitality of an ultraconservatism which had been under wraps before the war, but now, for the moment at least, was coming into the open and flourishing in an emotion-charged atmosphere which was discrediting the very thought of rebellion or revolution.

A step toward reviving the almost forgotten doctrine of "divine right"—the belief that established institutions are ordained by God, not popular will—was taken in 1863 by Henry W. Bellows in his important war sermon, "Unconditional Loyalty." This sermon, widely distributed as a patriotic pamphlet, took its text from Isaiah: "And the government shall be upon his shoulders." The burden of the message was that this text applies to "human governors," and that the time had come to reaffirm the Christian doctrine of the "divine right" of rulers. "We boast ourselves of having got beyond these political superstitions," said Bellows, "but if we have got beyond the profound truths they rudely covered, we have passed out of the sphere of safety and lost the anchorage of civil authority." The fact was that "the head of a nation *is* a sacred person." In what amounted to a defense of Lincoln, right or wrong, our leader, Bellows tried to show how the cause of Lincoln as chief executive was the "sacred cause of government itself" and that the critics of his apparently unconstitutional actions were following a dangerous path: "File at the staple which God fastens to his own throne, in the oaths of office which make a man chief ruler of a people, and you loosen thoughtlessly every link of the chain of law and order, which binds society together." The implication was that the oath of office makes a ruler directly responsible to God and not to the people who elected him. To criticize the nation's leader in time of crisis, as the Copperheads and some of the abolitionists were doing, was criminal; for "it is not the policy but the STRENGTH of the government that is to save us."[13]

Bellows was apparently trying to revive the political doctrines of the Puritan oligarchs of Massachusetts Bay, who had believed that a magistrate, although elected by the people, is responsible only to God for his conduct while in office. It is curious to see this venerable notion re-emerging during the Civil War, long after the

American Revolution and the apparent triumph of secular democratic theory. This view, which would have sounded heretical in
the prewar period, was now being expounded in the editorial
columns of a popular magazine like *Harper's*[14] and becoming a
commonplace of clerical discourse. It was stated in extreme form
in an 1863 sermon by Rev. Joseph T. Duryea of the Collegiate
Dutch Reformed Church in New York, who claimed that the war
was providing discipline for the "vast number of unintelligent
and lawless people from foreign sources" who constituted such a
large part of the American population. Duryea's principle was
that "law must be enforced by power, until the people are trained
to obey from principle"—a new version of John Winthrop's
theory that "civil liberty" as opposed to "natural liberty" is the
freedom to act in a way that the magistrates define as moral. The
war has been a valuable experience, concluded Duryea, because
it has taught the lesson that "government is ordained of God,
sanctioned and entrusted with power by him [*sic*]."[15]

The most articulate supporter of this theocratic view of politics
was Horace Bushnell. Attacking the notion of "the sovereignty
of the people" in 1864, Bushnell made it clear that in his view
"the magistrate is sovereign over the people, not they over him,
having even a divine right to bind their conscience by his rule."
One wonders if the Puritan oligarchy could have phrased it any
better.[16]

Bushnell's major contribution to the discussions of "loyalty"
and "divine right" came in July 1863, when he published an
article which attempted to define exactly what conservatives meant
by "loyalty" and what application this concept had to traditional
American habits of thought. He observed, first of all, that the
word "loyalty" as applied to American patriotism had only come
into existence as a result of the war: "Heretofore we have looked
upon this word, and, in fact, have even spoken of it, as a strictly
old-world's word, capable never of any fit application to the conditions of American society. It supposes, we have conceived, some
sort of hereditary magistracy. . . ."[17] For evidence of this traditional American view of "loyalty," Bushnell could have pointed
to the 1861 Fourth of July Oration of Henry James, Sr., in which
loyalty is defined pejoratively as "strictly a personal sentiment,"

the "purely blind and instinctive" homage granted to a ruler because of his office and not as a result of his "radiant human worth" or the benevolence of his rule. "Loyalty bears to patriotism the same relation that superstition bears to religion," James had concluded.[18]

Now, two years after James' oration, "loyalty" had become a respectable word, and Bushnell wanted to make certain that Americans understood what was implied by its use. He made it clear that American loyalty was not simply respect for forms or adherence to the constitution; quite the contrary, for "disloyal" elements were basing much of their case against the war policies on a strict constitutionalism. "One may even be a great stickler for the Constitution, at such a time, and be only one of the pestilent movers of sedition—more poisonously disloyal than he could be in the open renunciation of his allegiance." American loyalty in fact was "even older than the Constitution; a moral bond created by disposing Providence, and sanctified to be the matrix of the coming nationality and the Constitution to be"; it should therefore parallel the English allegiance which accepts royalty and nobility as "organs of a grand providential order, prior to all history, older than all statutes." In essence, then, Americans needed to think of themselves as subjects, having the blind duty to uphold a traditional way of life, rather than as free individuals claiming their rights under the constitution—especially now when a strong government was upholding this providential union against rebellion.[19]

In his efforts to define the "loyal sentiment" more precisely, Bushnell described it as similar to the "undiscriminating" instinct "which attaches us to our native locality and country," and more than this, as a manifestation of the instinctive desire of men to live in communities and be guided by institutions. "Our very nature is political, in short, just as it is domestic; configured to the state as to the family, craving after loyal emotion, even as after family love." Loyalty was the key to establishing the proper attitude toward the state and society, as "Christian nurture" in the family had been the key to religious faith. Indeed, family, church, and state were a kind of interdependent holy trinity to Bushnell, and loyalty had a religious as well as political dimension, which gave it its ultimate meaning. "We believe," he wrote, "that there is a relation so deep between true loyalty and religion that the loyal man will be inclined toward religion by his public devotion, and the religious man raised in the temper of his loyalty to his country, by his religious devotion."[20]

Bushnell's social organicism had been implied in his antebellum attack on the individualism of American religious practices, but it had taken a favorable wartime climate of opinion to bring it to full application. He now found it possible to integrate the state into his fabric of "providential" institutions and to see such institutional loyalties and feelings as patriotism and familial affection as similar manifestations of a socially oriented piety. Nothing could have been farther from the belief of the transcendentalists and the abolitionists that each individual has a direct relation to the divine which transcends his familial or patriotic obligations.

By 1864, Bushnell's hope that the pressures of war would lead to a strengthening of respect for established authority had led him to see his "Doctrine of Loyalty" as actually replacing what he considered the unreliable and qualified patriotic ideal of a people who believed in "government by consent." In a sermon called "Popular Government by Divine Right," he reiterated his 1861 attacks on the "pernicious nostrums" of secular democracy and found signs that the struggle had awakened a spirit of loyalty which would strengthen both the church and state, and lay to rest, once and for all, those theories which pictured men as "monads" with "natural rights" rather than social creatures with functional roles defined by history and tradition.[21] Preaching in the wake of a revival of religion in 1863 and 1864—which saw not only conversions but a great number of new church buildings and an expansion of Christian organizations like the YMCA[22]— Bushnell observed many hopeful signs of the strengthening of the institutional basis of Christianity in the United States and even found that political and religious institutions were coming into harmony. The federal government, he pointed out, had given official recognition to the existence of God for the first time by issuing a coin with the motto "In God We Trust." He hailed a movement which had sprung up to amend the Constitution to make "some fit acknowledgment of God and of the fact that human government stands in true authority only when it rules in the emphasis of religious sentiments and sanctions." The war, it seemed, was having a salutary influence on the dangerous American love of freedom which had brought on the conflict in the first place. One reason for this was the existence of the army, "a vast and mighty schooling of authority" where "nothing goes by consent, or trust, or individual sovereignty. . . . The power is not delegated here and liable to be recalled." It was military drill, he recalled, that had made the Romans "the great law nation of the earth." A similar lesson "we are taking by the million now, and the result will be a great moral intoning of our allegiance, such as we could never have had from any other discipline."[23]

In the course of his argument, Bushnell in effect challenged the whole concept of American nationality which had been generally accepted in the prewar years. Americans had believed they were unique, that only they had a truly legitimate government based on "the consent of the governed." The United States had been regarded as a Messiah among nations with a mission to proclaim its democratic doctrine as the future of mankind. Bushnell had begun his effort to undermine this idea in his Bull Run sermon when he had announced that "our popular vote . . . is only one way of designating rulers, and the succession of blood another, both equally good and right when the historic order makes them so."[24] In 1864, he continued this attack on the identification of American nationality with certain Enlightenment ideas. "What can be more preposterous for us," he said, "or a conceit more fatal to our moral sobriety than to assume that there is no legitimate government in the world and never has been, to the present hour, but our own, in the principle forsooth that all governments 'derive their just powers from the consent of the governed'?"[25] He went on to point out that "government by consent" was a meaningless abstraction; not even the American government, which in its inception had restricted the franchise to male property holders, had followed this formula to the letter. The unavoidable conclusion was that all governments are legitimate "when the historic order makes them so." "It will almost always be felt," he said of government in general, "that the government in power is in a sense historic, that it could not well be different from what it is. In that view, it will be accepted as a kind of Providential creation."[26]

If Bushnell was right, the war was actually transforming the nature of American patriotism from adherence to a set of abstract and utopian ideas with allegedly universal application to a kind of loyalty no different in its essential nature from the loyalty of an Englishman to his king or the Russian peasant to his czar. "The doctrine of loyalty," if taken seriously, could mean a fundamental change in the self-image of America.

Bushnell, Bellows, and many others who spoke of "divine right" were ministers, and their encouragement of a patriotic feeling which would contribute to religious devotion bore an obvious relation to their desire to increase the power and prestige of the clergy. Intellectuals of other backgrounds and ambitions could argue in a similar manner, however, as shown by the writing and addresses of Charles J. Stillé, who was a lawyer and an historian, in addition to being a wartime Sanitary Commissioner. Stillé's speculations received wide notice because they were based on a philosophy of law and a concept of American history which were particularly well suited to the ideological demands of the situation.

Stillé's view of history was first suggested in his famous pamphlet of 1862, *How a Free People Conduct a Long War*. This pamphlet, reprinted several times in 1863 to counter the growing "disloyalty" problem, eventually sold over 500,000 copies, making it probably the most widely distributed single piece of Northern patriotic literature.[27] In substance, it was an account of Britain's experiences in the Peninsular War with some reassuring contemporary parallels. What is interesting, however, is the assumption, uncommon in ante-bellum America, that United States and British history can be described in the same terms. Both are "free peoples" with a similar problem—defined at one point as "that hideous moral leprosy which seems to be the sad but invariable attendant upon all political discussions in a free government, corrupting the very sources of public life; breeding only the base spirit of faction." The British achievement in the Penin-

sular War had been that they had managed, despite the bicker-
ing of parties, to turn "the excited passions of the multitude,"
which had greeted the war, into "a stern endurance—that King-
quality of heroic constancy" which carried the nation through
temporary setbacks to ultimate victory.[28]

In an 1863 speech on "The Historical Development of American Civilization," Stillé spelled out what had been implied by his
British analogy. A conservative interpretation of the Northern
cause, he argued, was firmly rooted in the Anglo-Saxon political
and legal tradition. Where Bushnell had maintained that dangerous abstract ideas of liberty had been present in the foundation
of the nation, Stillé put forth the more palatable and filio-pietistic
view that the founders had really been conservative Englishmen,
whose views in the last analysis were more Burkean than Lockean,
and that subsequent generations, their minds clouded by sympathy
for the more radical nineteenth century European revolutions,
had distorted this heritage: "The glory of our system is, that there
is nothing revolutionary about it, and that when properly understood, it contains within itself every necessary means, founded on
a purely historical and legal basis, of perpetuating our national
life. We need then no revolutionary leaders, no appeals to revolutionary passions, none of those wild devices and expedients by
which enthusiasts abroad have from time to time sought to infuse
the spirit of liberty into the corrupt body of civilization on the
continent."[29]

In his attack on the view that Enlightenment ideas of liberty
had been an influence in American history, Stillé noted "how few
of the great principles of our liberty can be deduced in any way
from any pure and unmixed general theory of human rights."
Americans, it seemed, had always recognized that individual
liberty must be modified in terms of the needs of the historic
community; hence the early colonists, who had spoken of religious
liberty in England, had "wisely" placed "restraints . . . upon
the absolute right of religious worship." Many Federalists, he
continued, had justifiably opposed the Bill of Rights as an unnecessary infringement on an organic and historical tradition of
rights. Here Stillé was drawing on the common law legal philoso-

phy of Justice Story and Rufus Choate, and pervading his argument was the Hamiltonian view of American nationality—that America is another England, operating within Anglo-Saxon tradition and not a democratic utopia in the making.[30]

In his address, Stillé touched here and there on the definition of patriotism or loyalty implied by his interpretation of American history. American patriotism, he claimed, had never been, as some radicals would have it, an enthusiasm for certain abstract ideas; it was rather an "historical ground of affection." It sprang not from "an abstract conviction of the excellence of [the nation's] institutions," but, using the language of Burkean conservatism, from the "fixed habits" and "instincts" of a people grown used to a certain way of life.[31] What Stillé was describing was the kind of patriotism Tocqueville had defined as "that instinctive, disinterested, and indefinable feeling which connects the affections of man with his birth place"—a feeling which is "united with a taste for ancient customs and reverence for traditions of the past." In 1830, Tocqueville had found little enough of this kind of patriotism in an America where national feeling seemed less a blind instinct than a "rational" conviction of each individual that the government is his own because he both participates in it and benefits from it.[32] Although such "rational" patriotism may never have existed in the pure form described by Tocqueville, it was certainly the ideal toward which the theory of "government by consent" had always pointed. For Stillé, this ideal was an illusion of liberal theorists. No viable social order could ever be maintained on a basis of conditional loyalty.

If Stillé's "historical ground of affection" was akin to Bushnell's "loyalty," the Philadelphia lawyer also shared Bushnell's belief that the war would strengthen a conservative devotion to the God-given political and social order. As he summed up his hopes: "It is impossible to review the causes which have produced in these days of ardent pursuit of gain, the extraordinary spectacle of heroic devotion to the idea of country, without giving its real prominence to the influence of that sentiment which recognizes God in government, and founds our duty to defend our country upon the great truth, that it embodies a divinely appointed system for the supply of our wants as His creatures in this world."[38] Behind this apparently pre-Lockean theory of government with its appeal to "divine right," Stillé was also describing nationality as, for all practical purposes, based on history and geography. He was therefore in tune with nineteenth century historicism and romantic nationalism. The fact that the "divine right" view of the war was not simply the last gasp of a reactionary theory of society, but also a manifestation of the nineteenth century acceptance of "history" at the expense of the "reason" of the Enlightenment, is more evident in Stillé's historical address, with its emphasis on roots, its incipient "Anglo-Saxonism," than in the theocratic sermons and writings of Bushnell.

The attempt of thinkers like Stillé, Bushnell, Bellows, and Orestes Brownson to promote a conservative, organic view of society seemed realistic in terms of the "loyalty" and growing reverence for "tradition" which was a natural result of the war for the Union. Yet there was one great obstacle to the general acceptance of their doctrines. The history of the United States had begun with a revolution which had been justified by an appeal to abstract ideals of liberty. The Declaration of Independence was part of the national heritage and had to be reckoned with. Logically the belief that established power ruled by "divine right" prevented *any* appeal to the right of revolution. If one ruled out the right of revolution, however, how could one justify the revolutionary act which had brought about the foundation of the national entity to which conservatives were devoted? It was clear that some way must be found to legitimize the birth of the American nation, some way that would put the "radical" European revolutions clearly beyond the pale. It was a greater problem than had been faced by the more liberal nationalists like Lieber and Thompson who had been willing to endorse the European revolutionary movements.

Orestes Brownson was unique in categorically denying the right of revolution, whatever judgment this brought on the men of 1776. Since "the essential and necessary rights of authority under any and every form of government, are from God, held and exercized by divine right," it followed that government "can never be justly resisted by the people either collectively or individually. . . ." Brownson accepted the argument of men like Bassett and O'Sullivan that the South was perfectly justified by the "right of revolution," but to him this meant that the American people should give up the doctrines of the Declaration of Independence in order to put down the rebellion in good conscience: "Either the theory which you have insisted on in the case of all foreign revolutions is untenable and should be promptly disavowed, or you are wrong in attempting to enforce the laws of the Union over states that do not choose to obey them."[34]

Brownson's extreme views stemmed from his interest in defending reactionary Catholic governments of Europe against the progressive forces of the nineteenth century. Others who were more directly concerned with American history had to tread more cautiously lest their superpatriotism take an unpatriotic turn. Stillé also deplored the European revolutions, which had been fought, he maintained, for the "emptiest abstractions, not only wholly unsupported by history, but also wholly inapplicable to man as an historical being," but felt obliged to make a careful defense of the American revolt of 1776. He noted that the American revolution had not been a social revolution; inherited British institutions, "the whole body of English Common Law" had been left untouched: "Never was there a revolution in any country . . . in which so little change was wrought in the spirit of the organic life of the nation." Like some American historians who came after him, he was arguing that the American Revolution had not been a revolution at all; it was simply a lawyers' quarrel on the application of "the great doctrines of English constitutional liberty." As for the Declaration of Independence, it gained its validity not from its "general political axioms" but from its complaint about "the violation of positive laws." Stillé did not deny the right of revolution, but he limited its application to rare and unlikely situations where the legitimate source of authority was not clear and where rebels had a good "legal" argument in terms of prevailing precedents.[35] Ironically, it was on exactly such grounds that the more legalistic Southern secessionists had based their case. Stillé, however, was so sure that the Southern revolt was of the same class as the European revolutions which contradicted the historic claims of government that he asserted shamelessly in his *How a Free People Conduct a Long War* that "Poland, Hungary and Lombardy . . . were just as determined to be free as the South," but had been legitimately put down by the great powers of Europe. The *"ultima ratio,"* as he put it, was physical force. All that finally mattered was that the North, like the historic European states, had the strength and will to put down rebellion in its own territory.[36]

Ultimately then Stillé's worship of history boiled down, like so many historicist views, to a worship of force. Any government strong enough to enforce its rule over an unwilling populace was providential and therefore legitimate.

Bushnell held forth in a similar vein when he asserted in his "Divine Right" sermon of 1864: "If there is any right of revolution at all it is a right against a government that is really no government. . . ." As for the American Revolution, it was apparently just such a providential uprising against a government that was too weak to rule and command obedience. Like Stillé, he argued that the American Revolution had been a conservative affair because the basic system of laws which had governed the colonies had been left "still standing as before." To the extent that constituted authority had been resisted, "the case was peculiar"; for we "revolted transcendentally, for reasons deeper than we conceived." The American Revolution was a unique case of divine intervention; other revolts were apparently the result of man's rebellion against the laws of God. In resorting to obscurantism to justify the Revolution, Bushnell revealed how profoundly he had departed from the original American ideology.[37]

Speculations of this kind on the Revolution reflected the immediate desire to give an ironclad sanction to the Union cause; but, more than this, they were symptomatic of an important change in American historiography. The universalist theory of national origins, as put forth by an ante-bellum historian like George Bancroft, had made the American Revolution not only the fruit of a specific historical tradition, but also a creed of liberty for all mankind. This view was beginning to give way to the particularist approach of "Anglo-Saxonism."

III

The divine right theory of loyalty was more than the key to a conservative theory of the state; it was also the basis of a generalized "doctrine of institutions," such as the one proposed by Bellows before the war. This much was clear from Bushnell's claim that "loyalty" meant not only unqualified allegiance to the federal government but to all established institutions, especially the church and the family. The war gave impetus and direction to this kind of thinking and made it fashionable to condemn anti-institutional individualism in all its forms. The editors of *Harper's,* for example, now blasted away continually at the anti-institutional "doctrinaires." In January 1862, the inconsistency of the Garrisonian abolitionists, with their "charming doctrine of the power of just ideas to make their own way," was cited in the light of abolitionist support of the war with its inevitable "armies, navies, and fortresses." The military experience, it was claimed, brought "discipline," and discipline suggested an acceptance of "government as a divine institution under all its forms, domestic, civil and religious."[38]

A year later, in January 1863, *Harper's* editorialized on "Institutions and Men" and used the war as an occasion to defend institutions against "the individualism, the idealism, emotionalism, and revolutions that are sometimes arrayed against them." The time was deemed ripe for denying categorically the Emersonian notion that the isolated man has an importance apart from his participation in the organic life of the community, and much was made of the fact that "individuals are almost powerless unless they can come together under the auspices of institutions." The article concluded with the assertion that "the whole history of individualism, whether of the emotional or mystical school, strengthens our faith in institutions, and makes us less and less inclined to think ideas, feeling or impulses, a sufficient guide to a community." The meaning of the Civil War was summed up in the description of the Northerners as "loyal champions of institutions."[39]

If the wartime "loyalty" of 1863 and 1864 implied a vindication of "the doctrine of institutions," where did this leave Walt Whitman and his belief that the patriotic feeling of the American people was an anti-institutional force and a fulfillment rather than a repudiation of the prewar faith in the ability of "ideas, feeling or impulses" to guide the community? As the war dragged on, Whitman grew increasingly uneasy. He became uncertain about the value of mere "patriotism" and deeply concerned about the "discipline" which seemed to be teaching subordination to hierarchical organizations to an American citizenry which had once believed so strongly in a full measure of freedom and equality. By 1863, in fact, Whitman was fully aware that the schooling of the nation in military discipline was one result of the conflict that would never fit into his view of the war as a saturnalia of democracy. He made this clear when he tried to interest a publisher in a book of sketches which would promulgate the idea that "our national military system needs shifting, revolutionizing & made ready to tally with democracy, the people— The officers should almost invariably rise from the ranks—there is an absolute want of democratic spirit in the present system & officers—it is the feudal spirit exclusively—nearly the entire capacity, keenness & courage of our army are in the ranks."[40] It was no more appropriate for the democratic army to be led by an officer caste than for the democratic electorate to be managed by a class of professional politicians. For Whitman, a citizen army should be held together by a spirit of comradeship, not by subordination and discipline.

Comradeship became for Whitman not only the core spirit of the democratic army, but the ideal basis of society itself. He came to feel that conventional patriotic feeling and Unionism expressed in political terms were not profound and spiritual enough to be the true foundations of democracy. Showing that he may have been aware of some of the uses to which patriotism and Unionism were being put, Whitman asserted, in an 1864 draft introduction to *Leaves of Grass,* that American democracy would have to undergo many trials and suffer many failures before it "put into practice the idea of the sovereignty, license, sacredness of the individual." For Whitman, the organic community was desirable, but it had to come as the product of an inward urge, not an external force. It could only be "the idea of Love" that "fuses and combines the whole."[41] His war poem, "Over the Carnage Rose Prophetic a Voice," which some critics have read as a sublimation of homosexuality,[42] contended that male comradeship, "the love of lovers" shall "solve the problems of freedom yet," and that real union can be achieved only by strengthening the bonds of "affection." If this was the poem of a man gaining release from a forbidden impulse by transmuting it and universalizing it, it can also be seen as a quixotic answer to Whitman's intellectual problem—the still unanswered question of how to give a genuine sense of community to an individualistic, egalitarian democracy. If the members of such a society were to avoid external authority and at the same time be held together by something more cohesive than self-interest, there would presumably have to be some awakening of the social instincts, some growth of "love" or "comradeship."

Whatever general value Whitman's reflections may have, they tell us little about the impact of the war. Although he was uncomfortable in the "loyal" North of 1863 and 1864, he never fully faced up to the fact that the war was not going his way. He resorted to a belief that the comradeship of the soldiers was a more fundamental experience than the undemocratic discipline of armies and, according to his habit, substituted an ideal America for the one that was forming under his gaze.

The conservative idea of American nationality and patriotism did not originate in the Civil War. In a sense, Hamilton defended it in his debate with Jefferson by arguing that America should be judged by the traditional standards of national power, not as the embodiment of an Enlightenment theory of government. A sound financial system, manufacturing, and national defense were deemed more important than the protection of liberties or the practice of democracy. In a later period, men like Rufus Choate and Daniel Webster were, when the exigencies of practical politics permitted, conservatives in this sense; but the passage of time permitted them to do what had been denied to Hamilton: They could emphasize an American past and a national tradition, at the expense of the view that America was a promise for the future. Yet people who had such views were out of phase with the currents of national feeling before 1861. Whatever the real motives of American policies in these years, political discourse had a highly ideological cast: American democracy was seen as the model of the world's future, and American patriotism was synonymous with a belief in the liberty of the human race. The war gave new confidence to conservative nationalists by convincing them that the winds of history had changed direction and were blowing their way. They could present a strong case by exploiting obvious facts about the war, and some who had been dissatisfied with America without fully knowing why could develop and clarify a position which required no lip service to democratic idealism. The view of Lincoln or Whitman that Unionism was a pragmatic necessity for the future of international democracy was surprisingly uncommon in the more systematic reflections of the period. Given an opening by the unrealistic and confused thinking of most radicals and abolitionists, the advocates of "divine right" and "unconditional loyalty" could proclaim with some effect that the ultimate America to which allegiance was due was not some vague and improbable democratic utopia but the organized and disciplined North that was going to war before their eyes.

10

The Martyr and His Friends

THE SUMMER OF 1863 BROUGHT THE GREAT NORTHERN VIC-
tories which turned the tide of war and took the edge off the
anxiety about "disloyalty." It also saw the fruition of a favorite
project of the abolitionists—the enlistment and use of Negro
troops.

The glorious culmination of this effort began at six o'clock on
the morning of July 18, 1863, when a brigadier general as-
sembled the members of a Massachusetts regiment and asked if
they would like to lead the dangerous and difficult assault that
was planned for that day on Fort Wagner, a Confederate strong-
hold near Charleston, South Carolina. He was answered by a
cheer of affirmation, and preparations were immediately begun
for the attack. What made this incident different from the pre-
liminaries to dozens of other engagements was the fact that it was
a black regiment which was being asked to lead the charge. It
would be the first time Negro troops had gone into battle, and
they would carry with them not only the aspirations of their own
race for freedom and dignity, but also the hopes of abolitionists
for a vindication of their disputed claims about Negro character
and readiness for equality.[1]

The regiment was the Massachusetts Fifty-fourth, which had

been recruited earlier in the year by the indefatigable governor John Andrew of Massachusetts. It was made up of free Negroes from all over the nation. The officers, however, were white; in command was Robert Gould Shaw, who had been chosen, according to John Murray Forbes, with "reference not only to military capacity, but to personal character and social position." Forbes, the Boston merchant who had been a prime mover in the effort to gain government authorization for the use of black troops, knew that both the public and the government had reservations about the project, and that it was essential to give dignity and respectability to the regiment by providing officers of good family and high social status. Shaw, "the youthful looking, fair-haired commander—the very type and flower of the Anglo-Saxon race—" seemed an ideal choice for the colonelcy.[2] After the regiment had received its orders, on May 18, Governor Andrew, accompanied by Garrison, Phillips, Frederick Douglass, and three thousand other well-wishers, had gone to the training camp at Readville and presented the regimental flag to Shaw. The regiment had then marched to Boston to debark, and had found a cheering crowd of many thousands lining the streets.[3]

In the assault on Fort Wagner, the Fifty-fourth Massachusetts acquitted itself remarkably for a unit which had not previously been under heavy fire. Unfortunately, however, the assault was ill-conceived, poorly prepared, and had no real chance for success. The fair-haired commander struggled to the top of the parapet with a handful of his men, waved his sword and called for his troops to rally, and then, an instant later, was shot and killed. The Negroes continued to fight gallantly but were eventually driven back with heavy losses.[4]

Shaw inevitably became one of the most celebrated heroes of the war. He was more than simply another officer who had shown extraordinary courage. Both his identification with the cause of the Negro and the fact that his family was on friendly terms with most of the literary men and leading abolitionists of New England made him the subject of numerous eulogies. He inspired a flood of poetry, including efforts by Emerson and Lowell, most of which emphasized the fact that he had been "buried with his niggers" in a ditch. The family received letters of condolence from Garrison,

Mrs. Child, John Lothrop Motley, Henry James, Sr., Lowell, Mrs. Gaskell, Henry Ward Beecher, and many others of similar prominence.[5]

Reading the various tributes to Shaw, one is struck by the fact that two quite different meanings are suggested for his sacrifice. The first was in terms of abolitionist martyrology—in the tradition of Lovejoy, he gave his life for Negro freedom. According to Mrs. Child, for example, "he has gone to join the glorious army of martyrs."[6] The *Anti-Slavery Standard* noted that of all those spirits "who have ascended as free will offerings from the altar of the country . . . we think there are few whose names will be more distinctly borne in upon men's minds than that of Colonel Shaw." Shaw was unique because his name was "associated with the new era in the history of the Country, . . . when the black race was called in to the help and deliverance of the nation."[7] His example then had a special importance for abolitionists; it was exploits like his which kept alive the belief that antislavery idealism was an important element in the war. It was the kind of evidence that was badly needed in the face of the government's reluctance to give unqualified support for Negro equality.

Shaw's heroism, however, had another meaning, which for some was of equal, if not greater, importance. It was often emphasized that Shaw was a young man of wealth, refinement, and social position. His father, Francis G. Shaw, was a wealthy philanthropist, the heir of a Boston mercantile fortune, and the Shaws were important members of the exclusive Staten Island colony, composed largely of transplanted members of New England's "Brahmin Caste." As one aristocratic woman wrote to Shaw's parents, "I never knew a hero, a Christian hero such as we read of before. Nothing is wanting. Youth, beauty, birth, wealth, position,—the love of men and women."[8] Henry Ward Beecher wrote that he had been pleasantly surprised that the cultivated class could still produce Christian heroes: "Our young men seemed ignoble; the faith of old heroic times had died . . . but the trumpet of this war sounded the call and O! how joyful has been the sight of such unexpected nobleness in our young men!"[9] John Lothrop Motley, the historian, wrote to Shaw's father that if he had sons, "I had rather they had died such a death as your son's, than that they were living in safe and cowardly ease. . . ."[10]

The letters of this type reveal a deep-seated anxiety among the members of "the cultivated classes" about their own ability, or the ability of their successors, to meet some undefined challenge—a fear which recalls the prewar concern of Norton and Parkman about the effects of prosperity on the national character, and more specifically on the capabilities of "the intelligent and prosperous classes." The example of Shaw was reassuring; perhaps the American aristocracy had not been emasculated by luxury after all. The most famous representation of Shaw as the young gentleman saved from the temptations of wealth by the trumpet of war occurs in Emerson's poem "Voluntaries," written to commemorate Shaw and his Negro troops.

> In an age of fops and toys,
> Wanting wisdom, void of right,
> Who shall nerve heroic boys
> To hazard all in Freedom's fight,—
> Break sharply off their jolly games,
> Forsake their comrades gay
> And quit proud homes and youthful dames
> For famine, toil, and fray?
> Yet on the nimble air benign,
> Speed nimbler messages,
> That waft the breath of grace divine
> To hearts in sloth and ease,
> So nigh is grandeur to our dust,
> So near is God to man,
> When Duty whispers low, *Thou must,*
> The youth replies, *I can.*[11]

This sense of Shaw as a model for the "fops" with their "hearts in sloth and ease" reflects the long-held belief that the wealthy and refined classes had failed to meet the challenges of American life. They had turned from politics and civic duty to "jolly games." In these terms, George William Curtis had satirized the frivolous-minded upper class of New York in his *Potiphar Papers,* published in 1853. Now Shaw was the brightest star in a firmament of well-bred Harvard heroes whose deaths in battle had given new hope to those who believed in the possibility of an American aristocracy.

A writer in the *Atlantic* of September 1863, inspired by the heroism of Shaw and others, proposed the erection of a Memorial Hall at Harvard. It would be in the same spirit as the pulpit in St. Paul's Cathedral in London which was "erected by his surviving comrades in arms to a noble officer of the Indian Army." The author alluded with reverence to the old names which could be inscribed to show the persistence of valor and vitality in the historic families. He proposed that the windows of the hall "be filled, as in the glorious halls and chapels of England, with memorial glass." These men should be remembered, he concluded, because "they fought for culture, generous learning, noble arts, for all that makes a land great and glorious. . . ."[12]

This proposal reflected a real sense that young Brahmins like Shaw were similar to the gentlemen-heroes of British India and should be memorialized in the same fashion. In Shaw's case the analogy could have been more closely drawn; for one of the propaganda pamphlets of the New England Loyal Publication Society had recommended Negro troops as "American Sepoys without any disposition to treachery." This was a period in which Major Hodson's *Twelve Years of a Soldier's Life in India,* which gave a picture of the Christian gentleman fighting for civilization against hordes of barbarians, enjoyed a vogue in refined circles.[13] Warfare in India had trained several generations of British aristocrats to a stern sense of duty and obligation. It was hoped that the American Civil War could do the same thing for at least one generation of American gentlemen.

The class pride and sense of *noblesse oblige* which were encouraged by the example of Shaw and other Harvard heroes were summed up in Thomas Wentworth Higginson's preface to *Harvard Memorial Biographies,* a volume of eulogies published immediately after the war. It was the lesson of these lives of Harvard martyrs "that there is no class of men in this republic from whom the response of patriotism comes more promptly and surely than from its most highly educated class." This response had dispelled "those delusions . . . in regard to some supposed torpor or alienation prevailing among cultivated Americans." Higginson noted with pride that "the lives here narrated undoubtedly represent on the whole those classes, favored in worldly fortune, which would elsewhere form an aristocracy. . . . It is surprising to notice how large is the proportion of Puritan and Revolutionary descent." The record of these men demonstrated that American gentlemen were "governed, above all things else, by solid conviction and the absolute law of conscience. To have established incontestably this point, is worth the costly sacrifice. . . ."[14] The American aristocracy had redeemed itself by showing its unselfishness. Presumably it could now be granted additional opportunities to prove its patriotism and virtue.

II

One family of high social status was more impressed with the first meaning of Shaw's heroism—the antislavery or humanitarian emphasis—than with his role as a symbol of aristocracy. The younger Henry James recalled that the Jameses took a great interest in the raising of Negro troops: "Our sympathies . . . were all enlisted on behalf of the race that had sat in bondage. . . ." Wilkinson James, a younger brother of Henry and William, served under Shaw as adjutant of the Massachusetts Fifty-fourth and was seriously wounded in the assault on Fort Wagner—a circumstance which implicated the entire family in that heroic incident. An immediate result was that "Wilky" James temporarily replaced his noncombatant elder brothers as the center of attention in the household.[15]

At the beginning of hostilities, the elder Henry James had not wanted any of his sons to enlist in the army. Despite his hopes that the war would result in the American millennium, his distrust of governments and institutions was great enough to provide a rationalization for his paternal solicitude. "Affectionate old papas like me," he wrote in a letter of 1861, "are scudding all over the country to apprehend their patriotic offspring and restore them to the harmless embraces of their Mamas. I have had a firm grasp on the coat tails of my Willy and Harry, who both vituperate beyond measure because I won't let them go." He justified

his "paternal interference" by his theory that "no existing government, nor indeed any now possible government, is worth an
honest human life and a clean life like theirs; especially if that
government is likewise in danger of bringing back slavery again
under our banner. . . ." His abolitionist distrust of a Unionist
policy, which was as great as that of Moncure Conway, led him
to prefer "chaos itself" to a restoration of the Union on its old
basis, and he saw no place for his boys in the war as it was then
being fought.[16]

A different view of how abolitionist zeal should be expressed
eventually led the two younger brothers, Wilkinson and Robertson, to volunteer. "Wilky" was particularly inspired by the antislavery cause. When he was brought home to convalesce after
Fort Wagner, his father wrote with pride that "he is vastly at-
tached to the negro-soldier cause; believes that the world has
existed for it; and is sure that enormous results to civilization are
coming out of it."[17] William wrote to his cousin at the same time
that Wilkinson's "wound is a very large and bad one, . . ." but
"he bears it like a man. He is the best abolitionist you ever saw,
and makes a common one, as we are, feel very small and
shabby."[18] Henry, Jr., was also deeply touched by the home-
coming of the antislavery hero. He claimed in later years that
Wilky's convalescence in the James home was his most intense
experience of the war. "Clear as some object presented in high
relief against the evening sky of the west . . . is the presence for
me beside the stretcher on which my brother was to lie for so
many days before he could be moved. . . ." It was one of those
"small scraps of direct perception . . . that were all but touched
in themselves with the full experience [of the war]."[19]

The heroism of Wilkinson, related as it was to the martyrdom
of Shaw and the cause of Negro troops, brought home to both
Henry and William their own inadequacy when faced with the
call for manly action in the righteous cause. Both were the right
age for service, but both claimed exemption on account of health.
The validity of these claims has been much discussed. Leon Edel
has diagnosed Henry's "obscure hurt" as a reasonably serious back
ailment, but what emerges from Henry's own recollections is how
embarrassing it had been to claim invalidism at such a time,

especially since the nature of his trouble was not apparent to the casual observer.[20] William's troubles were perhaps even more "obscure." He had long been recognized within the family as something of a hypochondriac; his mother had written on one occasion before the war that his ailments seemed to be more the product of "a morbidly hopeless" temperament than of organic difficulties.[21] His father at one point had regarded his going to war as an unwelcome possibility, making no mention of health as a ground of exemption, and in 1865 William apparently felt well enough to start off on a strenuous expedition up the Amazon. The evidence is not sufficient to prove that he was actually fit for service, but it does suggest an emotional complication. A temperamental aversion to strenuous physical activity or a neurotic sense of his own insufficiency may have led him to cultivate or exaggerate his condition; or, if he was really as ill as he claimed, his habit of anxious self-analysis may have led him to think of himself unjustly as a malingerer. In any case, he was clearly dissatisfied with himself and what he called his "small and shabby" role in the war. How inadequate he must have felt in Newport in 1863 when he saw Shaw's regiment reviewed! He was, on this occasion, in the company of his friend Captain Charles Russell Lowell and Lowell's fiancée, Josephine Shaw, sister of the martyr-to-be; and an observer has actually described "Willie James," as he timidly watched the martial couple sitting "on their great war horses . . . [and seeming] so like a king and queen that he did not venture to speak to them."[22]

Whether they really wanted to fight or not, both brothers were plagued with the sense of missing a great experience. In 1863 they made a last attempt to get into the war as noncombatants, in a way that accorded with the family humanitarianism, by applying for a place with a volunteer group that was being organized to work among the "contrabands" or freedmen, but for some reason nothing came of this plan.[23]

In the case of Henry, we have some direct testimony on the psychological effects of missing the war. If his recollections of fifty years later are to be trusted, it would appear that his confidence in his ability to make literary use of the more sensational aspects of American life was undermined before he had written a line of publishable fiction—partly, at least, because of the limits on his perception of the war. Remembering a visit to "Wilky" in camp, he recalled how envious he had been "that this soft companion of my childhood should have such romantic chances and should have mastered . . . such mysteries, such engines, such arts." As he received letters from his brothers at the front, he was given a "sense of what I had missed, compared to what the authors of our bulletins gained, in wondrous opportunity of vision, that is *appreciation of the thing seen*—there being clearly such a lot of this, and all of it, by my conviction portentous and prodigious." He had found himself "seeing, sharing, envying, applauding, pitying, all from too far-off, and with the queer sense that, whether or no they would prove to have had the time of their lives, it seemed that the only time I should have had would stand or fall by theirs." As for observing the great change that was taking place in American life in general, what James described as hearing the "tune altogether fresh," he regretted in retrospect that "far more of the supposed total was I inevitably to miss than to gather to my use."[24]

It seems clear that the emphasis on an extremely heightened "sensibility" in James' writing, the willingness to make much of what in conventional terms would seem to be a pitifully small amount of human experience, was encouraged by what he called "my 'relation to' the war." The war, he indicated, had been the most intense experience of his life, but "the case has to be in a peculiar degree, alas, that of living inwardly—like so many of my other cases; in a peculiar degree compared, that is, to the immense and prolonged outwardness, outwardness naturally at the very highest pitch, that was the general sign of the situation." He was learning to live "inwardly" and to substitute sensibility and imagination for a direct confrontation with the raw "outwardness" of American life.[25]

William's failure to participate in the war also led to a greater reliance on inner resources. But this did not come until after he had tried to find a physical equivalent of the military experience by joining the Agassiz expedition, which departed for Brazil in the last month of the war. In a letter to his mother written just before the ship left New York, James showed his sense of the military parallel by describing Agassiz as "expatiating over the map of South America and making projects as if he had General Sherman's army at his disposal instead of the ten novices he really has." Several sentences later, in a different context, he wrote: "Offering your services to Agassiz is as absurd as it would be for a South Carolinian to invite General Sherman's soldiers to partake of some refreshment when they called at his house." This was more than humor. In the first letter from Rio, James identified himself quite seriously with his brothers in the army: "I have felt more sympathy with Bob and Wilk than ever," he wrote, "from the fact of my isolated circumstances being more like theirs than the life I have led hitherto."[26]

Before he could prove himself in the open air, however, James contracted smallpox and had a breakdown which was more than physical. In a letter to his father, he revealed the anguish caused by his failure to meet the demands of the active life. "I am convinced now, for good," he wrote, "that I am cut out for a speculative rather than an active life . . . I became convinced some time ago and reconciled to the notion, that I was the very lightest of featherweights. Now why not become reconciled with my deficiencies? . . . Men's activities are occupied in two ways: in grappling with external circumstance, and in striving to set things at one in their own topsy turvey minds. . . . The grit and energy of some men are called forth by the resistance of the world. But as for myself, I seem to have no spirit whatever of that kind. . . . But I have a mental pride and shame, which although they seem more egotistical than the other kind, are still the only things that can stir my blood. These lines seem to satisfy me, although to many, they would appear the height of indolence and contemptibleness."[27]

Other intellectuals have recorded a similar moment of decision, but few with the apologetic tone and self-depreciation which come out so strongly here. James' sense of himself as a "featherweight" who needs to be "reconciled" with his "deficiencies," and his defensiveness against the opinion of others, suggest that he almost agreed with the activists that the speculative life is "the height of indolence and contemptibleness." His problem was aggravated by the fact that he was an inactive member of an active generation—a generation which had just fought in the Civil War, and his breakdown in Brazil can be seen as the frustration of a last attempt to emulate his heroic brothers and friends. James may have chosen the contemplative life, but he never lost his admiration for "Wilky" and companions like "Rob" Shaw and "Charley" Lowell, who had exemplified the ideal of heroic action in a good cause. This ideal was to contribute in later years to his "strenuous" moral philosophy with its exultation of the will and its rhetoric of strife and battle.

James' sense of the Civil War and the full impression that the assault on Fort Wagner had made on him were not apparent until the day, many years after the conflict, when he gave an oration at the unveiling of the Robert Gould Shaw Memorial in Boston. Relying on Wilkinson's memories, he related the story of the desperate heroism of Shaw and his men in a graphic and compelling way. He also reasserted vigorously the antislavery meaning which Shaw, like the James family, had tried to give to the war. He held up Shaw as something more than another military hero. As a courageous soldier Shaw had demonstrated only a "common and gregarious courage." What James revered was "that more lonely courage" Shaw had shown when he undertook the unpopular task of commanding the first Negro regiment. It was this "lonely kind of valor . . . to which the monuments of nations should most of all be reared, for the survival of the fittest has not bred it into the bone of human beings as it has bred military valor." It was the courage of the abolitionist in arms. Shaw was a hero for James, not only because he had acted valiantly, but because, behind his action, was the moral vision which had led him to champion Negro freedom.[28]

III

To Francis Parkman, on the other hand, it was precisely "military valor" and other "aristocratic" qualities which made Shaw and the other Harvard heroes glorious. Parkman had always detested the abolitionists, and he had little concern for the Negro, but he was Shaw's cousin, and he took great pride in later years in pointing this out to distant correspondents. One suspects, however, that he was almost ashamed that Shaw had led Negroes, since he never mentioned this fact.[29]

In a series of letters written during the war to the Boston *Advertiser,* Parkman carried to great lengths the line of thought suggested by the second meaning given to Shaw's heroism—that he had died not for the Negroes but for his own class, for the cultivated Americans who sought to regain their self-confidence and their role in society.

Parkman's letters were in the form of patriotic exhortations and constituted his way of participating in the struggle. They were a way of working off the frustrations he experienced because his health prevented him from joining the Shaws and the Lowells. As he wrote to his cousin Mary in September 1862, he could not watch troops in training without thinking of "the banners I was not to follow,—the men I was not to lead, the fine fellows of whom I could not be one." His previous "deprivation," in being unable to pursue the outdoor life that he craved, had been nothing compared to this.[30] His most mortifying experience came the following year, however, when his improved health gave him new hopes of a normal life. Carrying out a long-held resolve, he went to ask for the hand of Ida Agassiz, daughter of the scientist, only to be told that she had just become engaged to Major Henry Lee Higginson, who had recently been brought home from the front, wounded and covered with glory. As Parkman wrote of the successful suitor: "The rebels who sabred and shot him were the best friends he ever had. Last winter she refused him decidedly, he went to war, . . . came back wounded, moved her compassion, & gained his wish."[31]

Parkman's own frustrated desire to fight made him very hard on young men of good or even fair health who avoided military service. In his letters to the *Advertiser,* he sternly called others of his class to the duty that he himself could not perform. His trumpet blasts evoke the atmosphere that made life so uncomfortable for young civilians like William and Henry James, who were not such obvious invalids as the nearly blind and partially crippled Parkman.

Parkman also used his war letters as a means of promulgating his general social doctrines. With a new sense of urgency he laid before the public his complaint that a democratic America had shoved aside its "natural" patrician leadership. His letter of January 1862, for example, stormed against the "mediocrity" of the "multitudes" and deplored the fact that the leaders of the nation were "men of the people, that is to say, men in no way raised above the ordinary level of humanity." As for "the best culture," it had not only "been banished from the arena of public life," but, in the absence of the "exercise and stimulus" that public life provided, it had become, "in great part, nerveless and emasculate."[32]

By August 1862, however, the war exploits of men with names like Peabody, Putnam, and Lowell had given Parkman a renewed confidence in "the best culture." He exulted in the "prompt courage" and "unflinching hardihood" displayed by the young men, "trained in ease, and perhaps in luxury, which New England has sent from colleges, from 'learned professions', or from homes of abundance." He still felt, however, that too many young men of leisure were continuing to follow their "round of amusement and ease."[33]

His letter of October 1862 showed that his expectations were continuing to rise. He noted happily that New England regiments were generally officered by gentlemen—a fact which demonstrated once and for all that "the fallacies of ultra-democracy cannot safely be applied to the organization of armies." The troops, he indicated, were fortunate in having officers "who by nurture, by associations, by acquirements, by character," had "an inherent claim to their respect." As a result of this great lesson in social subordination, "democracy has learned the weak points of her armor. . . . In peace, as in war, she cannot dispense with competent and right minded leaders." Parkman's pessimism was rapidly disappearing; he was beginning to believe that the American people were learning the value and necessity of aristocracy.[34]

Parkman's joy in the military prowess of cultivated New Englanders was related to the inferiority feeling that would-be New England aristocrats had always experienced when confronted with the myth of Southern chivalry. As William R. Taylor has shown, prewar Northerners with a concern for "gentility" had often smarted under Southern attacks on the commercial basis of

Northern society and had been disturbed by the comparison of the "Yankee," allegedly obsessed with the pursuit of wealth, with the Southern "Cavalier," who had a true sense of the aristocratic life.[35] Parkman had always accepted much of the Southern argument, and in June 1863, he once again took the North to task for its traditional emphasis on commerce and its neglect of "the war-like instinct and the military point of honor." The South, "a community essentially military," had done well, he suggested, in making "military honor" a part of the training of its ruling caste.[36]

The next month, in two letters, he further developed the odd propaganda line that the best way to whip the South was to emulate certain aspects of its civilization. He went from praising the military education of the Southern aristocrat to praising his political education. Compared to the North, where an "organized scramble of mean men for petty spoils" had driven the better elements from politics, the South had made politics "a battleground" for the well-born, "where passion, self-interest, self-preservation, urge to intensest action every power of their nature." This explained "the vigor of their development." By comparison, the education of Northern gentlemen had been too academic. Now, however, the war was altering the picture. The South, which had identified the North with three classes, the merchants, the politicians, and the "abolitionist agitators" and, therefore, with "extravagance, fanaticism and obstreperous weakness," was learning how, "under a surface of froth and scum, the great national heart still beat with the pulsations of patriotic manhood." In other words, they had underestimated the ability of the Northern gentry to adapt to the military life.[37]

It was in his letter of July 21, 1863, published only three days after the death of Shaw, that Parkman revealed most fully what was really on his mind. Repeating his charge that "the culture of the nation" had become a "political nullity," Parkman referred specifically to the " 'Brahmin caste'," which had "yielded a progeny of gentlemen and scholars from the days of the Puritans," but had "long ceased to play any active part in the dusty arena of political turmoil." This class, however, had at last found an outlet for its energies. Brahmins had been tested in battle at places like Ball's Bluff, Antietam, Fredericksburg, and Gettysburg and removed all doubts about their vigor and character. Pointing to the "necrology of Harvard University" as an example to the nation, Parkman clearly suggested that the American people had no further excuse for rejecting the political and social authority of what was now a tried and true aristocracy. Perhaps a patrician could finally say that the age of "ultra-democratic fallacies" was coming to an end.[38]

Parkman's willingness to view the war almost solely in terms of class interest was somewhat unusual. There were very genteel New Englanders who professed to see the war as a vindication of democracy and egalitarianism. Charles Eliot Norton and others claimed that their wavering belief in democracy had been revived by the proofs of obedience and endurance shown by the common people and by the Negroes in the struggle.[39] This commitment to equality, however, was obviously conditional. It depended on the preservation of a model which had been suggested by the assault on Fort Wagner. If the "inferior elements," whether Negro or white, consented to be led by "the best culture," then their rights were assured; if, however, they struck out in directions of their own, democracy and equality might again be questioned. In a similar manner, the abolitionists were lionized by their former detractors, on the assumption that they would behave like Garrison and accept the *status quo* of Northern society as perfection itself, closing their eyes to the need for additional reforms. In such an atmosphere of cant, the outspoken elitism of Parkman was refreshing. Only a small number of cultivated Americans shared the honest humanitarianism of the James family.

11

The Strenuous Life

PARKMAN'S BELIEF IN THE THERAPEUTIC VALUES OF MILI-
tary life was shared to some degree by young men of patrician
background who actually got into the fighting. But the soldiers
inevitably saw the war in a different perspective from even the
most military-minded civilians. A sense of glory and achievement,
such as Parkman expected officers and gentlemen to derive from
the fighting, was hard to sustain through months and years of
difficult campaigning and tedious picket duty. As for the great
battles in which the aristocrats had allegedly proved themselves,
they seemed to the participants too overwhelmingly confused and
bloody to provide opportunities for individual distinction and
personal courage in the chivalric tradition. As the war continued
into 1864 and the hopes for quick victory raised by the Northern
triumphs at Gettysburg and Vicksburg were dashed by new evidence of Southern intransigency, even the young Northerners
who were temperamentally most suited to the military life had
their moments of despair and defeatism. Charles Francis Adams,
Jr., who loved the outdoor life and the arena for manly exertion
which the war provided, wrote to his brother Henry in July 1864
that he was thoroughly "tired of the Carnival of Death," and had
no desire to see the war continue.[1] The 1864 letters of Oliver

Wendell Holmes, Jr., are filled with the bitter complaints of a man who is physically and spiritually exhausted by three years of war.[2] When necessary, these men could bolster themselves with a grim determination to see the struggle to the end, but their over-all experience was one of pain, tedium, and frustration. If they recognized an ideal of heroism, it was not in the tradition of Sir Walter Scott; it was defined less by glorious exploits than by sheer endurance and tenacity.

The battle sketches of Captain John W. De Forest, the Connecticut novelist who became a hard-bitten soldier, are saturated with this sense of war as a very nasty business, thoroughly unheroic in the traditional sense of heroism. Making no concession to his readers' sensibilities, De Forest took the mask off war, providing detailed description of foot ailments caused by forced marching and other equally unpleasant aspects of daily life at the front. In his account of the assault on Fort Hudson, Louisiana, in May 1863, De Forest criticized "certain military authors who have never heard a bullet whistle" and could therefore claim that "fighting is delightful." The truth was that it was "just tolerable; you can put up with it; but you can't honestly praise it." There were "a few flashes of elation," but on the whole it was "much like being in a rich cholera district in the height of the season." De Forest had a particular distaste for those desperate assaults with little chance of success which demanded "some unusual high cockalorum of heroism," and he admitted realistically that "self-preservation is the first law of nature." On the other hand, however, he was the last man in the world to sanction cowardice. When going into battle, De Forest kept his pistol ready in case any of his men tried to run away. "The man who does not dread to die or to be mutilated is a lunatic," but "the man who, dreading these things, still faces them for the sake of duty and honor is a hero."[3] This new ideal of heroism was grim and stoical; it partook little of the dashing and chivalric and conveyed no image of the hero of romance. It is not surprising, therefore, that De Forest's war experiences pushed him in the direction of literary "realism" and that his Civil War novel, *Miss Ravenel's Conversion from Secession to Loyalty*, completed in 1865, inaugurated the movement for "realistic" fiction in the United States. The novel's much praised battle descriptions laid bare the ugly and unglamorous aspects of fighting and broke all the conventions of literary treatment of war.

De Forest's view of the war had come easily and naturally; he had always been willing, even, curiously enough, eager, to face hardship of the most prosaic kind. As a young man, he had sought to improve his health by undergoing the incredibly rigorous cold water bath treatments offered by certain European "health" resorts, and he described the various discomforts and "heroic" cures in painstaking detail in his letters.[4] He apparently regarded going to war as a similar experience. He had little understanding of those who volunteered with more exalted hopes than simply to test their ability to stand up under mundane hardships, who felt that the war would be glorious because they were fighting for a glorious cause. De Forest was unusual in thus lacking susceptibility, even early in the conflict, to any of the "holy war" theories which were meant to give the soldiers a joyful sense of participating in a crusade. Although "a free-soiler," De Forest had shown his contempt for the Negro race on several occasions during a period of residence in South Carolina in the mid-1850s, and in 1862 turned down the chance to command a Negro regiment.[5] He was fully convinced that the North was right on the slavery question, as on all matters; he was simply not given to ideological enthusiasm and this coolness was increased by the war. He was like his hero, Colburne, in *Miss Ravenel's Conversion,* who, after returning home from battle, found himself labeled a "Copperhead," because he refused to join in the frenzied popular denunciation of the Southern soldiers, whom he had learned to respect as military opponents.[6]

The war's impact on the eager young officer of patrician background was revealed more fully in the experience of Oliver Wendell Holmes, Jr. Holmes had grown up at a time when the antislavery movement had some appeal for young aristocrats; for in the years just before the war, abolitionism in Massachusetts had seemed to call for men willing to risk their lives in manly combat against "border ruffians" in Kansas or "slave-hunters" in Boston. Representative of the abolitionists of this time was a dashing, quasi-military figure like Thomas Wentworth Higginson. Holmes, naturally enough, had been touched by the excitement. In later years, he remembered the time, "before the Civil War when I was deeply moved by the Abolition cause—so deeply that a Negro minstrel show shocked me and the morality of Pickwick seemed to me painfully blunt."[7] His own brief involvement had reflected a youthful thirst for dangerous service in a worthy cause. He had been one of a number of young zealots who had formed a bodyguard for Wendell Phillips when he spoke to a hostile audience in Tremont Temple on January 24, 1861. With such a background, Holmes undoubtedly went to war with some sense that he was engaging in a humanitarian crusade.[8]

Holmes was only twenty at the beginning of the war, and therefore his three years of fighting came at a very impressionable time of life. In the glare of battle, his antislavery idealism proved to be the conventional and superficial enthusiasm of youth rather than a tested faith. When he lay seriously wounded on the field at Ball's Bluff in October 1861, he was not sustained in his ordeal by the thought of the "holy" cause in which he was fighting, but rather by the desire to prove to himself that he had the heroic qualities of a Sir Philip Sydney. It was essentially a matter of living up to an aristocratic code—a code which Holmes had described earlier the same year, in his eulogistic comments on a friend who had died. "Courage and courtesy . . . high breeding restraining all needless display of bravery"; the qualities of "a truly chivalrous gentleman"—these, and not the humanitarian precepts of Wendell Phillips, were the ideals to which Holmes appealed when the chips were down.[9]

Holmes' growing distrust of "causes" and ideology was strengthened by his discovery that some of the most efficient and courageous officers in his regiment had Copperhead sentiments. The gallantry of young Brahmins who sympathized with the South gave Holmes the sense that the personal qualities he admired came from breeding and class pride rather than from a commitment to the abstractions for which antislavery men claimed to be fighting.[10] As the war went on, Holmes himself defined the purpose of the conflict more and more in exclusively military terms, and developed a tough-minded and stoical philosophy of life which revealed how the war could kill all vestiges of humanitarian optimism. For the kind of heroism that comes to the believer who is fighting in a religious cause, Holmes substituted the heroic ideal he was later to advocate in one of his most famous observations: "that the faith is true and adorable, which leads a soldier to throw away his life in obedience to a blindly accepted duty, in a cause which he little understands, in a plan of campaign of which he has no notion, under tactics of which he does not see the use."[11] Applied to civil life, this heroism suggests the determination of a patrician to stick to his traditional code of behavior while functioning in a world in which the orders are being given by plebeians. This view could lead to a belief that the gentleman does not become an iconoclast, a wilderness traveler, or an expatriate, but tries to do his "duty" within the context provided by society, however little his prejudices suit him to the conditions of that society. Just such an affirmation of America by duty and not by inclination came out in one of Holmes' letters of 1862. ". . . I'm an out and outer of a democrat in theory," he wrote, "but for contact, except at the polls, I loathe the thick-fingered clowns we call the people—especially as the beasts are represented at political centres—vulgar, selfish & base. . . ."[12] To men with such opinions, public service in peacetime, like military duty in time of war, was a matter of stern self-discipline, an ability to stand unpleasantness, pain, and frustration.

With his distrust of home-front ideology and his sense of himself as a professional soldier rather than a citizen volunteer, Holmes diverged increasingly from his correspondents in Boston. The elder Holmes, who, like almost all the members of the older generation of intellectuals, expected national salvation from the war, was dismayed by the unenthusiastic tones of his soldier son, whom he accused of losing faith in the Northern cause.[13]

Another instance of the breakdown of communications between the men at the front and the people at home occurred in the Adams family. Charles Francis Adams, Jr., in a way very much like Holmes, was taught by the war to speak a nonideological language that his father could not understand. The father in this case was Charles Francis Adams, Sr., a man of stern principle who had been a leading free-soiler. During the war, when he served as American minister to England, he never wavered in his belief in the antislavery meaning of the conflict. When his son and namesake wrote for permission to enter the army, in June 1861, he felt obliged to put his plea in terms of the family commitment to antislavery. "For years our family has talked of slavery and of the South, and been most prominent in the contest of words, and now that it has come to blows, does it become us to stand aloof from the conflict?" Once in the army, however, young Adams, like Holmes, cultivated the professional soldier's view that the war should be conducted on a purely military basis and became increasingly critical of those who tried to give a humanitarian meaning to the conflict. "Philanthropy is a nuisance in time of war . . . ," he wrote from South Carolina in 1862, after observing Northern abolitionists who had come to work among the freed Negroes. Here he went squarely against the views of the Adamses in England, who were putting great hopes in such experiments with the freedmen.[14]

Charles Francis, Jr., to the horror of his father and brother, came to take a very dim view of Negro prospects in general. This became apparent later in 1862 when Henry wrote from England that he and his father supported General Hunter in his proposal to enlist Negroes in the Union Army; only to have his brother write back: "Our ultra-friends, including General Hunter, seem to have gone crazy." Charles felt that the scheme was based on an overestimation of the freedmen. "It will be years," he wrote, "before they can be made to stand before their old masters." In support of his views, he cited the "low cunning" of the Negro and even predicted that the race "will be destroyed the moment the world realizes what a field for white emigration the South affords. The inferior will disappear . . . before the more vigorous race." He went on to say that "this war, I think, begins a new era from which . . . the African has little to hope." In his opinion the only way to make the Negro into a useful citizen would be a transitional status between slavery and freedom, "proportioned in length to the length of their captivity," for which he offered some parallels from the later stages of feudalism.[15]

The Adams in uniform did not really differ profoundly from

the rest of the family in basic values. It was simply that military experience had narrowed his perspective and given him the sense of a particular interest in which civilians could not share. Also his direct contact with poor and uneducated Negroes had brought out the latent snobbishness and horror of equality which upper-class New Englanders living in the safety of Boston or London did not have to acknowledge. His growing distaste for the "ultras" who led the antislavery forces in New England reflected the same disenchantment with ideology and concern for limited practical objectives which has been observed in the case of Holmes.[16] The war was shaping a generation which would have little respect for the broad enthusiasms of their elders, which would think in more practical or "pragmatic" terms. These men were not likely to be deficient in duty, but their concept of "duty" would be defined less in relation to great causes, and more as a matter of doing necessary tasks in an efficient way.

It was more, however, than a love of "causes" that was being shed—it was the whole Emersonian style of intellectuality. This was evident in the case of Holmes, who was to recall, in a way that suggested a previous existence, that Emerson had set him "on fire" before the war.[17] The most dramatic example of a conversion from the exalted faith of transcendentalism to a more "realistic" definition of the purpose of life was that of Charles Russell Lowell. Lowell, who had tried before 1861 to plan his life in a way that fulfilled all the Emersonian demands, signified, before he was killed in late 1864, that the war had freed him from the ambitions and desires which Emerson had inculcated. In a letter of June 1863 to his fiancée, Josephine Shaw, Lowell described his conversion: "I wonder whether my theories about self-culture, &c., would ever have been modified so much, whether I should ever have seen what a necessary failure they lead to, had it not been for this war: now I feel every day more and more that a man has no right to himself at all. . . ."[18] By "self-culture" Emerson had meant the right of an individual to cultivate his inner life without regard for the demands of society. Lowell, who had previously tried so hard to reconcile this ideal with an active existence, had been convinced by the war that such individualism was futile and selfish. In the fall of 1864, he promulgated his new faith in the form of advice to a close friend who had also been under the spell of Emerson. "I hope you have outgrown all foolish ambitions," he wrote, "and are now content to become a 'useful citizen'. . . . The useful citizen is a mighty unpretending hero. But we are not going to have any country very long unless such heroism is developed. . . . By jove! what I have wasted through crude and stupid theories. . . . How I do envy (or rather *admire*) the young fellows who have something to do now without theories to do it."[19] For Lowell, Emersonian self-consciousness and transcendentalist theorizing had led nowhere. The war, as an experience of doing without thinking, had suggested that an unreflective activism was the best escape from the burden of self.

A little more than a month after this letter was written, Lowell was killed in battle. The circumstances were unusually heroic, and his death made almost as great an impression as that of Shaw. Henry Lee Higginson, the recipient of Lowell's advice, treasured the letter and was fond of quoting it in later years as a kind of personal creed. As Higginson's biographer has indicated, Lowell's description of "useful citizenship" is "essential to an understanding of the controlling motive of Higginson's later life."[20] Specifically it made it easier for him to give up his musical ambitions to accept a place in the family business. The concept of "the useful citizen" helped the former Emersonian idealist to become the civic-minded State Street banker who would show his respect for the artistic life in a peculiarly institutional way by founding the Boston Symphony Orchestra.

Higginson's decision to turn his back on a solitary life of art or scholarship was a characteristic response to the military experience. Higginson's cousin, Thomas Wentworth Higginson, the militant abolitionist and genteel man of letters, recalled in his autobiography that when he left the service in 1864, "two years of army life . . . had so checked the desire for active literary pursuits . . . that I should actually have been contented not to return to them." He indicated that "the charge and government of men, as for instance in the position of agent of a large mill or railway enterprise," would have suited him better. "This mood of mind was really identical with that which led some volunteer officers to enter the regular army, and others to undertake cotton raising at the South."[21] As examples, he could have pointed to Henry Lee Higginson, who, before returning to the business world of Boston, *did* try cotton raising in the South; to Charles Francis Adams, Jr., who suspended his literary ambitions to become a railroad man; or to De Forest, who remained for several years in the army, trying to combine a literary and an active life.

This disposition to live an active and "useful" life on whatever terms American society offered was described most fully at the conclusion of De Forest's *Miss Ravenel's Conversion*. At this point in the narrative, Captain Colburne, the genteel hero, has returned from a military career which had been neither glorious nor well rewarded, in which deserved promotion had been continually blocked by "politics." Yet Colburne's mood at the end of the war is not defeatist; it is not the attitude of the aristocrat who is about to retreat from the contamination of democratic society. He accepts the view of Dr. Ravenel, the philosopher of the novel, who claims that the Northern victory is a triumph of industry and progress, which has demonstrated that the slaveholding aristocracy must "make room for something more consonant with the railroad, electric telegraph, printing-press, inductive philosophy, and practical Christianity." Dr. Ravenel's prescription for the young intellectual in the new Yankee-ized America is that he must "go to work" like everyone else; he should not try to "make his living by his pen." It is now imperative that "every university man as well as every other man should learn a profession, or a business, or a trade. Then, when he has something solid to fall back upon, he may if he chooses try what he can do as a scholar or author." Young Colburne takes this advice and decides to reopen his law office, much in the spirit of Oliver Wendell Holmes, Jr., who felt impelled after the conflict to follow the practical career of law rather than studying philosophy or writing poetry. At the end of the book, Colburne's prospects are summed up: "His responsibilities will take all the dreaminess out of him, and make him practical, industrious, able to arrive at results." He has learned "the patience of a soldier, and a soldier's fortitude under discouragement. He is a better and stronger man for having fought three years, outfacing death and suffering . . . he will succeed in the duties of life and control other men's lives, labors, opinions, successes."[22]

The young intellectuals who fought seem to have agreed that the war had rescued them from an aimless literary or scholarly existence.[23] In adopting this view, they were fulfilling an 1862 prediction of John Lothrop Motley, who had written of Oliver Wendell Holmes, Jr., that "the young poet, philosopher, artist has become a man, *robustus acri militia puer* . . . when a whole community suddenly transforms itself into an army . . . what a change must be made in the national character."[24] It was not so much a change in the national character that was signified, however, as a change in the attitude of the gentleman-intellectual toward society and the active life. He was prepared to be a "practical" man, working in an institutional setting. He was ready to make an heroic effort to find his place in the America that was coming into being. In a curious way, this experience was a reversal of what was to happen to intellectuals in the First World War. Men like De Forest, Holmes, H. L. Higginson, Charles Francis Adams, and Charles Lowell had been, in a sense, a "lost generation" at the beginning of the war. At its end, if they survived, they had a feeling that they had found themselves—that they had become a generation that was committed to working in useful ways in a dynamic, activist society with little place for the purely intellectual or artistic existence.

What was occurring was the transformation of the ideal of the "strenuous life"—which had previously meant a retreat into the wilderness—into a social ideal. Rather than following the path of Francis Parkman and Theodore Winthrop and seeking adventures outside the confines of civilization, it was now deemed more suitable to do one's duty in a strenuous way within society. Anything that would stand in the way of useful activity, such as radical speculation on the value of institutions, was put beyond the pale. The military experience, which had taught the young patrician intellectuals to take pride in a life of service and to emphasize professional skills and professional objectives, had destroyed whatever respect they might have had for anti-institutional thinking, radical individualism, or transcendental hopes of self-fulfillment.

II

While young men in the army were rebelling in their various ways against what Emerson had come to represent, Emerson was adjusting his own views. As early as August 1861, Emerson acknowledged that the national situation was threatening his ideal of the detached scholar-philosopher. "The war," he wrote, ". . . has assumed such huge proportions that it threatens to engulf us all—no preoccupation can exclude it, & no hermitage hide us. . . ." He was not unhappy, however, about this violation of the privacy that he had once prized, and he expressed his hope "that 'scholar' & 'hermit' will no longer be exempts, neither by the country's permission nor their own, from the public duty."[25]

Emerson was pushed toward valuing activity over contemplation by something in him that responded to calls for manly exertion of the kind being made by Parkman, and his journal of the years 1861 to 1865 is filled with praise of war in general as an expression of vitality and energy. As might be expected, however, he took a less aristocratic line than Parkman. As he indicated in 1862, he had lost his respect for the abolitionists "who give their money or give their voices for liberty from long habit and the feminine predominance of sentiment," but he had a new regard for "the rough Democrat who hates Garrison, but detests these Southern traitors."[26] Statements of this kind, which placed the unreflective man of energy over the man of thought or sentiment, had occasionally cropped up in Emerson's earlier works; and we have noted his ambivalence on the question of the relative merit of the scholar and practical man of affairs. Now, however, there is no ambivalence; the practical man has won out completely.

Even more startling is Emerson's new commitment to "government" and "civilization" as ideals which take precedence over the interests of "the private man." In his "American Scholar" address of 1837, Emerson had said of men who aspire to political

office: "Wake them and they shall quit the false good and leap
to the true, and leave governments to clerks and desks."[27] In his
1862 address on "American Civilization," Emerson affirmed
almost the exact contrary: "Government must not be a parish
clerk, a justice of the peace. It has, of necessity, in any crisis of
the state, the absolute powers of a dictator."[28] In April of the
same year, he wrote an article for the *Atlantic* on the same subject
and defended "civilization" as "the result of highly complex
organization," endorsing the conventional Northern view of the
war as a struggle between Yankee "civilization" and Southern
"barbarism."[29]

In the process of praising "government" and "civilization" as
abstract ideals, Emerson's characteristic emphasis on individualism
and anarchism disappeared. He now exulted in the fact that
"war organizes" and "forces individuals and states to combine
and act with larger views."[30] Institutions were no longer regarded
as enemies or obstacles to human perfection; indeed, he saw the
defense of institutions as the essence of the Northern cause. As
one of Emerson's biographers has put it, the effect of the war
on his thought "was remarkable; the anti-social and anarchistic
sentiments which were to be plentifully found in his writing before this time cease; and in their place there is a powerful grasp
of the social unities embodied in the state as a main source of the
blessings of civilization."[31] This statement may require modification in the light of Stephen E. Whicher's discovery that the sense
of a social and historical whole which transcends the individual
was implicit in Emerson's later prewar thought and was gradually
undermining his "radical egoism" of the 1830s.[32] But it remains
true that this organic sense had not reached the level of political
and social doctrine before 1861. Emerson's political statements
on the eve of the conflict were still extremely anarchistic and
individualistic. It took the war itself to bring out fully the anti-
individualistic tendency of his later thought and give it a relation
to questions of public policy. A vague sense of limitation was
replaced by a positive commitment to a social order shaped by
history and tradition. Emerson in effect now embraced the "doctrine of institutions" which Bellows had offered as an alternative
to Emersonianism in 1859.

Having altered his basic social philosophy, Emerson could be sympathetic to the spirit of his young friends and former disciples in the army. As he wrote of the military experience of the younger generation in 1863: "What a teacher! What a field! What results! . . . how grave a searching this ordeal is. How it has taught courage!" He thought of the "youth, sensible, tender, from school, college, counting room, with no experience beyond football game, or school yard quarrel, now to leap on a battery, or a rank of bayonets. He says . . . I can well die,—oh, yes,— but I cannot afford to misbehave."[33] Despite the exuberance characteristic of a civilian observing the war from afar, these reflections, with their emphasis on a code of conduct, show a sense of the war surprisingly close to that of Oliver Wendell Holmes, Jr.

Emerson's response to the mood of the younger generation went even further. As he indicated in his journal of 1864, he had even come to understand their ideal of military professionalism: "Captain O. W. Holmes tells me that the Army of the Potomac is acquiring a professional feeling, and that they have neither panics nor excitements, but more self-reliance."[34] The ideal of "self-reliance" which had originally meant nonconformity could now suggest the steady, obedient professional soldier.

Emerson's growing respect for the military took a practical form in 1863 when he accepted an appointment as an official visitor to West Point. For Moncure Conway, formerly one of Emerson's most devoted followers, this was the ultimate disillusionment. Emerson had not only surrendered to institutions but had apparently become a militarist.[35] On his first visit to the military academy, Emerson found entirely to his liking the emphasis on discipline and order. He saw in professional military training the possible basis of a "true aristocracy or 'the power of the Best,'—best scholars, best soldiers, best engineers, best commanders, best men."[36]

Acceptance of the West Point appointment was only one of many indications that a growing belief in the value of institutions was leading the former hermit to give up his solitary life. Emerson, who had always shunned social commitments and public activity, even to the point of avoiding town affairs in the village of Concord, became during the war an influential and active citizen. He used political influence to get his friends government jobs or army commissions, and he became chairman of the Concord School Committee. In 1863, he joined the Union League Club of Boston and the following year was elected a fellow of the American Academy of Arts and Sciences.[37] He became in short the very model of the "useful citizen" as described by Charles Russell Lowell and John W. De Forest.

The most surprising and significant evidence of Emerson's commitment to institutions was his growing belief in the need for a literary establishment, which led him in the closing months of the war to endorse a proposal for a National Academy of Literature and Art. His reasons for advocating such an institution suggested a meaning of "culture" which was far from his former ideal of "self-culture"—an experience of the soul which was impeded rather than helped by tradition, form, and organization. In December 1864, Emerson wrote to Charles Sumner, who was sponsoring the Senate bill, to report his discussions of the idea with James Russell Lowell and Oliver Wendell Holmes, Sr.: "We agreed on the general objects of such a society; as for the conservation of the English language; a constituted jury to which questions of taste & fitness in literature might be carried; a jury to sit upon abnormal anomalous pretensions to genius, such as puzzle the public mind now and then. Custodians of sense & elegance—these colleagues are to be,—in literature."[38]

The poet and philosopher who had once been the great champion of unbridled individualism and originality in the arts—even more than elsewhere—now believed in submitting "abnormal and anomalous pretensions to genius" to a committee of elders who would set standards of taste. This willingness to shackle the "American genius" of Emerson's early essays was accompanied by the sense that formalism and an emphasis on "organizations" were suitable responses to the historical conditions and opportunities resulting from the war. "What recommended to us a cordial sympathy with the proposition," he wrote, "was the belief shared by us and we believe the community, that, we are at an important point of national history, & one from which very great expansion of thought & moral & political activity in all kinds is likely to follow; & that organizations hitherto sterile may easily hereafter come to be of greater scope & utility."[39]

Emerson thus seemed to accept the fact that many of his old ideals were without application in the new America foreshadowed by the war experience. Authority and discipline, he suggested, were as necessary in the arts as in the army and the government. If the Northern thought of the Civil War represented, in a sense, a repudiation of Emerson, it was the old Emerson of the 1830s and 1840s. The new Emerson, like the Yankee lad he described in "Self-Reliance," fell on his feet like a cat and ended in harmony with the intellectuals who denied his individualistic, anti-institutional philosophy. The change in American thinking which occurred during the Civil War was perfectly summed up by the changing views of Emerson himself.

PART III

The Legacy

12

The Twilight of Humanitarianism

MOST OF THE HOPES FOR THE REFORMATION OF AMERICAN society by the discipline of war proved to be illusory. Instead of purging the nation once and for all of self-seeking, materialism, and corruption, the war opened the floodgates for the greatest tide of personal and political selfishness the nation had ever seen. The Gilded Age was equally remote from the utopian and the conservative-nationalist views of the ideal America. Emerson, who was one of the first to realize this, commented in his journal of November 1865 that nothing important had really changed: "The energy of the nation seems to have expended itself in the war, and every interest is found as sectional and timorous as before."[1] This was the first of many similar statements by the committed writers and publicists of the war years, who registered growing disappointment with the turn of the events that seemed to isolate them more than ever from the main currents of American life. As the Republican Party of the Grant era ceased to reward intellectuals with offices and recognition, and as the party's narrow concerns and corrupt methods became apparent, the intellectuals began to drift into their characteristic late nineteenth century position as "independents" or "mugwumps."

While it failed to transform politics and society in the anticipated manner, the war did bring significant adjustments in ideology and social thought. By accelerating some tendencies and awakening others, it promoted a sudden and dramatic change in the intellectual landscape.

As early as 1865, there were thinkers who understood that such an intellectual revolution had taken place. As Francis Lieber put it: "The heat of a civil war of such magnitude would alone be sufficient to ripen thoughts and characteristics which may have been in a state of incipiency before; a contest so comprehensive and so prolonged makes people abandon many things, to which they had clung by mere tradition without feeling their sharp reality. . . ."[2] Lieber saw this change primarily in terms of a greater commitment to a strong federal government and to the imperatives of nationalism. A like view of the effects of the war was expounded by Samuel Fowler in the *North American Review* of October 1865. "The Civil War which has changed the current of our ideas, and crowded into a few years the emotions of a lifetime," Fowler wrote, "has in measure given to the preceding period of our history the character of a remote state of political existence." Fowler described the way in which the war, a triumph of nationalism and a demonstration of "the universal tendency to combination," had provided the *coup de grâce* for the Jeffersonian philosophy of government with its emphasis on decentralization and the protection of local and individual liberties.[3]

The new respect for nationalism and the positive state which was engendered by the war is reflected not only in the theoretical writings of 1865, but also in two of the most significant poetic efforts of that year—the "Commemoration Ode" of James Russell Lowell and the *Battle Pieces* of Herman Melville. Lowell, in his celebrated "Ode," delivered at the Harvard Commemoration of July 21, 1865, brought together several strains of New England thinking about the war. In conformity with the new activism, he rejoiced that young scholars had been drawn from their vain search for truth "amid the dust of books" to learn about truth by fighting for it. The martial valor of these former scholars, he proclaimed proudly, had disproved the belief of Southern "Cavaliers" in the plebeian origins of Yankee "Roundheads" and demonstrated once again that "the best blood" is that which

"hath the most iron in it." Throughout the poem, the nationalistic meaning of the war is emphasized. If there is any sense
of the conflict as an antislavery crusade, it is covered by a few
vague references to "freedom." In the famous section on Lincoln,
the former abolitionist makes no mention of Lincoln's role as an
emancipator; he is described simply as a great patriot. For Lowell,
the most valuable effect of the war was that it increased the power
and confidence of the nation and certified "to earth a new imperial
race."[4]

The poems in Melville's *Battle Pieces,* most of which were
written in 1865 after the fall of Richmond, also make little of
antislavery humanitarianism as an element in the conflict. In
"America," Melville described the country as facing the future at
the end of the war with "law on her brow and empire in her
eyes."[5] The struggle for "law" and "empire" is the central theme
of the entire collection (in several of the poems, it is simply
"law" for which the North is fighting). Unlike Lowell, therefore,
Melville did not invoke "freedom" even as a subsidiary aim, but
preferred to view the conflict exclusively as a triumph of authority
and national ambition. Reflected in these nationalistic poems, with
their strange staccato toughness, was the fact that the Melville of
1865 was a disillusioned democrat, who had seen through what
he considered the absurd pretensions of American democracy. He
had come to agree with men like Bellows and Bushnell that the
principal need of society is the maintenance of order, an end best
accomplished by the combined forces of law and religion.[6] Melville's distrust of the democratic masses was buttressed by his
belief in a form of original sin. This came out strongly in his
poem on the New York draft riots, which describes the incident as
"corroborating Calvin's Creed." Recalling the suppression of the
disorder by federal troops, Melville charged that the entire affair
was a "grimy slur on the Republic's faith implied,"

> Which holds that man is naturally good.
> And more—is Nature's Roman, never to be scourged.[7]

It was not merely the draft riots, however, which demonstrated
to Melville the fatuity of some old American beliefs. The Northern victory itself implied that the nation must outgrow its original

ideology, a prospect which Melville noted without misgivings, because he himself had rejected what he believed to have been the theory of human nature which had inspired the founding fathers. He summed up his views in a poem about prophecies which might have been made at the beginning of the war:

> Power unanointed may come—
> Dominion (unsought by the free)
> And the Iron Dome,
> Stronger for stress and strain,
> Fling her huge shadow athwart the main;
> But the Founders' dream shall flee.
> Age after age shall be
> As age after age had been,
> (From man's changeless heart their way they win).[8]

Melville was suggesting that the war would bring power and responsibilities which could not be exercised in accordance with the "founders' dream" of individual freedom and human perfectibility. America's new imperial role would require a general acceptance of the conservative doctrine that the passions of the masses must be held in check by the strong hand of authority.

It was left to Orestes Brownson, however, to make the most complete analysis of what the war had done to "the founders' dream." Brownson argued in his *American Republic* of 1866 that the war had permanently discredited the ideology of the Declaration of Independence, and its latter-day apostles, the abolitionists. Before the rebellion, he noted once again, the philosophy of "government by consent" had led "nearly every American" to assert " 'the sacred right of insurrection' or revolution" and to sympathize with "insurrectionists, rebels, and revolutionists, wherever they made their appearance." In such a situation, "loyalty was held to be the correlative of royalty, treason was regarded as virtue, and traitors were honored, feasted, and eulogized as patriots, ardent lovers of liberty, and champions of the people." He now felt, however, that "the fearful struggle of the nation against a rebellion which threatened its very existence may have changed this."[9] Americans, in the course of putting down a popular uprising in their own country, had perhaps learned by painful experience that sovereignty must be defined and acknowledged, so that governments can govern and citizens obey. It was now merely a question of "dissipating the mists that still linger, of brushing away these wild theories and fancies"—the "floating mists of [the nation's] earlier morning."[10]

There was evidence in the postwar years that the "mists" did dissipate to some extent. One of the first signs was an article in the *Nation* of July 17, 1865. This "journal of liberal opinion" took Americans to task for their "holy rage" at the oppression of foreign nationalities. Excusing the Russian massacres in Poland, the magazine pointed out that Russia's autocratic "institutions are as legitimate an expression of the national thought and feelings as our institutions are of ours, and just as suitable to her stage of culture."[11] This indifference to foreign tyrannies became widespread. In 1870, when the French took to the barricades again, overthrowing the Second Empire and setting up a new republic, the oratory and demonstrations which had greeted the earlier revolutions were noticeably absent from the American scene.[12] One of the many factors behind this decline of sympathy for foreign revolutions was the tradition of wartime Unionism with its denial of the unconditional right of a people to choose its own government. The Civil War, by making the very concept of "revolution" or "rebellion" anathema to many Northerners, had widened the gulf that separated nineteenth century Americans from their revolutionary heritage.

Another important argument of Brownson's *American Republic* was that the war represented a repudiation of the abolitionists, who, like the secessionists, had been legatees of the outmoded theories of the Enlightenment. Brownson first attacked the abolitionists for their belief in "humanitarian" or "socialistic democracy." To this concept of an ideal egalitarian and democratic society, he opposed his own theory of "territorial democracy," a formally republican system based on particular historical facts and national traditions, not on universal principles applicable to all humanity. He even claimed that the true mission of the American republic "is not so much the realization of liberty as the realization of the true idea of the state." Recognizing that the "humanitarian" democrats had claimed a victory when the slaves had been emancipated, Brownson pointed out "that slavery had been abolished, not for humanitarian or socialistic reasons, but solely for reasons of state, in order to save the territorial democracy." The war was a triumph for conservative nationalism, not for the utopian view of American society for which some abolitionists thought they were fighting—"as if it had been socialism, not patriotism, that fired the hearts and nerved the arms of the brave men led by McClellan, Grant and Sherman." Not content with showing that the war was no abolitionist crusade, Brownson went on to characterize it as a clear defeat for the abolitionists and their social theories. Those, he wrote, who have "sought to dissolve patriotism into a watery sentimentality called philanthropy" have "been crushingly defeated." By calling forth the masculine emotions of patriotism and love of glory, the war had weakened the feminine or humanitarian sentiments which the antislavery movement had tried to drum up. To Brownson's mind, the abolitionists may have gained some temporary prestige, but the long-run effect of the war experience would be to weaken the national impulse toward humanitarian reform and decrease the prospects of radical democracy.[13]

Brownson probably overstated his case. Few New Englanders would admit that the war represented a defeat for the abolitionists. Yet it was apparent in the years that followed that the drive for radical reform had lost momentum. The fact was that the nation had turned a corner; the triumph of Unionism and nationalism had led to assumptions which obviated the anti-institutional philosophy that had been the basis of abolitionism. It had turned the genuine radicalism of the prewar period into an obvious anachronism.

The fate of the radical of the Garrisonian type is vividly illustrated in the writings of Lysander Spooner, a prewar extremist who refused to modify his views. Spooner, who is remembered primarily as an advocate of theoretical anarchism, had at one time been of some influence in the antislavery movement. In the 1840s, he had been known as a moderate, the author of an important pamphlet designed to prove that slavery was unconstitutional; but by the 1850s, he had jettisoned his legal arguments and become an extreme radical, a thoroughgoing revolutionary. In 1858 he had tried to interest Wendell Phillips in a circular calling for a slave uprising in the South.[14] Despite this commitment to anti-slavery violence, however, Spooner had found the Civil War an unacceptable way to free the slaves. In a series of pamphlets which started to appear in 1867, he described the war as a defeat for men like himself. The North, he argued, had fought for the principle that "men may rightfully be compelled to submit to, and support a government they do not want; and that resistance, on their part, makes them traitors and criminals." The result was that "chattel slavery" had been replaced by "political slavery." Before the war the government had been "in theory at least" based on popular consent. "But nothing of that kind can be said now, if the principle on which the war was carried on by the North is irrevocably established."[15] As for the argument that emancipation had changed the nature of the war, Spooner pointed to the well-established fact that slavery had been abolished "not from any love of liberty in general—not as an act of justice to the black himself, but only 'as a war measure'."[16] Spooner may have been something of a crank, but he was also an authentic American radical of the prewar era. He shared his "no government" notions with men like Garrison and Thoreau. He rightly sensed in the late 1860s that history had passed him by. The war had made it less likely than ever that his ideas would prevail.

II

Spooner and other ante-bellum agitators had assumed that humanitarian radicalism is indissolubly linked to anarchism or the rejection of all constituted authority. But it is possible, especially in a democracy, to believe in strong government as an expression of the popular will and an instrument of egalitarian reform. For Northern humanitarians of 1865, the great immediate necessity was guaranteeing equal rights to Southern Negroes, and this seemed to require vigorous federal action. Such reliance on government for the protection of the rights of the freedmen could be reconciled with the humanitarian impulse only by re-evaluating the role of the state and abandoning all vestiges of doctrinaire anti-institutionalism.

This concept of a popular will working through a strong

government might have been suggested by Lincoln's presidential addresses with their defense of extraordinary measures for the preservation of "government of the people, by the people, and for the people." Such a doctrine was also implied in the efforts of Radical Republicans in Congress to follow up emancipation with a drastic program for transforming the South into an egalitarian society, and even before the end of the war, some conservatives had begun to fear that Radical Republicanism would develop a thoroughgoing philosophy of democratic centralization. Brownson, for one, was beset in 1864 by fears of an impending "Jacobin democracy." In *The American Republic* he sought to avert such a catastrophe by winning adherence to his theory of "territorial democracy." The war, he believed, had discredited not only the belief that any substantial portion of a people has a God-given right to revolution, but also the theory of state sovereignty and the constitutional right of secession. But there was still one dangerous theory in the air—the view that a national majority had an almost unlimited right to make use of the federal government for its own purposes. To nip in the bud any thoughts of this kind Brownson outlined a constitutional theory, reminiscent of Lieber's "institutional liberty," which vested sovereignty neither in the individual states nor in the people taken as simple population, but in the "organic" or "territorial" people—the people as organized politically and socially in corporate bodies. Since the corporate entities he had in mind were the states, it might appear that he was back on the road to state sovereignty. But for Brownson it was the states acting *together* which had sovereignty over the mass of the people or the national majority, not the states acting separately. With such a theory as this, conservatives could resist any federal efforts to implement radical social reform. "State sovereignty" had gone down to defeat in the Civil War, but "states' rights" in some form might still be useful. An escape hatch was provided for conservative nationalists who feared that the agents of "humanitarian" or "socialistic democracy" might take advantage of the nation's new attitude toward power and authority.[17]

According to a standard view of the Radical Republicans, Brownson's fears were justified. The common description of the

Radicals as "Jacobins" suggests that they had a belief in the unlimited power of the central government to legislate the general
will and, what was more, a sense of themselves as uniquely
embodying and transmitting that will. There is some basis for this
theory. The proposals of men like Thaddeus Stevens and Wendell
Phillips for the confiscation of Southern estates and division of
the land among the freedmen undeniably defied the cherished
rights of property in the name of a national democracy. By 1867,
according to a recent and sympathetic biographer of Phillips, "he
and a little band of abolitionists he represented, like Robespierre
and the Jacobins, believed that their will was the General Will"
and looked for the federal government to establish and maintain
an equal political and social position for the Negro in the South,
by as much force as proved necessary.[18] In reality, however,
Stevens and Phillips offered no consistent and fully developed
theory of state action and national planning in 1867. They even
lacked a carefully thought-out and workable plan for the social
and economic transformation of the South.[19] They were groping
for something like the modern concept of the welfare state—
foreshadowed as it was by pragmatic programs of the time like
the Freedman's Bureau—but their intense hatred of the white
South prevented a rational approach. In the end, they settled for
the panacea of moderate Republicans—the purely political solution of giving the Negro the vote, denying it to certain classes
of whites, and then leaving the freedman to fight his own battles,
protected only by a sporadic and inconsistent use of federal troops.
As a result, "Radical Reconstruction," as it finally emerged from
the Congressional caldron, was a set of half-measures, which
did not represent any triumph for the theory of centralized democracy that Brownson feared as an outgrowth of the war. It was a
triumph for the more cautious "radicals" like Carl Schurz, who
had written in the *Atlantic* of March 1867 that reconstruction
must be based on local self-government in the South rather than
on long-term federal control. Dangerous "centralization" was to
be avoided by relying on Negro suffrage for the protection of
Negro rights.[20] Not faced was the problem of how a despised,
impoverished, and largely illiterate minority was to maintain its

rights in the face of a determined majority in full possession of economic and social power. The fiasco of Radical Reconstruction had begun.

The shortsightedness of the late 1860s was due to many factors. Republican opportunism was important: There was a desire to get the Southern states readmitted to the Union under Republican control in time to deliver critical votes in 1868 and thereafter. For intellectuals, however, there was a "scientific" reason for avoiding national planning. The new "Darwinist" view of social processes warned against a paternalistic approach to the Negro problem. Albion Tourgée, the novelist and "carpetbagger," who was a friend of the Negro and a radical critic of Radical Reconstruction, suggested in 1879 that evolutionary thinking may have had some impact on Northern theories of Reconstruction. Looking back on the plan that was put into effect a decade earlier, Tourgée charged that the federal government had left the contending parties in the South "like cocks in a pit, to fight out the question of predominance without the possibility of national interference." This decision, he felt, amounted to a triumph of the philosophy of "root-hog-or-die."[21] But in using this phrase, which was to become a Social Darwinist slogan, Tourgée was referring to a climate of opinion and not to a coherent system of thought. Social Darwinism, as a fully articulated doctrine, had not really taken hold in America by 1868: Herbert Spencer, the English exponent of the theory, had been published in the United States, but William Graham Sumner, the great American Social Darwinist, had not yet begun to write. Darwin himself was known to an intellectual elite but had made no great impression on the general public. Yet Social Darwinism, if not fully formulated or accepted as a popular creed, was nevertheless in the air, and some applied it explicitly to Reconstruction and the Negro. In 1869, for example, Georges Clemenceau, a visitor from France and its future Premier, described the Reconstruction legislation as an application of Darwinism. Now that certain rights for "the blacks" have been written into the constitution, he wrote, the rest is up to them. "They must gird up their loins and struggle for their existence, in Darwin's phrase, for their physical as well as their moral existence.

In a word, they must become men." He was not at all certain they would succeed: "In this ruthless struggle for existence carried on by human society, those who are weaker physically, intellectually, or morally must in the end yield to the stronger. . . . If, then, the black man cannot successfully compete with the white man, he is fated to be the victim of that natural selection which is constantly operating under our eyes in spite of everything, and he must eventually go under, in the more or less distant future."[22] Clemenceau gave the black man a fighting chance. More pessimistic was John W. De Forest, who was on duty in South Carolina as a Freedman's Bureau officer from 1866 to 1868. Convinced that "the Negro as he is, no matter how educated, is not the mental equal of the European," he saw the "low down Negro" as passing "into sure and deserved oblivion." The superior Negro, however, "will struggle longer with the law of natural selection; and he may eventually hold a portion of this continent against the vigorous and terrible Caucasian race; that portion being probably those lowlands where the white can not or will not labor."[23]

If the set of attitudes summed up in the phrase "Social Darwinism" did not really rule the thoughts of the architects of Reconstruction, it can hardly be denied that it contributed to the later Northern decision to permit the fall of the Southern radical governments and the return to the "natural condition" of white supremacy. By 1883, white rule was firmly re-established in Dixie, and William Graham Sumner spoke for the "enlightened" opinion of the North when he asserted that freedom meant greater personal hardship for the Negro than slavery, but that such suffering was the price of evolution. Outside interference with the Negro's struggle for existence was incompatible with the "modern free system of industry."[24]

The failure of the nation to plan for Negro freedom and construct the necessary bridge from slavery to citizenship suggests that the ideal of a strong central government encouraged by the war had a limited application. It was acceptable to use federal power to put down a rebellion, and proper to encourage economic developments with land grants to railroads and a protective tariff for industry, but the line was drawn when the government was called upon to act in the field of social welfare and humanitarian reform. In this area, the principles of Social Darwinism and *laissez faire* ruled supreme.

The intellectuals of the Liberal Republican or "mugwump" type were more consistent than the national policy makers. They opposed government aid for business as well as government assistance for the poor or newly emancipated. In the early 1870s, as they turned away from the ideal of a strong government that had been encouraged by the war and the commitment to a defense of Negro rights that had been characteristic of the beginning of Reconstruction, they found a compelling platform—the crusade against political corruption. Their unwillingness to use the federal government as an instrument of humanitarian reform was made adamant by the sordid spectacle of political jobbery represented by the Grant administration, and their hopes for Negro equality were blasted for good by the corruption of the Grant-supported Reconstruction governments in the South.

While idealists like Carl Schurz, Charles Sumner, Charles Francis Adams, and Horace Greeley were deserting the Republican Party and the Reconstruction program to set up the abortive Liberal Republican movement of 1872, the cause of the Southern Negro was taken up and further discredited by political opportunists of the regular party organization. The issues of the war were kept alive in the seventies and eighties as a Republican campaign technique—a way of recalling the "disloyalty" of the Democrats by "waving the bloody shirt."[25] In the character of Senator Dilworthy in *The Gilded Age*, Mark Twain has provided an unforgettable portrait of the Republican politician making unscrupulous use of the "Negro question" for his own ends. Robert G. Ingersoll, although apparently a sincere believer in Negro equality, became the most eloquent of the "bloody shirt" orators and even prostituted his vivid sense of the horrors of war by turning it into the basis of a partisan attack on the Democrats. In the famous "vision of war" passage from his Indianapolis speech of 1876, he repeated his 1862 observations about the intolerable nature of war, but in a way that put all the blame for the maimed bodies and bereaved wives and mothers squarely on the head of the Democratic Party.[26]

The Reconstruction era was a perplexing time for intellectuals who had been antislavery militants before and during the war. Unable to support the sordid Grant administration and filled with doubts about the form that Radical Reconstruction was taking in the South, they had little to offer in the way of insight or inspiration. Many, especially those with literary ambitions, ignored the whole problem and turned to other things. William Dean Howells, who had once been a fervent abolitionist, intimated as editor of the *Atlantic Monthly* in 1869 that he was tired of the Negro question. In a review of Thomas Wentworth Higginson's *Army Life in a Black Regiment,* Howells wrote that "we should . . . not venture to commend Colonel Higginson's book if it were a celebration of the negro in any of his familiar aspects of martyr or hero, or his present 'transition state' of bore, however we might praise it as excellent and charming literature."[27] Howells' diminishing interest in the Negro, which reflected the disenchantment of the New England literary community in general, was further manifested in subsequent issues of the *Atlantic.* This journal, which had been an important antislavery forum, devoted less and less space to public issues and became almost exclusively a literary organ. Even Colonel Higginson, guilty as he was of the untimely publication of a book about the Negro in 1869, took surprisingly little interest in the problems of Reconstruction after 1868. Finding that his time was taken up by his new role as a genteel man of letters, he made no significant contribution to the discussion of events in the South until 1878, when he made a tour of South Carolina to inquire into the condition of the freedmen under "conservative" rule. Higginson found all going well enough for the Negro, despite the fact that he was now at the mercy of the Southern whites. His final answer to the great problem to which he had devoted many years as an abolitionist and commander of Negro troops was "local self-government" for the Southern states, trusting to the benevolence of Southern gentlemen like Governor Wade Hampton to protect the Negro, or, in the event matters got out of hand, to the ability of the Negro to emigrate from areas where his life was intolerable.[28]

Among those who had been imbued with the millennialist spirit of New England abolitionism, however, there were at least two who steadfastly refused to forget the Negro or deliver him up to his former masters. Wendell Phillips and one of his greatest admirers, the Congregational minister Jesse H. Jones, persisted in their agitation for Negro rights. For Phillips, the acid test came in 1875 when he was forced to choose between the corrupt Reconstruction governments of the South and the restoration of white rule. In a meeting in Faneuil Hall, which had been called to protest the sending of troops to Louisiana to prop up a tottering radical regime, Phillips gained the floor and amid hissing and disorder defended the government's action and berated the audience for forgetting the Negro and his predicament. This extremely unpopular speech, which was repudiated by many of Phillips' old supporters, was an inspiration to the Reverend Jesse H. Jones, who published it after the death of Phillips under the title *His Last Battle and One of his Greatest Victories*.[29]

Defense of Grant's Reconstruction policy did not mean, however, that men like Phillips and Jones were satisfied with the Republican Party of the 1870s. In 1871, Jones published a curious book entitled *The Kingdom of Heaven* which condemned the Republicans and proposed a new political party as the vehicle of radical reform. What Jones was seeking was a new outlet for his long-standing Christian millennialism. Before the war, he had come under the influence of Charles Grandison Finney and had seen in revivalism the signs of the approaching millennium. When the war had broken out, Jones had volunteered as a chaplain, but his abolitionist zeal, his belief that this was a "holy war," had soon led him to find a more active role as a captain of infantry. As a result of the Emancipation Proclamation and the rise of Radical Republicanism, Jones' hopes for the American millennium had been invested for a time in the Republican Party; in his tract of 1871, he could still write that, on the slavery issue, the Republican Party had been "wholly for Jesus Christ and Humanity." But he now noted sadly that "the Republican Party is growing steadily more and more corrupt." The time had come to form "A NEW POLITICAL PARTY, TO BE CALLED JESUS CHRIST'S PARTY." This new party would work for absolute political and social equality—an end to all distinctions based on race, sex, or class. It could even prepare the way for economic equality. His millennial consummation would be a return to primitive Christian practice of "UNIVERSAL COMMUNISM."[30]

Jones' extravagance and the fact that his book was privately printed give him the appearance of an isolated eccentric, a man raving to himself. Yet his speculations did have a kind of fruition. In 1872, he was instrumental in founding the Christian Labor Union, the first Christian Socialist organization of the postwar period. He lived on to contribute to the Christian Socialism of the 1890s, a living link between Civil War millennialism and the Social Gospel movement.[31] His interest as a transitional figure in the history of American radicalism lies in his rejection of the Christian perfectionist concept of "moral reform" which had held sway before the war. Jones was perfectly willing to use the state as an instrument of social revolution, and his temporary faith in the Republican Party had taught him the value of organized political activity. *The Kingdom of Heaven* includes elaborate plans for organizing "The Party of Jesus Christ" on a local level. Unlike the ante-bellum "come-outers," he saw the value of working within the church and using it as a pressure group for egalitarian causes. In a sense, he was both the last of the ante-bellum Christian perfectionists and one of the first "institutional" radicals of the new "age of reform."

For all this, however, there is a mystical enthusiasm, a half-mad prophetic quality, about the writings of Jones that makes him inappropriate as the prototype of the modern reformer. Wendell Phillips moved in the same direction as Jones but with a more precise and plausible definition of purpose. Phillips had also flirted with Republican politics and had expected great things from the radical leadership of the late 1860s. In 1870, however, when he ran for governor of Massachusetts, it was not as a Radical Republican. His decision to make his first race for political office as the candidate for the Labor Reform Party revealed the new outlet for his humanitarian energies. As a crusader for the rights of labor, Phillips was fully convinced of the value of political action. He advocated legislation to improve the conditions of labor and control the activities of corporations. He emerged as an early advocate of what Sydney Fine has called the theory of "the General Welfare State" which developed in opposition to the dominant *laissez faire* philosophy in the 1880s and 1890s.[32] Perhaps the obvious necessity of strong government to protect the Negroes in the South had taught Phillips that the cooperation of the state was necessary to the cause of social reform in general. In any case, his old faith in "moral reform" had been shattered, and he confronted economic and social problems of the new age with the kind of programs that future generations would consider appropriate.

The ideas of Phillips and Jones, however, were rare and exotic growths in the Social Darwinist jungle of the 1870s. Consequently their efforts were little noticed or appreciated. Jones' Christian Labor Union attracted almost no support and went out of existence in 1878.[33] Phillips polled only 12 per cent of the votes in 1870, and the Labor Reform movement soon collapsed. Phillips interested himself in other matters, such as the greenback movement and the plight of the Chinese in California, besides retaining his unflagging concern for the Southern Negro. But by the time of his Phi Beta Kappa Oration at Harvard in 1881, in which he made a blanket defense of radicals, agitators, and "nihilists," he was regarded primarily as an oddity.[34] The isolation of Phillips, the growing belief that he was a voice from the past, proved that Brownson was basically right in contending that the war had thwarted the drive for "humanitarian democracy."

13

Science and the New Intellectuals

ALTHOUGH THE NATION TURNED ITS BACK ON HUMANITARIAN reform, the war brought no clear victory for the ultraconservative ideology of Bellows, Brownson, and Bushnell. Acceptance of their "divine right" theories required a return to the social ideals of an age of established churches and acknowledged clerical authority, and the necessary conditions for such a theocratic order were no more present in American society of 1865 than before. Contributing to the irresistible progress of secularism was the fact that the prestige of traditional religion was already beginning to decline as a result of the impact of new scientific ideas, principally Darwinism. The younger intellectual figures who were coming into prominence were likely to have little respect for ecclesiastical pretensions.

A spokesman for those who believed that the new age was going to be an age of science and not of faith was John W. Draper, scientist and historian, who is remembered primarily as the American thinker who did most to define "the conflict of science and religion." Vitally interested in the meaning of the Civil War, Draper managed to describe the conflict in a way that combined the conservative emphasis on elitism and authoritarian principles with the new reverence for science and scientists. In his *Thoughts on the Future Civil Policy of America,* published in 1865, Draper argued that "War, civil war . . . is not without its uses. In no other school . . . can society learn subordination; in no other can it be made to appreciate order. It may be true, as has been affirmed, that men secretly love to obey those whom they feel to be their superiors intellectually. In military life they learn to practice that obedience openly."[1] Although this statement could almost have been made by a Christian conservative like Brownson or Bushnell, its context reveals that Draper had a kind of authority in mind which would hardly have been acceptable to supporters of clericalism. Draper, like the conservatives, admitted to a respect for the medieval church; he believed that "all political institutions . . . should tend to the improvement and organization of National Intellect," and that the church in earlier times had served the political function of opening influential careers to the talented and intelligent. But, in the manner of Comte or Saint-Simon, who had also believed in the inevitability of a spiritual or intellectual elite, Draper maintained that the role once performed by the clergy must now be assumed by the new race of scientists and technicians.[2]

Draper fitted the Civil War into his theory of social evolution in a three-volume history of the conflict which began to appear in 1867. In his view, the war had been caused by a number of interrelated factors. The North and South had begun with different motives of settlement, different climates, and other varying physical circumstances. These variations gave rise to two different civilizations—indeed "two races": the Northern way based on "individualism" and the Southern on "independence." In accordance with the irresistible natural tendency of all societies to "centralization" or "concentration," the North demanded greater strength and cohesiveness in national institutions, and the South resisted. Slavery entered the picture only as a platform on which Southern leaders could rally their section. In the end, the futile Southern resistance to centralization was the proximate cause of the war. But Draper was not entirely consistent on this point. As a patriotic Northerner, he wanted to put the South in the role of resistant to progress; but in the first volume he gave sympathetic attention to ante-bellum Southern claims that Northern society was coming apart at the seams as a result of the reign of "individualism." In the conclusion to the third volume, he proclaimed that "it was Individualism that brought on this Civil War—the individual setting up his interest in opposition to the public good." Since individualism was the Northern disease, one wonders if Draper is not implicitly blaming the North as much as the South for the resistance to "centralization" and "concentration" which was the main cause of hostilities—particularly since he had defined "centralization" as "the inevitable retreat of power from the Individual or from the Party."[3]

In any case, the lesson was clear. The war was a punishment for someone, probably both sections, for fighting against the laws of nature. It had demonstrated the scientific law that "centralization is an inevitable issue in the life of nations," or, put another way, that "all animated nature displays a progress to the domination of a central intelligence." The idea of a "central intelligence," which implies an intellectual elite, needed special emphasis, Draper thought, because "in democratic countries the political application of these doctrines is received with disfavor; in America, even with condemnation." Draper was giving a quasi-scientific explanation to the same movement away from ultrademocratic dogmas and practices that had been perceived and hailed by Brownson, Bushnell, and Stillé. But his stress was different; in seeking to substitute "the controlling influence of reason" for that of faith, Draper indicated that he was a nationalist on what he believed to be scientific and liberal rather than religious and conservative grounds. He broke with some of his Enlightenment roots, however, in his assertion that rule by the people themselves is impossible: "If the people will open their eyes, they will see that it is few who govern."[4] To Draper, the movement toward "the domination of a central intelligence" meant the rise of a new elitism based on the organized intellect of a scientific age.

II

Draper's basic beliefs were shared by several young veterans who found that the ideal of "organized intelligence" suited their own aspirations. Driven by a growing faith in science and the

war-born desire to be "useful citizens," they hastened to offer
themselves as candidates for the scientific elite. Since the postwar
era saw a rising interest in "social science," it was natural that
this should be the favored area. It was not the pursuit of social
knowledge for its own sake, however, that inspired young intellectuals who had come out of the army with high rank and a love
of action and responsibility. They sought the "laws" underlying
social, economic, or legal phenomena in the hope of finding ways
to discipline society and control events. Armed with the knowledge of how to deal "scientifically" with national problems, they
could lay claim to new positions of power and influence. By the
nature of these ambitions, the new intellectuals could have no
truck with iconoclastic individualism or anti-institutionalism. They
were committed to working with and through available institutions and sources of authority. As thinkers, they could not allow
themselves to be isolated from the workaday world, and as "reformers," they felt the need to depart drastically from the ante-
bellum reform tradition with its reliance on conscience and
emotion. Following the lead of Liberal Republicans like Whitelaw
Reid, they affirmed that the age of "sentimental politics" was
over and that the complicated economic problems facing the nation could not be solved by humanitarian zeal. As Reid put it;
". . . these are problems worthy of the best thought of our best-
trained thinkers; and in handling them a government of the people
has the right of the aid of the finest culture and highest intellectual power that the people has been able to develop."[5] These men
also subscribed to a definition of "the new reform" which was
put forth by Francis Parkman in 1878. Whereas, "conviction and
enthusiasm, with very little besides, served the purpose of the
abolition agitators," the zeal of the new reformers, according to
Parkman, "must be tempered with judgment and armed with
knowledge."[6]

Representative of the new intellectual as social scientist and
scientific reformer was General Francis A. Walker. His distinguished career as Civil War staff officer, statistician and bureau
chief in the federal government, professor of political economy
at Yale, and president of Massachusetts Institute of Technology
suggests the range of interests and institutional commitments of

the generation that came on the scene at the end of the Civil War. Walker's importance in the new university-centered intellectual milieu is suggested by the fact that he received degrees from more institutions of learning than any other American of his time.[7]

Although Walker seemed to follow in the footsteps of his father, Amasa Walker, who was also a famous economist, he was actually in rebellion against his father's world. Amasa Walker was the kind of ante-bellum optimist who had seen no contradiction between *laissez faire* economics and the active support of humanitarian causes. As a Jacksonian Democrat, a strong supporter of the peace crusade, and an early convert to Garrisonian abolitionism, he had been an archetypical product of the prewar reform milieu, and his theory of economics, like his view of politics and reform, had been abstract and doctrinaire. With other representatives of the "classical" school, he had focused not on actual conditions, but on a theoretical model.[8] His son, on the other hand, was both more empirical in his approach to economics, and more conservative and "scientific" in his concept of reform.

The younger Walker had perhaps learned to be an empiricist while on duty as a staff officer during the war. As a result of his uncanny ability to analyze the most confused battle situations, he had risen to the rank of brevet brigadier general at the age of twenty-five. He has been described as the ideal staff officer—pragmatic, methodical, and efficient in the handling of a bewildering mass of detail.[9] Four years after the war, Walker found a natural position for a man who had learned to value precise and accurate intelligence. He became chief of the Federal Bureau of Statistics and Superintendent of the United States Census. In this period of government service, however, Walker did not operate simply as a compiler of information. He was one of a coterie of "working practical reformers" striving within the government for the elimination of corrupt practices.[10] The character of the Grant administration being what it was, he faced a difficult and frustrating task. Walker, however, had a war-inspired ideal of service, not unlike that of Oliver Wendell Holmes. While dedicating a soldiers' monument in 1870, he described the duty of a soldier to obey an incompetent commander—"to go without shrinking into what you know to be not a battle but a butchery."[11] The man who had entered government service had a similar duty. He must be loyal to his superiors, however corrupt, while at the same time doing what was possible for the cause, of reform.

In 1871, however, Walker took on an additional task which exhausted his patience with the administration. Taking over as Commissioner for Indian Affairs, he attempted to clean up one of the most scandal-ridden bureaus of the federal government, as the first step in establishing an enlightened and "scientific" Indian policy. Failing to get the necessary cooperation from Grant and the Congress, he became discouraged and resigned his post in 1872 to become a professor of political economy at Yale.[12]

In his subsequent career as an economist, Walker emerged as the first important American critic of the classical or *laissez faire* school of economics which had been so well represented by his father. His greatest contribution was a refutation of "the wages fund theory" which had been used to justify subsistence wages. Yet his revision of *laissez faire* economics did not make him an advocate of sweeping welfare legislation. As a dogma, *laissez faire* lacked scientific validity, but as a practical basis of policy it was safer than state intervention in the economy.[13]

It was on another subject entirely that Walker's thought became the basis of a "reform" movement. His studies of American population as Superintendent of the Census led to an interest in the question of immigration. Feeling that the "vast masses of peasantry" which were being "decanted upon our soil" represented a threat to the Anglo-Saxon civilization in the United States, he became an early advocate of immigration restriction, and was later recognized as the philosopher of the restriction movement.[14] Here he departed most sharply from his father's optimistic mixture of liberal humanitarianism and *laissez faire*. Amasa Walker had been a notable champion of unrestricted immigration, both for the economic reason that it gave a dynamic quality to the economy, and on the political ground that American institutions were fully capable of elevating the most debased of peoples.[15] This faith in the perfectibility of all men under a democratic system was lacking in the younger Walker's generation. Disillusioned first with the Negro, they were now giving up on the immigrant. Immigration restriction was Walker's idea of social planning, and it was a kind of planning remote in spirit from that vainly advocated in the seventies by Wendell Phillips. For Phillips, planning was a new method of reaching the egalitarian goals which had been the inspiration of the abolitionist movement; for Walker, it was a way of legislating the supremacy of the Anglo-Saxon race.

Walker was not the only young brevet brigadier who turned his postwar energies to social science, public administration, and nonhumanitarian reform. Charles Francis Adams, Jr., had a similar career, and, in good Adams fashion, was highly self-conscious about seeking and finding a role. More explicitly than Walker, he thought in terms of the Comtean scientific elite that Draper had seen foreshadowed by the wartime emphasis on subordination and efficiency. In these thoughts, he was in apparent agreement with his brother Henry, who noted in his history of the Jefferson administration that one of the young republic's great disadvantages had been the absence of a "scientific class to lead the way" and give direction to technological progress. Henry, however, was a congenital spectator, and sitting out the war in England as his father's secretary, toying all the while with the possibility of going into the army, had accentuated his Hamlet-like incapacity for action.[16] Charles, on the other hand, was one of the officers to whom the war had given a restless desire for practical activity and public service. In a letter of 1869, Henry explained to Charles the difference between them: "Your ideas and mine don't agree, but they never have agreed. You like the strife of the world. I detest and despise it. You work for power. I work for my own satisfaction."[17] While Henry could write about America's historic need for an elite of scientists and technicians, Charles had the will to train himself as a scientific expert on one of the complex problems of the new age and to offer himself as a leader in his chosen field.

When he was mustered out of the service in 1865, however, Adams was, physically speaking, "a mere wreck," in no condition to undertake an active career. It was while recuperating in Europe that he came upon the philosophy of Auguste Comte, in the form of Mill's essay on the father of positivism. "My intellectual faculties had been then lying fallow for nearly four years," he recalled in his autobiography, "and I was in a most recipient condition; and that essay of Mill's revolutionized in a single morning my whole mental attitude. I emerged from the theological stage, in which I had been nurtured, and passed into the scientific."[18] This new intellectual orientation, however, did not immediately suggest a career. It was not until his return to America the following year (1866), that Adams found a field of activity in which he might exercise not only his new scientific approach but also the love of power that had been awakened by the experience of commanding a regiment: "I fixed on the railroad system as the most developing and largest field of the day, and determined to attach myself to it."[19] He quickly became an expert on railroads and in a series of books and articles attempted to describe the "scientific laws" which underlay the incredibly rapid and apparently chaotic development of railroading during the Gilded Age.[20] Not content with being a publicist, Adams lobbied successfully for the setting up of a state railroad commission and had himself appointed to it. As chairman of the Massachusetts Board of Railroad Commissioners for seven years and "the controlling mind" of the board for the full ten years of his membership, he sought to put into practice the principles he had uncovered in his empirical studies.[21]

In conformity with the intellectual fashion of the time, Adams was a Spencerian and had no real faith in legislation: In railroading, as in other areas, the evolutionary process should be allowed to take its course, unimpeded by coercive state regulation. His method for dealing with strikes and public grievances against the railroads was investigation and publicity, not rate-fixing and compulsory arbitration. Originally an advocate of competition in railroading, Adams eventually concluded that combinations or "pools" were not only inevitable but beneficial and should not be resisted by public authority. As a result of this loss of faith in governmental action, Adams resigned from the state railroad commission in 1879 to go into private life as chairman of the Board of Arbitration of the Trunk Line Railroads. In this capacity, he presided over an ill-fated attempt by the railroads themselves to bring about rational combination and self-regulation. In 1884, he embarked on his ultimate effort to control railroading from within by accepting the presidency of Union Pacific.[22]

Adams' evolutionary economics and his lack of faith in government raise the question of how he could be a Spencerian and a Comtean at the same time. If society was to be ruled by an elite of scientists and technicians, how could this be done without the state as the foundation of authority? Adams provided an answer in a lecture of 1880, entitled "Individuality in Politics." As an "independent" in politics, he attacked centralization of power in the federal government because the state of American politics made the government the inevitable haven of the spoilsman. ". . . the future of this country," he said, "is in the hands of our universities, our schools, our specialists, our scientific men, and our writers. Taken in the grand results what does Washington do but impede? As an obstacle to intelligent Progress, the National Government is an undisputed success." Real progress, then, came not from government and politicians, but from "we specialists, educators, scientific men, merchants, bankers, farmers, mechanics." Adams' scientific elite would function principally within the great network of private institutions which was developing during the Gilded Age. From positions in the new universities and great industrial enterprises, the intellectuals could give guidance to social and economic development. The government should be no more than a caretaker maintaining "order and submission to law"; while "we who manage the schools, the press, the shops, the railroads, and exchanges will take care of the rest. . . ."[23]

In his tenure as Trunk Line mediator and president of Union Pacific, Adams put his *laissez faire* Comteanism to a great test. As a specialist in railroad economics trying to control railroads without the aid of government, he confronted the American businessman, who *ought* to have been a scientific, managerial type, but unfortunately was often a short-sighted buccaneer. Adams' failure to teach businessmen to seek long-range evolutionary goals resulted in his being forced out of the presidency of Union Pacific in 1890. In a famous observation in his autobiography, he wrote of the " 'successful' men—'big' financially" with whom he had come in contact, as a "set of mere money-getters and traders."[24] If these were the kind of men who were running the country under the Adams doctrine of *laissez faire,* then his whole dream of an extragovernmental elite had turned into a sham and a mockery.

If Adams had to become a businessman to apply scientific laws to economic development, Oliver Wendell Holmes, Jr., had to become a judge to apply his science of the law. Holmes, however, took the safer path. The judge is not dependent on the approval of his associates. Neither an administrator nor a reformer, the judge encounters the complexities of social and economic life only in the form of the limited and precisely defined issues which come before him for adjudication. Yet, with all his enjoyment of a certain Olympian detachment, Holmes, like other former Union officers, could never be satisfied with an intellectual life which had no relevance to the practical affairs of ordinary men or gave no recognition to the limiting conditions of man's social environment. His attempt to find and apply an empirical jurisprudence— a definition of law which was grounded in the realities of power and history—was the natural enterprise of a man who had grown tired of the millennial expectations and abstract moralism of the war years.[25] Where he differed from Adams was in his realistic and stoical acceptance of the fact that no educated elite could really control the evolution of society. The primary function of the elite was to record changes and point out unalterable trends. Judges made the law, but only in the sense that they recognized the evolving sentiments of the majority. Men of the law, like men at war, were at the mercy of history.

Holmes' legal thought of the 1870s and 1880s contained a view of reform which was similar to that of Walker and Adams. He endorsed Spencer's theory that legislation for social welfare merely shifts burdens from one part of the population to another and contributes in no significant way to the general well-being.[26] Later, as a judge, he was to uphold humanitarian legislation not because he was a humanitarian or believed the legislation beneficial, but because the will of the community was behind it.

If Walker, Adams, and Holmes were representative of the new intellectuals, "reform" must have had a very limited meaning in this period. As a matter of fact, there was only one popular reform movement which really touched the war generation. This was civil service reform, which was acceptable because it was consistent both with a *laissez faire* view of government and with the concept of a scientific elite. As Edward Kirkland has suggested, the civil service reformers desired a government of men trained in social science, who would know enough not to meddle with the evolutionary currents which determined the nature of social and economic life.[27] If the power elite, as described by Adams, was really outside the government, it was still necessary to have an inside elite which would, paradoxically enough, act in a positive way to keep government from expanding beyond its "natural sphere" as defined by the economics and sociology of the day.

The civil service reform movement was also congenial for another reason: It suggested the ideal of military professionalism that had such a strong hold on the soldier-intellectuals. As Dorman B. Eaton, one of the civil service reformers, indicated in 1881, the Civil War army was the real prototype of the proposed civil service. In recommending the military model, Eaton described the army as "the pride of our statesmen and the dread only of our demagogues and our enemies," and hailed "the perfection of its education and its discipline, which has kept it out of politics and given it victory on the battlefield."[28] This image of the civil service as an army of educated public servants was perfectly expressive of the belief of the new intellectuals in science, professionalism, and limited government. It is true that some civil service reformers, notably George William Curtis, saw the movement as an attempt to recapture the spirit of the abolitionists, but in point of fact, it departed from the antislavery movement in motives, methods, and objectives. It aimed not at the extension of democratic or humanitarian ideas, as these had been understood in ante-bellum America, but at something quite different— the creation of an efficient and disciplined administrative elite, an elite which would be relatively free of popular and political pressure and immune from the temptation to initiate basic social reforms.

The only danger in this program was the possibility that some government experts or scientific bureaucrats would be empirical enough to see beyond the Social Darwinist smokescreen and recognize the American "struggle for existence" for what it was —a chaotic and wasteful scramble of special interests. Conclusions of this sort could lead to a heretical belief in central planning. The career of Major John Wesley Powell showed the new and unexpected directions in which government by experts could go. Powell, who like Walker and Adams had gone from military service to one of the new careers in government, learned to act consistently on the basis of a more comprehensive view of the state and its functions than the civil service reformers were willing to allow.

Powell, a brilliant military engineer who had seen enough battleline service to lose an arm at Shiloh, took a position after the war as a government geologist concerned with the arid regions of the West. In an age of expanding government science, Powell saw his role as more than that of a compiler of scientific information, and the peculiar problems of the West forced him in the direction of social planning. In his famous *Report on the Arid Regions of the United States* of 1878, he argued that the remaining Western lands could not be peopled by the traditional method of unregulated migration and settlement, and he proceeded to make a proposal which revealed an interesting combination of scientific empiricism and democratic principle. He advocated setting up, under federal sponsorship, a network of cooperative irrigation and grazing districts as a first step in instituting a new land policy which would fulfill the promise of the Homestead Act by making certain that the public land would "provide homes for poor men" rather than profit for the special interests which were gobbling up the public domain.[29] In 1888, Powell got his chance to plan for Western development when legislation was passed which authorized an irrigation survey of the public lands. This enactment implicitly permitted withdrawal of the lands from settlement and vested in Powell, as director of the United States Geological Survey, the power to determine when and under what conditions they would be reopened. In 1890, however, Congress woke up to what it had done. Powell's right to reserve lands was taken away, and his appropriations were cut drastically. The nation at this point in its history was not willing to admit the benefit of scientific planning for the general welfare.[30]

Powell's approach to the problems that he faced was essentially pragmatic. While not bound by the clichés of Social Darwinism and *laissez faire,* he had neither the time nor the inclination to work out a broad social philosophy to justify his heresies. This task was left to Powell's friend and associate, Lester Ward. Ward, a self-educated genius who had been an enlisted man during the war, worked under Powell in the Geological Survey and, thanks to the indulgence of his superior, was able to write parts of his *Dynamic Sociology* on government time. Ward repudiated the sociology of Spencer, with its view that social evolution was governed by the law of the jungle, and offered a powerful defense of intelligent and scientific planning as the basis of human progress. His concept of "sociocracy" envisioned a government of scientific legislators acting for the greatest good of society. What Ward seemed to have done was to develop and expand Draper's theory of "organized intelligence." But like his mentor, John Wesley Powell, Ward had a streak of democratic idealism. He proposed a vast improvement of the national educational system, in order to insure that men of the humblest origin would have full access to the highest positions in the new scientific aristocracy.[31]

III

If the military experience contributed to the new ideal of the intellectual as scientific expert, practical administrator, and pragmatic reformer, service with the Sanitary Commission led to a similar emphasis on professionalism and scientific principles in the field of philanthropy. It was a group of former Sanitarians, mostly women, who brought about a revolution in the philosophy and methods of charity work, especially in the area of urban poor relief. Louisa Lee Schuyler, who as corresponding secretary of the Woman's Central Association of Relief had been in charge of gathering supplies for the Sanitary Commission in the New York area, turned her energies after the war to organizing the New York State Charities Aid Association, founded in 1872.[32] This organization, modeled after the Sanitary Commission, was a semi-official body of prominent citizens who inspected public institutions such as poor houses and work houses—much in the way the Sanitary Commissioners had inspected the camps—and made recommendations, based on "scientific" principles. Like the commission, it placed members of the upper classes in positions of influence which were immune from the pressures of democratic politics. If the Sanitary Commission had been devoted to military efficiency at the expense of purely humanitarian ends, the State Charities Aid Association was apparently more interested in the efficiency of the labor force than in the relief of suffering. It opposed public relief as "undermining the self-respect of recipients, fostering a spirit of dependence opposed to self-support, and interfering with the laws governing wages and labor."[33] The belief that the poor, like the soldiers of the Union Army, should learn to stand up under necessary hardship for the general good was a basic tenet of Miss Schuyler's concept of charity.

Another important innovator in this field was Josephine Shaw Lowell, the regal figure of William James' youth. As the sister of Robert Gould Shaw and the bride—and widow—of Charles Russell Lowell, she was one woman who had experienced the afflatus of the Civil War patricians in a unique and personal way. During the war she had suffered because her sex kept her from going into battle and had turned to the Sanitary Commission as an outlet for her patriotism. This work had suggested a postwar career in philanthropy—a field in which she could live up to her husband's ideal of the "useful citizen."[34] She soon became recognized as a representative figure of the war generation. Oliver Wendell Holmes, Jr., in his Memorial Day Oration of 1884, referred to Mrs. Lowell as typifying those "lovely, lonely women," the war widows, "whose sex forbade them to offer their lives," but who had gone on to useful tasks. He paid her homage as "one whom the poor of a great city know as their benefactress and friend."[35] With her background, it is not surprising that she was driven by an exacting sense of duty, a desire to do something worthwhile on her own, and the willingness to demand the same "heroic" soldierly virtues from the urban poor that her brother had demanded from the Negroes at Fort Wagner.

After working with Miss Schuyler in the State Charities Aid Association, Mrs. Lowell made her own great contribution by founding the Charity Organization Society of New York in 1882, and she soon emerged as the philosopher of the American charity organization movement—the great philanthropic innovation of the postwar era. This movement, which was influenced by British philanthropy, had as its purpose the "scientific" coordination and regulation of existing charities, not to provoke greater giving but to prevent duplication and to cut off aid to the "unworthy poor" or those who refused to help themselves. The movement demanded abolition of all public and most private relief as having a demoralizing effect on the recipients. For charitably inclined members of the upper classes, it substituted "friendly visiting" for alms-giving. "Friendly visiting" meant that the volunteer charity worker went to visit poor families, not to give them material aid, but solely to provide practical advice, about the possibility of a job, for example, and give moral and spiritual instruction to inspire self-reliance and self-improvement.[36]

"Friendly visiting" had some prewar American precedents, but never had the visitor been so firmly discouraged from relieving directly the suffering that he saw before him. Joseph Tuckerman, who had instituted a form of friendly visiting in Boston in the 1830s, had opposed public outdoor relief on the basis of the "scientific" ideas of political economy which had led to the abolition of the poor laws in England, but he had always insisted that "Christian benevolence" demanded the immediate relief of genuine deprivation by private charity.[37] The charity organization societies discarded all emphasis on benevolent feelings. In tune with the Social Darwinism of the age, they made it their business to prevent "irresponsible" expressions of pity and compassion from emasculating the poor and interfering with the struggle for existence; and they did all in their power to prevent the various private charities from giving alms of any kind. An obvious precedent was the Sanitary Commission with its "scientific" approach to philanthropy, its distrust of the benevolent public, and its exaltation of the expert over the "good Samaritan."

In social motivation, as well as in method, the charity organization movement echoed the Sanitary experience of the Civil War;

for, as Mrs. Lowell indicated, one of its purposes was to give important and redeeming roles to idle members of the upper classes. What was needed in the field of philanthropy, she wrote in a letter of 1882, was "more men of leisure with the tradition of public service like so many of the 'nobility and gentry' of England"—a statement which recalls the class consciousness on the British model which had come out during the war in the tributes to the Harvard heroes.[38] But how was it possible for Mrs. Lowell to be at one and the same time a Social Darwinist, or a believer in struggle as the law of life, and the advocate of a privileged class which had no need to fight for its existence?

In an address of 1890, she made an heroic effort to synthesize class consciousness and Social Darwinism. In discussing "the economic and moral effects of outdoor relief," she condemned relief in her usual way as destructive of the manhood of the poor. Considering what would happen if every person over twenty were given a substantial sum of money, she concluded that people would very soon "become less energetic, less skilled in money making directions, less able to succeed." Some, she admitted, "would devote themselves to higher pursuits than earning a living, to study, to art, to philanthropy," but others would "spend their substance in riotous living." If bare subsistence relief was given to all, however, the ordinary man would not work, and those with higher inclinations would still not have "the quiet and peace, the power to live for worthier objects than mere physical support, which an assured income supplies." Culture in the form of "higher" pursuits is therefore dependent on leisure and "an assured income," but only a few can be trusted "to live for worthier objects"; for the opportunity for dissipation that comes from suspending the iron law of necessity offers "what to any but a heroic nature must be an overwhelming temptation." One can only conclude that the leisure class, if they live for "worthier objects," are even more heroic than the poor who must fight for a living or fall by the wayside.[39] The goal for Mrs. Lowell was a hard-working capitalistic society, saved from materialism, corruption, and bad taste by an aristocracy subservient to the highest principles. The best model for such a society was the North of the war years with its patrician heroes and general spirit of self-sacrifice.

It would not be far from the mark to describe Mrs. Lowell's concept of charity entirely in patrician military terms. The urban environment, as pictured in her writings, resembles nothing so much as a war, with vice and poverty as the enemy, the virtuous poor as infantry, and the upper-class charity workers as generals or "natural" leaders, giving strategic and tactical guidance. The charity worker, like the military commander or the Sanitary Commissioner, was never to give way to "sentimental" humanitarian impulses, but was to consider the army as a whole and the "cause" rather than the immediate comfort of individuals. The suitability of this analogy makes it clear how the Civil War tradition could contribute to an acceptance of Social Darwinism, even among old-family "aristocrats" who were not overly friendly to the business interests that were most directly served by the new philosophy. The wartime sense of the inevitability of mass suffering had prepared many people to adopt a callous view of the troubles of the poor, in the belief that progress comes only at a great human cost. Those who had stoically accepted the massive toll of dead and wounded, who had shown an "heroic" willingness to send brothers and husbands to their deaths, were fully prepared for the almost pitiless approach to poverty revealed in the new charity movements.

Mrs. Lowell had come from a strong antislavery background; so had Oliver Wendell Holmes, Jr.; Charles Francis Adams, Jr.; and Francis A. Walker. In their different ways, they had all rejected this heritage. The war had weaned them from an inheritance of utopian idealism and pointed them in the direction of a more conservative, "realistic," or practical approach to reform, which could be justified on "scientific" grounds. The social pessimism, the acceptance of limiting historical conditions, which came to characterize these figures, had few roots in the ante-bellum period. What they were demanding was the continuance, not of the prewar reform impulse, but of the crisis mentality of the war. They wished to preserve a wartime sense of strenuous social duty, not only for themselves, but for everyone else, to be expended on the pursuit of comparatively conservative goals. The intellectual who stood outside the institutions and was either a student of his own transcendental consciousness or a utopian reformer had no place in the new order. Only in the thought of Lester Ward and in the policy-making of John Wesley Powell did the war generation suggest the possibility of middle ground—a social philosophy grounded in the belief that science, organization, and planning could be enlisted on the side of humanitarian reform.

14

The Moral Equivalent of War

MRS. LOWELL AND ALL THE OTHERS WHO WORKED UN-
ceasingly to keep alive a wartime spirit of strenuous service must
have known that they were facing an almost hopeless task. Ordinary peacetime existence simply did not provide the stimulus
to self-sacrifice that was present in a moment of national crisis.
In the 1880s and 1890s, as the mood that swept the North after
the firing on Fort Sumter receded farther and farther into the past,
the members of the war generation began to look for new ways
to stir the souls of their countrymen and impel them to selfless
action. In their search for an "equivalent of war," they were
forced once again to confront their war experience and to seek
an explanation of that one glorious moment when the nation had
forgotten its love of the short cut and the easy life. For many,
therefore, the late nineteenth century effort to define and promote
"the strenuous life" was inseparably bound up with the continuing
search for the meaning of the Civil War.

The obvious way to cure the national lethargy and recapture
the spirit of 1861 was to clamor for new wars. But for those who
had lived through the Civil War there was much that would not
bear repeating; men who knew what it was like to go into battle
were certain to think twice before calling for new military ad-

ventures. Francis A. Walker was one veteran who was quick to condemn the hotheads of 1869 for their willingness to go to war with England over the Alabama claims. In an article in *Lippincott's,* Walker voiced strong disapproval of anyone "who assumes, or acts on the assumption, that he can make slaughter and devastation minister to human happiness and well being." "War is, and remains utterly unjustifiable until it becomes actually inevitable. Nor can there be any worse condition for judging of its necessity than a readiness to accept it as something grand and heroical."[1] Oliver Wendell Holmes had a similar, battle-born sense of the dark side of war. For years after the conflict he could not bear to read anything about it, and in later life, he referred frequently to his personal loathing of war, his belief that there was nothing romantic about it, especially for one who had been in the infantry and "stood the great slaughter." Yet men like Walker and Holmes were not pacifists. As Walker's statement reveals, they recognized that armed conflict in some circumstances was inevitable. In the letter which stated most strongly his hatred of war, Holmes wrote that "force, mitigated as far as may be by good manners, is the *ultima ratio,* and between two groups that want to make inconsistent kinds of worlds I see no remedy but force."[2] War then was not to be risked for inconsequential reasons, but where there were competing ways of life struggling for dominion—as in the case of the North and the South—war might be the only resolution and a necessary episode in the evolutionary struggle.

To say that war was never justifiable would have required an admission that the Civil War experience had been not only painful and unromantic but without ultimate value. Perhaps the only ex-Northern patriot who was willing to say this was Moncure Conway. By the time he came to write his memoirs, in 1897, he had become a thoroughgoing pacifist, and he made his *Autobiography* a *mea culpa,* full of repentance for any support he had given the war. His contrition came out most vividly in the recollection of a young man whom his antislavery preaching had sent into battle: "Rest in your peaceful unknown grave beside the Rappahannock, O my friend! For you no tears, no heartbreaks, no harrowing reflection that your chivalry was in vain, and the war mere manslaughter! These are for me, who found you a happy youth clinging to me with boyish affection, and from my pulpit helped to lay on you the burden of the world."³ Conway had arrived at such a view after the soul-searching which had followed his disillusionment with Northern war motives, and his intellectual pilgrimage had led not only to pacifism, but to agnosticism and "the religion of humanity." Conway's revolt against Christianity had been inspired in part by a retrospective horror at the providential interpretation of the war—a theory which had been so favored by abolitionists like himself. Beset with doubts about the kind of God who would permit catastrophes like the Civil War, Conway found that he had to cease being a Christian, or even a theist, in order to remain a humanitarian.⁴

Oliver Wendell Holmes, Jr., was also an agnostic, but, unlike Conway, he could contemplate the pain and agony of existence without protest because he had substituted a stoical acceptance of nature and the universe for a belief in Divine Providence. For Holmes, man was "an inseparable part of an unimaginable whole"⁵—a situation which gave no cause for despair and no excuse for inactivity. If as "private soldiers" we "have not been told the plan of campaign," he wrote in one of his essays, ". . . we still shall fight—all of us—because we want to live, some at least, because we want to realize our spontaneity and prove our power for the joy of it, and we may leave to the unknown the supposed final evaluation of that which in any event has value for us."⁶

It was in terms of this "fighting faith" that Holmes looked back on the Civil War in his famous Memorial Day Addresses of 1884 and 1895—the most profound statements of what the war had come to mean to those who had lived through it as young men. The heart of his message was that "war, when you are at it, is horrible and dull. It is only when time has passed that you see that its message was divine."⁷ With all the eloquence he could muster Holmes insisted that "the generation that carried on the war has been set apart by its experience. Through our great good fortune, in our youth our hearts were touched with fire. It was given to us to learn at the outset that life is a profound and passionate thing." This passionate sense of life had nothing to do with ideology. The Southerners had learned the same lesson from fighting as their Northern brothers; they had "held as sacred convictions that were the opposite of ours, and we respected them as every man with a heart must respect those who give all for their belief." Despite the South's commitment to slavery, then, it had been the duty of every eligible Southern man to fight for his section: ". . . as life is action and passion, it is required of a man that he should share the passion and action of his time at peril of being judged not to have lived."[8] The nature of the cause was unimportant; what mattered was the kind of devotion given to it. Indeed, there was no release from duty in the fact that neither the detached observer nor the soldier in the field could determine the ultimate validity of the claim made by one side or the other. "I do not know what is true," Holmes confessed, "I do not know the meaning of the universe. But in the midst of doubt, in the collapse of creeds, there is one thing I do not doubt . . . and that is that the faith is true and adorable which leads a soldier to throw away his life in obedience to a blindly accepted duty, in a cause which he little understands, in a plan of campaign of which he has no notion, under tactics of which he does not see the use."[9] For Holmes, strenuousness and courage were not means to an end, but ends in themselves; personal moral choice as to whether a cause is worth defending has no justification in a murky universe where history is made by the collision of blind forces. Both his disillusionment with Northern Civil War ideology and his belief in science had led Holmes toward relativism, yet it was a relativism that instead of rejecting blind faith of all kinds tended to endorse impartially all beliefs that generated the heroic fighting qualities.

Holmes' nonideological interpretation of the Civil War may have had its own profundities, but in many respects it was in tune with the feeling of the American people in the 1880s and 1890s. By then, the nation was well along on what Paul Buck has called "the road to reunion." In 1889, *Scribner's* noted the increased observance of Memorial Day in both the North and the South: "the veterans' memories of the conflict that called them to arms are on both sides turning to a single noble ideal—martial heroism. Surely the worshippers of that ideal will know no North and no South while turning chaplets to immortalize the brave."[10]

Besides reflecting a loss of interest in the ideological or moral issues of the Civil War, Holmes' orations were characterized by a concern for the state of American society during the Gilded Age. In his 1895 address, he pointedly called attention to the martial virtues at a time when "commerce is the great power" and men long for a society "in which they may be comfortable and may shine without much trouble or any danger." Holmes hoped, however, that it would not be war itself that would be required to redeem the nation: "I hope it may be long before we are called again to sit at that master's feet." But he was quick to add that "some teacher of the kind we all need. In this snug, over-safe corner of the world we need it, that we may realize that our comfortable routine is no eternal necessity of things, but merely a little space of calm in the midst of the tempestuous untamed streaming of the world, and in order that we may be ready for danger."[11] Here Holmes revealed how deeply he was imbued with the patrician ethic of a Francis Parkman. He shared Parkman's contempt for the values of businessmen and philanthropists alike, and some of his comments even suggested Parkman's desire to bring back the age of chivalry and the testing of men by physical struggle. If Parkman had hoped that the Civil War would save the nation from commercialism, Holmes confronted a later America in which he could hear a man say, "Where Vanderbilt sits, there is the head of the table. I teach my son to be rich"—a society in which "the man who commands the attention of his fellows" is not the soldier or the patrician as member of a learned profession, but "the man of wealth."[12] Perhaps Holmes was suffering from the "status revolution" described by Richard Hofstadter, but more likely he was concerned with the fact that so many of his fellow Brahmins had retained their status at the price of joining the Gilded Age as successful businessmen, thereby denying themselves the possibility of being a noncommercial aristocracy.[13] In any case, he was one with Parkman in his emphasis on the aristocratic virtues, and he believed that the example of "high breeding, romantic chivalry" provided by the Brahmin war heroes might yet save the educated classes from the slough of materialism.[14] As a veteran, however, he was less willing than Parkman had been to call for war itself as the immediate remedy. He seemed to be searching for some equivalent of war—some other way in which young men could be tested and readied for "heroic," noncommercial roles.

Holmes' concern for the backbone of America's youth was shared by many contemporaries, and there were various ideas of how the martial qualities could be encouraged short of war. One was suggested in 1888 by General Horace Porter, who is remembered as the author of the lively narrative *Campaigning with Grant*. In the course of a discussion of soldierly courage and how it could be developed in the young men of the time, Porter pointed as Parkman had once done to the frontier: "Take two youngsters born with equal degrees of courage; let one remain in a quiet city, playing the milksop in a modern Capua, leading an unambitious, namby-pamby life, surrounded by all the safeguards of civilization, while the other goes out on the frontier, runs his chance in encounters with wild animals, finds that to make his way he must take his life in his hands, and assert his rights, if necessary, with deadly weapons, and knows he will be drummed out of the community if once he is caught showing the white feather. In the one particular trait of personal courage, the frontiersman must undoubtedly become the superior of the lad who has remained at home."[15] Teddy Roosevelt became the living exemplar of this doctrine. Going West to hunt grizzlies and herd cattle was one way to live "the strenuous life" without actually going to war.

An even more popular remedy was one suggested by Holmes himself in the "Soldier's Faith." In the course of illustrating his famous contention—"Out of heroism grows faith in heroism"—Holmes pointed to "dangerous sport" as an excellent way of developing courage: "The students at Heidelberg, with their sword-slashed faces, inspire me with sincere respect. I gaze with delight upon our polo players. If once in a while in our rough riding a neck is broken, I regard it, not as a waste, but as a price well paid for the breeding of a race fit for headship and command."[16] It was strange that Holmes did not mention football, the most popular "dangerous sport" of the time, which was then being played with such enthusiasm at places like Harvard and Yale, despite the primitive rules and absence of padding which made it fully as "dangerous" as polo. But the value of football and other college sports as a means of reviving the Civil War spirit was amply acknowledged by Henry Lee Higginson in one of his benefactions to Harvard College. By donating a large plot of land for athletics, to be called "The Soldier's Field," in honor of his comrades who had been killed in the war, Higginson hoped to contribute to the rearing of a new generation of patrician heroes, who would carry on in the tradition of Charles Russell Lowell and Robert Gould Shaw. His 1896 presentation speech to the Harvard undergraduates sounded the call for strenuous social service. Sports would make "full-grown, well-developed men, able and ready to do good work of all kinds." And there was much work for "the useful citizen" to do: "The world on all sides is moving fast, and you have only to accept this fact, making the best of everything—helping, sympathizing, and so guiding and restraining others, who have less education, perhaps, than you."[17]

Francis A. Walker made the fullest statement of the new importance of collegiate athletics in his Phi Beta Kappa address at Harvard in 1893. Walker began in a humorous vein by caricaturing the undergraduate of the ante-bellum period—an era in which athletics was not encouraged—"He was self-conscious, introspective, and indulged in moods as became a child of genius. He had yearnings and aspirations, and not infrequently mistook physical lassitude for intellectuality, and the gnawings of dyspepsia for spiritual cravings. He would have gravely distrusted his mission and his calling had he found himself at any time playing ball." Walker revealed something of the intellectual revolution that had taken place when he attributed this unhealthy condition to "the transcendentalism and sentimentalism of the last quarter of the eighteenth and the first quarter of the nineteenth century, which had created false and pernicious opinions concerning personal character and conduct." Fortunately, however, the Civil War had come along "to produce a vast change in popular sentiments and ideals, as it showed how much nobler are strength of will, firmness of purpose, resolution to endure, and capacity for action than are the qualities of the speech-maker and the fine writer, which the nation had once agreed chiefly to admire." Thus Walker summed up the values which his generation had acquired from serving in the Civil War and went on to find the best hope of preserving these values in "the competitive contests of our colleges." On the playing fields, "something akin to patriotism and public spirit is developed," which counteracts "the selfish, individualistic tendencies of the age." "It is a good thing," he concluded, "that the body of students should now and then be stirred to the very depths of their souls; that they should have something outside themselves to care for; that they should learn to love passionately, even if a little animosity toward rivals must mingle with their patriotic fervor. . . ."[18] Football had a tremendous burden to carry; it would have to be a miniature Civil War, without, it was hoped, the carnage, in which young men of coming generations could learn the lessons which Holmes, Higginson, and Walker had learned in a harder school.

Walker was especially eager to make sports the equivalent of war because he had an honest revulsion from war itself. In his address on athletics he registered his opposition to "pugnacity" in international affairs and his gratification that America had seemingly outgrown its former "jingoism."[19] Yet five years after Walker's speech and one year after his death, jingoism had triumphed and the United States had gone to war against Spain. The career of Theodore Roosevelt illustrated that the "strenuous life" doctrine, with its emphasis on physical courage, was less a harmless substitute for war than an invitation to get into one. For Roosevelt, college athletics or frontier life was a training for bigger adventures. In leading "the rough riders" up San Juan Hill, he led a regiment composed primarily of Ivy League athletes and Western cowboys.[20] Roosevelt, who had been a mere toddler during the Civil War, had learned what members of the war generation had to teach about the manly virtues, but he had not absorbed their unromantic view of war, their belief in keeping the peace if possible.

By 1899, Roosevelt had made "the strenuous life" synonymous with American imperialism. In the address of that title, "The Strenuous Life," he suggested that anyone unwilling to help in the suppression of a popular revolt in the Philippines was not worthy of manhood. In this defense of an expansionist foreign policy, Roosevelt drew heavily on the example of the Civil War, speaking of the "iron in the blood of our fathers, the men who upheld the wisdom of Lincoln, and bore the sword or rifle in the armies of Grant!" Grant and Lincoln were the greatest exemplars of the strenuous life, because they "recognized the law of work, the law of strife."[21] With Roosevelt, the "strenuous life" ideal had come full circle. Beginning with Parkman's glorification of physical strife as drawing out the masculine fighting qualities, it had been transmuted by young men who were tired of war into the ideal of "useful citizenship" in time of peace; in the eighties and early nineties, it had regained its emphasis on physical courage—to be demonstrated, however, in the West or on the playing field rather than on the battlefield. In the age of imperialism, we are back to an essentially military ideal. Yet Roosevelt's formulation was as much a summing up of the entire "strenuous life" tradition as a reversion to its primitive form. There was still, as it turned out, a domestic role for "the useful citizen": He could be the nationalist who would support a build-up of the army and navy and other policies suitable to America's new role in the world. Even more revealing was Roosevelt's justification of imperialism in terms of America's "responsibility" for "uplifting" backward peoples. Here was Higginson's "useful citizenship" on a world scale.

II

The Civil War experience could be an inspiration for thinkers with aims differing sharply from Roosevelt's. For Edward Bellamy, the utopian novelist, the search for an equivalent of war was one aspect of the effort to envision a socialist America.

Although only a boy in his early teens during the national convulsion which followed the firing on Fort Sumter, Bellamy had been deeply affected by it. In a school composition of 1861, he had marveled at the way the North had responded to the rebellion, at how ". . . this great nation gathered determination with God's help to forever crush treason from this continent."[22] The outbreak of the war had found Bellamy already enthralled by the thought of a military career, and his jottings of the time reveal an obsession with military discipline, organization, and tactics.

This interest outlived the war years, and in 1867, Bellamy attempted to enroll in West Point. His rejection on grounds of health was a traumatic disappointment.[23]

His hopes for a military life frustrated, Bellamy went on to a career as a journalist and writer of fiction, which culminated in the fantastic international success of his socialist romance, *Looking Backward*. Behind Bellamy's socialism was a philosophy of life which he called "the Religion of Solidarity." He described this faith in an early essay, revealing a heavy debt to the transcendentalists. Like Emerson, Bellamy believed that man is the fragment of an "Oversoul" or, in his own terms, an "all soul." In addition to a phenomenal self or "personality" which cannot escape the limitations of personal existence, he possesses an "impersonal consciousness," "an inner serene and passionless ego," which is a reflection of the divine "All." Bellamy, however, resembled Henry James, Sr., or the "fraternity" school of transcendentalism, in finding the ultimate expression of the "impersonal self" not in the isolation of the Emersonian individualist, but in a sense of human solidarity. It was "the moral intuitions that impel to self-sacrifice"—as manifested in "loyalty or patriotism, philanthropy or sympathy"—which gave the individual his most sustained experience of the infinite.[24]

In some ways, Bellamy's socialism was a latter-day manifestation of the spirit that had led some of the ante-bellum transcendentalists to engage in utopian experiments as a way of realizing their vision of human perfection. Putting himself explicitly in this tradition, Bellamy acknowledged Brook Farm and other communitarian enthusiasms of the 1840s as the antecedents of his Nationalist movement.[25] Yet the war had also made its contribution to his image of the ideal society. This legacy was revealed in his Civil War story, "An Echo of Antietam," published in 1889. In this tale, Bellamy described the men of a New England village marching off to join the Union ranks. "The imposing mass," he wrote, ". . . gives the impression of a single organism. One forgets to look for the individuals in it, forgets that there are individuals. Even those who have brothers, sons, lovers there, for a moment almost forget them in the impression of a mighty whole." Relying undoubtedly on boyhood memories, Bellamy noted how the spectators responded to the "afflatus of heroism given forth by this host of self-devoted men," how "the booming of the drum fills the brain, and the blood in the brain leaps to the rhythm," how the sight of the flag inspires "a thrill of voluptuous sweetness in the thought of dying for it." Later in the story, the men go into battle, and their willingness to die "testifies to a conviction, deeper than reason, that man is greater than his seeming self." "What a pity," Bellamy concluded, "that the tonic air of battlefields . . . cannot be gathered up and preserved as a precious elixir to reinvigorate the atmosphere in times of peace, when men grow faint of heart and cowardly, and quake at the thought of death."[26]

It is clear that Bellamy agreed with Holmes on the need to stir a nation of cowards and self-seekers by recalling the heroic mood of the war years. In using war to exemplify man's ability to be "greater than his seeming self," he made it appear that marching to battle was the very culmination of "the religion of solidarity." Elsewhere in his writings, however, Bellamy showed an awareness of the horror, cruelty, and suffering that went along with the heroism. He may have valued some of the emotions associated with war, but he regretted the cost in blood and tears.[27] In his utopian novel, *Looking Backward,* which was published in 1888, he offered the blueprint for a society in which patriotic fervor and self-sacrifice would cease to be the concomitants of slaughter and would become, instead, the normal motives of social and economic life.

In *Looking Backward,* Bellamy drew heavily on the example of wartime patriotism as the cement of society and revealed that same love of military organization and discipline which had contributed to his youthful desire to be a soldier. His society of the year 2000 is characterized not only by absolute economic equality, but also by the organization of the working force as an army. Under this system, the workers go up through the ranks until they reach the mandatory retirement age of forty-five. Since this is supposed to result in rule by the most competent in each field or profession, it inevitably calls up an image of the efficiency-minded technocratic elite—an impression which is reinforced by Bellamy's great emphasis on scientific and technological progress. Behind it all, however, was an idealistic concern for motives, a belief that men will work for something nobler than money. As Dr. Leete, Bellamy's spokesman from the future, explains it: "Now that industry of whatever sort is no longer self-sacrifice, but service of the nation, patriotism, passion for humanity, impel the worker as in your day the soldier. The army of industry is an army, not alone by virtue of its perfect organization, but by reason also of the ardor of self-devotion which animates its members."[28] The industrial army, therefore, constitutes both a use of the military form in the service of peaceful progress and an outlet for all the heroic emotions associated with war.

Bellamy, however, was a gradualist who realized that the perfect society of his hopes might be far in the future. The question that remained was how to keep the heroic instincts alive during the long interim. There was no recognition of this problem in *Looking Backward*, but in *Equality*, a sequel of 1897, Bellamy made a startling admission which suggests how narrow a line could divide the socialist with a military ideal from the out-and-out militarist of the 1890s. "As we look back on your era," Dr. Leete tells Julian, the pilgrim from the present, as they examine the ruins of old fortifications, "the sort of fighting those old forts down there stood for seems almost noble and barely tragical at all, as compared with the awful struggle for existence. We even are able to sympathize with the declaration of some of the professional soldiers of your age that occasional wars with their appeals, however false, to the generous and self-devoting passions, were absolutely necessary to prevent your society otherwise so utterly sordid and selfish in its ideals, from dissolving into absolute putrescence."[29] This statement comes surprisingly close to the "splendid little war" theory of Theodore Roosevelt and John Hay. What Bellamy seems to be saying is that until utopia arrives, war will continue to be a necessary exercise in virtue and self-sacrifice. Here again the partial glorification of war seems to lead, for immediate and practical purposes, not to a peaceful equivalent at all, but back to war itself.

III

The most significant search for a way of sublimating the emotions of war was that of William James. For James, the seeking of an equivalent of war was virtually a psychological necessity. It was at the center of his entire effort to define himself in relation to the "strenuous life" ideal and its exponents.

In the years immediately after the Civil War, James continued to suffer from the sense of inadequacy that had been aggravated by his inability to play a role in the great national drama. It was at this time that he cultivated his curious friendship with Oliver Wendell Holmes, Jr., that highly articulate spokesman for "the strenuous life." In 1867 and 1868, when James was studying in Berlin, he wrote a series of letters to Holmes in which he complained of the illness and inactivity which were driving him to despair—as if in the hope of borrowing some of the veteran's self-reliance. He addressed Holmes as "the one emergent peak, to which I cling when all the rest of the world has sunk beneath the wave." When he wrote about his "stagnation," his "crass indolence," his life which "resembles that of a sea-anemone," Holmes replied, as might be expected, with a Holmesian sermon on courage. Somehow correspondence with Holmes only increased James' inferiority feeling. He gave himself away in his last Berlin letter by admitting that Holmes' way of thinking had induced in him "a reaction caused by some subtle deviltry of egotism and jealousy" which put him "involuntarily into a position of self-defense as if you threatened to overrun my territory and injure my own proprietorship." Ultimately, as he wrote to his brother Henry in 1869, he was repelled by Holmes' "cold-blooded conscious egotism." Holmes had done him good "more in presenting me something to kick away from or react against than to follow and embrace."[30]

This antagonism was as much philosophical as personal. If Holmes' hard-boiled stoicism and "cold-blooded egotism" represented a triumph of the self-contained will, it was not the kind of will that finally interested James. It was not the "will to believe," but the will to carry on without believing. The war may have changed Holmes from an idealist into a tough-minded anti-utopian who valued a "fight" solely for the chance it provided for a release of human energy in an amoral universe: but for James, who had seen the struggle from a civilian abolitionist's point of view, it had encouraged a thirst for moral intensity, a desire to find some basis of human participation in a cosmic struggle between good and evil. James in fact differed significantly from most of his generation in retaining a respect for the uncompromising moralism and crusading humanitarianism of the ante-bellum reformers. At the same time, however, he rejected their belief in an intuitive moral sense as the foundation of right conduct and embraced a form of utilitarianism. In one of his letters to Holmes, he revealed his early musings on the need to put the old wine in new bottles. "If happiness is our Good," he wrote, "ought we not to try to foment a passionate and bold will to attain that happiness among the multitudes? Can we not conduct off upon our purposes from the moralities and the theologies, a beam which will invest us with some of the proud absoluteness which made them so venerable, by preaching the doctrine that Man is his own providence, and every individual a real God to his race. . . . The sentiment of philanthropy is now so firmly established and apparently its permanence so guaranteed by its beneficent nature, that it would be bold to say it could not take its place as the ultimate motive for human action."[31] Here is the beginning of James' attempt to reconcile a basically utilitarian ethics with the zeal of an absolute moralism. His hopes for the triumph of "the sentiment of philanthropy" echo the millennial hopes of his father and the righteous spirit of the abolitionists. Holmes' impressions are not recorded. One can hardly believe that he was sympathetic.

With Holmes offering no help, James had to overcome by himself the sense of powerlessness that had been accentuated by sitting out the war. He tried a purely scientific career, but it did not fulfill his emotional needs. "I sometimes feel pretty discouraged by the inanity of my activity," he wrote to a friend in 1868. "The fact is that I am about as little fitted by nature to be a worker in science of any sort as anyone can be. . . ." How he envied the kind of man who went beyond science and its positivistic ideas of truth—"the well constructed whelps who travel on their free-will and moral responsibility." They were, he thought, "the greatest success of any of us, the most susceptible of happiness." How fine it would be to "get at something absolute without get-ting out of your skin! To measure yourself by what you strive for and not by what you reach."[32]

James would have been in safe water if he could have agreed with Holmes that "to act affirms, for the moment at least, the worth of an end." But he demanded a real sense that action had potential meaning—that it was based on "free will and respon-sibility." Unfortunately, the philosophers to whom he was closest, men like his friend Chauncey Wright, tended to define truth as scientific truth and to proclaim "the neutrality of science" in ethical and religious questions. In the same letter in which he suggested that utilitarianism could be a fighting faith, James admitted to Holmes that he was really "but little interested in any particular battle or movement of progress. . . ." His sense of personal insufficiency joined with his philosophical uncertainty to keep him from being the active partisan, the moral warrior he would have liked to be.[33]

In 1870, at the height of his intellectual and spiritual crisis, James recorded in his diary how far he had fallen and what he saw as the only way out: "Today I about touched bottom, and perceive plainly that I must face the choice with open eyes: shall I *frankly* throw the whole moral business overboard, as one un-suited to my innate aptitudes, or shall I follow it, and it alone, making everything else merely stuff for it? I will give the latter alternative a fair trial. Who knows but the moral interest may become developed. . . ." The story of how he staked his life on the "moral business" is well known: as a first step in building a philosophy that would pull him out of the pit of melancholia, he asserted his belief in free will as an act of faith. Lacking interest in a specific cause, an antislavery movement to which he could commit himself, he turned to a defense of the moral interest itself. There were, he convinced himself, real danger and personal risk in committing oneself by a deliberate act of will to a set of basic beliefs which were beyond scientific verification. As he was to

write in "The Will to Believe," believing or not in the religious
and moral significance of the universe is "in either case" to "*act,
taking our life in our hands.*"[34] Action, therefore, could be defined as an internal effort which had little to do with physical
activity. It was the kind of heroism that keeps sensitive and
thoughtful men from suicide, not the kind that wins battles.

Despite his apparent success in making himself a man of action
by defining action in terms of an inner struggle—a war with
doubt—James could never conceal his respect for those who
could conquer doubt completely and turn beliefs into vigorous
physical activity. In "The Moral Philosopher and the Moral
Life," an address of 1891, he described the "strenuous mood"
which impels religious men to fight for a good cause on "the
battlefield of human history": "When . . . we believe that a
God is there, and that he is one of the claimants, the infinite
perspective opens out. . . . The more imperative ideals now
begin to speak with an altogether new objectivity and significance, and to utter the penetrating, shattering, tragically challeng-
ing note of appeal. . . . All through history, in the periodic
conflicts of puritanism with the don't care temper, we see the
antagonism of the strenuous and genial moods. . . . Every sort
of energy and endurance, of courage and capacity for handling
life's evils, is set free in those who have religious faith."[35] This
was clearly an invocation of the spirit of the abolitionists, and the
reference to an embattled puritanism is indicative of the awe James
felt when confronting the kind of moral fervor that helped bring
on the Civil War. Writing in the heroic vein was a way of making
up in imagination for something he had missed in life.

James' glorification of moral struggle, however, did not lead
to a glorification of war in the physical sense. In fact his sympathy with the spirit of the ante-bellum reformers was accompanied by the view that the Civil War had been a tragic setback
for many of their hopes and expectations. In his oration on Robert
Gould Shaw in 1897, he acknowledged that the war "had freed
the country from the social plague which until then had made
political development impossible in the United States," but went
on to say that emancipation had come too late to bring about the
redemption of the nation. The abolitionists, as "the voice of the

world's conscience" and the most loyal adherents of "the American religion . . . the faith that a man requires no master to take care of him," had pointed the way to national salvation, but the nation had refused to follow. In a manner that almost echoed Moncure Conway, James claimed that the necessity of war had meant that genuine moral reform was no longer possible. "The lesson that our war ought most of all to teach us," he said, "is the lesson that evils must be checked in time, before they grow so great. The Almighty cannot love such long-postponed accounts or such tremendous settlements. . . . Our present situation, with its rancors and its delusions, what is it but the direct outcome of the added powers of the government, the corruptions and inflations of the war? Every war leaves such miserable legacies, fatal seeds of future war and revolution, unless the civic virtues of the people save the State in time."[36]

James' views contrast sharply with the Holmesian judgment that the war itself had been a valuable experience but that the abolitionist agitation had been unlovely and perhaps even unjustified. It is possible that his oration was an indirect rebuttal of Holmes. We know that James read Holmes' speeches and disapproved of them. In 1900, he was to complain of Holmes' "one set speech" with its defense of "mere vital excitement" as an end in itself.[37] What appears to be an attack on the crude physical version of "the strenuous life" comes out in the dedication speech in James' explanation of the greatness of Shaw. While conceding some value to "the common and gregarious courage" of Shaw as a soldier in battle, he saved his real praise for "that more lonely courage" Shaw had demonstrated when he went against the view of some of his peers and agreed to take command of the first Negro regiment.[38]

James' view that the Civil War had left "the fatal seeds" of future war seemed borne out the year after the Shaw oration when the United States went to war against Spain. James himself responded to some extent to the "excitement" of the crusade to liberate Cuba,[39] but in 1899, when the United States began to suppress the Philippine revolt, he realized that an ugly spirit of militarism and imperialism had developed, and he quickly became a leading "anti-imperialist."

James was particularly incensed by the "Strenuous Life" address of Theodore Roosevelt. In his speech, Roosevelt had denounced anti-imperialists like James and had spoken with contempt of the "over-civilized man, who has lost the great fighting, masterful virtues" in the course of living "that cloistered life which saps the hardy virtues in a nation, as it saps them in the individual." Particularly annoying to Roosevelt was the manner in which the cloistered critics would "cant about 'liberty' and 'the consent of the governed'."[40] James responded to this speech with the kind of anger one reserves for a personal affront. What disturbed him most about "The Strenuous Life" was its appeal to strenuousness as an end in itself: "Not a word of the cause," he complained, "—one foe is as good as another" even if this meant to "enslave a weak but heroic people."[41]

If, as James saw it, the Civil War provided a precedent for American imperialism and bellicosity, it had also bequeathed examples of the "strenuous mood" in the constructive form of "civic virtue" and "civic courage," as demonstrated by Robert Gould Shaw; and it was presumably from this tradition that the anti-imperialists should draw inspiration. The abolitionists, however, whether they had been agitators like Wendell Phillips or antislavery soldiers like Shaw and Wilkinson James, had possessed an energy and vitality which seemed lacking in the "mugwumps" and "anti-imperialists" of 1900. In 1902, James noted sadly that the liberals of his own time were "the party of pale reflection" with a lamentable "lack of speed and passion." It was the imperialists who constituted "the party of red blood."[42] Roosevelt, it seemed, had struck a raw nerve in his strictures on the manliness of the opposition, and had stated the irrefutable in maintaining that the sons of the rich must save themselves from a life of "pale reflection." James did not go along with Roosevelt's belief in imperialism as the remedy, but he did agree that something had to be done to inspire and invigorate the nation's youth. In his own essays of 1899 and thereafter, he described the "important forms of energizing" and "potential forms of activity" which had been "sealed up by the critical atmosphere in which we have been reared," and suggested that "we of the highly educated classes" who are "far away from nature" need to be "imprisoned or shipwrecked or forced into the army" to "find the good of life" and banish morbid fears. With his sense of having missed a great energizing experience—he spoke of the idea of "the Union" in the Civil War as one of the great "energy-releasing ideas"—James was certain that the younger generation needed something like war to call out their "vital reserves"; they needed to experience the vigorous, active life that he himself had never really known.[43]

James' attitude, however, was complicated by his particularly strong sense that war itself was a barbaric survival, incompatible with the best ideals of modern civilization. As the aftermath of the Civil War revealed, it invariably did more harm than good to a nation. The problem was how to combine the enthusiasm, courage, and spirit of self-sacrifice called forth by war with peaceful and constructive activities. The best answer that James could find is revealed in his famous essay of 1910, "The Moral Equivalent of War."

"The Moral Equivalent of War" is the culmination of all James' thinking about war and "the strenuous mood." That the heritage of the Civil War was at the root of his concerns is clear from the first paragraph, in which he begins his call for the preservation of the war spirit in a peaceable society by citing "our war for the Union" as "the most ideal part of what we now own together" and "a sacred spiritual possession worth more than all the blood poured out." Recollection of the Civil War—"Those ancestors, those efforts, those memories and legends"—was behind James' belief that there is some good in war when the cause is just, and that warfare will never disappear until pacifists can suggest a moral equivalent. His solution was to draft "an army against nature," composed of the youth of the country to do the hard and disagreeable work of society: "To coal and iron mines, to freight trains, to fishing fleets in December, to dishwashing, clothes-washing, and window-washing, to road-building and tunnel-making, to foundries and stoke-holes, and the frames of skyscrapers would our gilded youths be drafted off . . . to get the childishness knocked out of them, and to come back into society with healthier sympathies and soberer ideas."[44]

What fascinates a modern reader of "The Moral Equivalent of

War" is that only in its conclusion does the essay differ from the militaristic writings and speeches of the same period. James gave vent to the usual warnings about the spiritual dangers of plenty and the "softness" of living only by the "ups and downs of politics and the vicissitudes of trade." He went so far as to affirm that "martial virtues must be the enduring cement; intrepidity, contempt of softness, surrender of private interest, obedience to command, must still remain the rock upon which states are built" —a statement which shows how close James could come to "the strenuous life" ideal as promulgated by patrician intellectuals and exemplified in the purely military side of the Civil War. The essay even reflects the Parkman or Roosevelt belief in strenuous activity as a means of toughening up "the cultivated classes" for social leadership. It was "the gilded youths" whom James wanted to enlist in "the war against nature" to make them "better fathers and teachers of the following generation."[45] In statements like this, James revealed that he was a man of his own class and his own time. To leave it at that, however, would be to miss the true James. The nature of his proposal is of critical importance. His "gilded youths" are not to be taught the sense of status and command that comes from being army officers; they are to become better democrats, more sympathetic with the problems of the working population for having been workers themselves. His proposal later came to fruition in the programs of two liberal American Presidents—in the Civilian Conservation Corps of Franklin D. Roosevelt and, most strikingly, in the Peace Corps of John F. Kennedy. James' deepest response to the Civil War had been not to the examples of military heroism, but to the democratic and humanitarian spirit which had flared up from time to time, but which, as a result of the "rancors" and "delusions" of war, had been almost extinguished. "Faiths and utopias are the noblest exercise of human reason," he once wrote, and "democracy is a kind of religion. We are bound not to admit its failure."[46]

In his effort to find a moral equivalent of the Civil War, James had succeeded in yoking the best of two traditions—the unworldly tradition of millennial reform and the all-too-worldly tradition of "strenuous" social service. This, however, was only one aspect of his struggle to preserve enough of the spirit of the ante-bellum idealists to counteract the tough-mindedness and authoritarianism of postwar thought. In addition to finding a place in his scheme of things for moral crusading, James went against the grain of his generation by making a general defense of the individualist or anti-institutional attitude. In *The Varieties of Religious Experience,* he wrote sympathetically of the zealot, the mystic, and the "twice-born" Christian, in a way which, as critics like Santayana were quick to point out, ignored the traditional and institutional nature of religion. James, to the horror of many, believed with the revivalists and transcendentalists that religion was nothing if not an intense, personal experience. But his anti-institutionalism extended beyond the religious sphere. In 1905, he asserted his "faith in personal freedom and its spontaneities," and claimed he could never be "unqualifiedly respectful . . . of 'civilization' with its herding and branding, licensing and degree-giving, authorizing and appointing, and in general regulating and administering by system the lives of human beings." In his view, "the individual, the person in the singular number, is the more fundamental phenomenon, and the social institution, of whatever grade, is but the secondary and ministerial. Many as are the interests which social systems satisfy, always unsatisfied interests remain over, and among them are interests to which system, as such, does violence whenever it lays its hand upon us. The best commonwealth will always be the one that most cherishes the men who represent the residual interests, the one that leaves the largest scope to their peculiarities."[47]

In this statement, James defined his role as an intellectual mediator. He was not denying the value and necessity of institutions. Indeed, his "army against nature" was an institution on a distinctly authoritarian model. But if it was the individual's fate to live in a structured and ordered society, it should be his aspiration to realize at the same time his uniqueness and individuality. If the radical abolitionists and transcendentalists had gone too far in one direction by denying the social side of man's nature, their critics had often gone to the opposite extreme and would have given the man with a vision no right at all to rebel against history, circumstance, or a given social system. This being the case, the duty of the American Scholar was clear: He was to learn to distinguish what was valid and human in the "proud absolutes" which have struggled for dominion over the American mind.

NOTES

PROLOGUE

1. Henry James, *Hawthorne* (London, 1879), p. 144.
2. *Ibid.*, pp. 142–144.
3. Merle Curti, *The Growth of American Thought* (New York and London, 1943), p. 469.
4. Nathaniel Hawthorne, "Chiefly about War Matters," *Atlantic*, X (July 1862), p. 56.
5. Letter of Hawthorne to Francis Bennock, cited in Moncure Conway, *Emerson at Home and Abroad* (Boston, 1882), p. 273.

CHAPTER ONE.   PROPHETS OF PERFECTION

1. Wendell Phillips, *Speeches, Lectures, and Letters, First Series* (Boston, 1902), p. 264.
2. Letter of Carl Schurz to Malwida Von Meysenbug, *Speeches, Correspondence, and Political Papers of Carl Schurz*, ed. Frederic Bancroft (New York and London, 1913), I, 7–8.
3. This entire chapter owes much to the illuminating discussion of Northern intellectuals and slavery in Chapter IV of Elkins, *Slavery: A Problem of American Institutional and Intellectual Life* (Chicago, 1959).
4. See John William Ward, *Andrew Jackson: Symbol for an Age*

(New York, 1955), Chapter IV; and Richard Hofstadter, *Anti-intellectualism in American Life* (New York, 1963), Chapter VI.

5. Ralph Waldo Emerson, "The American Scholar," in *Nature, Lectures, and Addresses,* The Complete Works of Ralph Waldo Emerson, I (Boston and New York, 1903), pp. 102–103, 107.

6. See Stephen F. Whicher, *Freedom and Fate: An Inner Life of Ralph Waldo Emerson* (Philadelphia, 1953), *passim.*

7. Emerson, "The American Scholar," in *Nature, etc.,* p. 100.

8. *Ibid.,* p. 94.

9. Whicher, *Freedom and Fate,* pp. 29–33.

10. Emerson, *Nature, etc.,* pp. 349, 353–354.

11. Ralph Waldo Emerson, "New England Reformers" (1844), *Essays, Second Series,* Works, III, 253, 255, 260–261.

12. Theodore Parker, Letter to the Members of the Twenty-Eighth Congregational Society, April 19, 1859, entitled, "Theodore Parker's Experience as a Minister," in John Weiss, *Life and Correspondence of Theodore Parker* (New York, 1864), II, 454–455.

13. Theodore Parker, "Emerson," *American Scholar* (Boston, 1907), p. 98. This review was originally published in the *Massachusetts Review* (March 1850), under the title, "The Writings of Ralph Waldo Emerson."

14. Mary E. Burtis, *Moncure Conway* (New Brunswick, N.J., 1952), pp. 3–12; Moncure Conway, *Autobiography, Memories, and Experiences* (Boston and New York, 1904), I, 91.

15. Burtis, *Conway,* pp. 32–38; Conway, *Autobiography,* I, 192, 127.

16. My interpretation of Garrison and his followers derives largely from Elkins, *Slavery,* Chapter IV, and from John L. Thomas, *The Liberator: William Lloyd Garrison* (Boston, 1963).

17. Wendell Phillips, *Speeches, Lectures, and Letters, First Series,* pp. 98–153, especially pp. 152–153; Phillips' theory of agitation is well described in Irving Bartlett, *Wendell Phillips: Brahmin Radical* (Boston, 1961), and in Richard Hofstadter, *The American Political Tradition* (New York, 1948), Chapter VI.

18. Phillips, *Speeches, etc., First Series,* pp. 243–244, 318.

19. Gay Wilson Allen, *The Solitary Singer: A Critical Biography of Walt Whitman* (New York, 1955), pp. 73–74, 83–88; Walt Whitman, "The Eighteenth Presidency," in *Walt Whitman's Workshop: A Collection of Unpublished Manuscripts,* ed. Clifton Joseph Furness (Cambridge, Mass., 1928), p. 104.

20. *Ibid.,* pp. 99–100, 62.

CHAPTER TWO. CONSERVATIVES IN A RADICAL AGE

1. See Stanley M. Elkins, *Slavery: A Problem of American Institutional and Intellectual Life* (Chicago, 1959), p. 141.

2. Frank Freidel, *Francis Lieber: Nineteenth Century Liberal* (Baton Rouge, La., 1947), *passim;* Francis Lieber, *On Civil Liberty and Self-Government,* Enlarged Edition (Philadelphia, 1859), *passim,* especially, pp. 285–290, 304–324, 362–363, 405–416.

3. Mary A. Cheney, *The Life and Letters of Horace Bushnell* (New York, 1880), p. 284.

4. Barbara M. Cross, *Horace Bushnell: Minister to a Changing America* (Chicago, 1958), pp. 78–80; Horace Bushnell, "The Age of Homespun," *Work and Play; or Literary Varieties* (New York, 1886), p. 401.

5. Henry W. Bellows, *The Suspense of Faith, An Address to the Alumni of the Divinity School of Harvard University, Cambridge, Mass., July 19, 1859* (New York, 1859), pp. 24, 30, 32; see also George Willis Cooke, *Unitarianism in America* (Boston, 1902), *passim,* especially Chapter VIII; and John W. Chadwick, *Henry W. Bellows* (New York, 1882), pp. 8, 10–11.

6. Bellows, *Suspense of Faith,* p. 37.

7. Letter of Bellows to Charles Eliot Norton, Sept. 29, 1859, Norton Papers, Harvard University Library; Chadwick, *Bellows,* pp. 13–14; Cooke, *Unitarianism,* pp. 240–241.

8. This account of Brownson's early career follows that of Arthur M. Schlesinger, Jr., *Orestes A. Brownson: A Pilgrim's Progress* (Boston, 1939).

9. *The Works of Orestes Brownson,* ed. Henry F. Brownson (Detroit, 1882–1887), XVII, 8–9.

10. "Charles Russell Lowell," in *Harvard Memorial Biographies* (Cambridge, Mass., 1866), I, 298–300; Charles Russell Lowell, Letters of April 15, 1855, June 24, 1855, and Sept. 28, 1856, in Edward W. Emerson, *Life and Letters of Charles Russell Lowell* (Boston and New York, 1907), pp. 80, 87, 120.

11. *Memorial Biographies,* I, 301–304; Letters of May 27, 1858, and Oct. 11, 1859, *Life and Letters of Charles Russell Lowell,* pp. 160, 182.

12. Bliss Perry, *The Life and Letters of Henry Lee Higginson* (Boston, 1921), pp. 90, 108, 138.

13. Kermit Vanderbilt, *Charles Eliot Norton: Apostle of Culture*

in a Democracy (Cambridge, Mass., 1959), pp. 7–66, *passim*. For an account of the Bowen affair, see the entry on Bowen in the *Dictionary of American Biography.* Bowen's heretical views were expressed in the *North American Review,* LXX (1850), pp. 78–136, and LXXI (1850), pp. 464–479.

14. Charles Eliot Norton, *Considerations on Some Recent Social Theories* (Boston, 1853), pp. 19–20.

15. *Ibid.,* pp. 23, 130–131, 158.

16. Letter of Francis Parkman to Martin Brimmer, 1886, in Henry Dwight Sedgwick, *Francis Parkman* (Boston and New York, 1904), p. 330.

17. Quoted in Howard Doughty, *Francis Parkman* (New York, 1962), p. 126.

18. Oliver Wendell Holmes, *The Autocrat of the Breakfast Table,* The Writings of Oliver Wendell Holmes, I (Boston and New York, 1895), pp. 260–261.

19. Francis Parkman, *The Oregon Trail: Sketches of Prairie and Rocky Mountain Life,* The Works of Francis Parkman (Boston, 1927), p. 334 (originally published in 1849 under the title *The California and Oregon Trail*).

20. Letter of Parkman, Nov. 10, 1850, *Letters of Francis Parkman,* ed. W. R. Jacobs (Norman, Okla., 1960), I, 79.

21. "Adventure," Lecture of March 14, 1856, Winthrop Manuscripts, New York Public Library; see also Eliot Ellsworth, Jr., *Theodore Winthrop* (New Haven, 1938); and Theodore Winthrop, *Life in the Open Air* (Boston, 1863).

CHAPTER THREE.   THE IMPENDING CRISIS

1. Henry Adams, *The Education of Henry Adams* (New York, Modern Library Edition, 1931), p. 43.

2. See *Letters and Journals of Thomas Wentworth Higginson,* ed. Mary Thacher Higginson (Boston and New York, 1921), pp. 140–144.

3. John Weiss, *Life and Correspondence of Theodore Parker* (New York, 1864), II, 170–171.

4. *Ibid.,* pp. 172, 177–178.

5. Ralph Waldo Emerson, *Miscellanies,* Complete Works of Ralph Waldo Emerson, XI (Boston and New York, 1904), pp. 258, 261–262.

6. *Ibid.,* p. 270; *The Journals of Ralph Waldo Emerson,* ed. Edward W. Emerson and Waldo E. Forbes (Boston and New York, 1909–1914), IX, 245–246.

7. *The Writings of Henry David Thoreau: Journal,* ed. Bradford Torrey (Boston and New York, 1906), XII, 420, 408, 438–439.

8. Ralph Waldo Emerson, *Essays, Second Series,* Works, III (Boston and New York, 1903), pp. 85–86.

9. W. P. and F. J. Garrison, *William Lloyd Garrison: The Story of His Life as Told by His Children* (New York, 1885–1889), III, 437–441.

10. Irving H. Bartlett, *Wendell Phillips: Brahmin Radical* (Boston, 1961), p. 200.

11. W. P. and F. J. Garrison, *William Lloyd Garrison,* III, 419, 440–441.

12. *Ibid.,* p. 473.

13. *Ibid.,* pp. 486, 491–492.

14. *Ibid.,* p. 492.

15. Wendell Phillips, *Speeches, Lectures and Letters, Second Series* (Boston, 1902), p. 308; Bartlett, *Phillips,* p. 218.

16. Wendell Phillips, *Speeches, Lectures and Letters, First Series* (Boston, 1902), pp. 269, 292.

17. *Ibid.,* p. 293.

18. Mary Elizabeth Burtis, *Moncure Conway* (New Brunswick, N.J., 1952), p. 75; Moncure Conway, *Autobiography, Memories and Experiences* (Boston and New York, 1904), I, 299–304.

19. *The Works of Orestes Brownson,* ed. Henry F. Brownson (Detroit, 1882–1887), XVII, 42 (from *Brownson's Quarterly Review of July 1851*).

20. *Ibid.,* pp. 54–55.

21. Charles C. Cole, Jr., "Horace Bushnell and the Slavery Question," *New England Quarterly,* XXIII (March 1950), pp. 19–30.

22. Norton to J. R. Lowell, April 6, 1855, *Letters of Charles Eliot Norton,* ed. Sara Norton and M. A. De Wolfe Howe (Boston and New York, 1913), I, 126–127.

23. Norton to A. H. Clough, Aug. 22, 1857, *ibid.,* pp. 183–184.

24. Norton's review of *The Laws of Race as Connected with Slavery,* in *Atlantic,* VII (February 1861), pp. 252–254.

25. Letter of Charles Eliot Norton to Mrs. Edward Twisleton, Dec. 13, 1859, *Letters,* I, p. 201.

26. Charles Eliot Norton, review of *The Public Life of John Brown,* by James Redpath, in *Atlantic,* V (March 1860), p. 380.

27. Quoted in Frank Freidel, *Francis Lieber, Nineteenth Century Liberal* (Baton Rouge, La., 1947), p. 298.

28. Letter of Lieber, Thomas Sergeant Perry, *The Life and Letters of Francis Lieber* (Boston, 1882), p. 315.

29. *Ibid.,* p. 314.

30. Letter of Howe to Theodore Parker, Jan. 22, 1860, *Journals and Letters of Samuel Gridley Howe,* ed. Laura E. Richards (Boston, 1909), II, p. 446.

31. James Russell Lowell, *Political Essays,* The Writings of James Russell Lowell, V (Boston, 1892), pp. 36–37.

CHAPTER FOUR. SECESSION, REBELLION, AND IDEOLOGY

1. *Northern Editorials on Secession,* ed. Howard C. Perkins (New York and London, 1942), I, 331–383, *passim.*

2. Quoted from an unpublished lecture in James E. Cabot, *A Memoir of Ralph Waldo Emerson* (Boston and New York, 1887), II, 603–604.

3. H. W. Bellows to C. A. Bartol, Dec. 12, 1860, and H. W. Bellows to his sister, Dec. 12, 1860, Bellows Papers, Massachusetts Historical Society, Boston, Mass.

4. Henry W. Bellows, *The Advantage of Testing Our Principles, Compensatory of the Evils of Serious Times, a Discourse of February 17, 1861* (Philadelphia, 1861), p. 4. Sermon in the Harvard University Library.

5. *Ibid.,* pp. 11, 15, 16–17, 19–20.

6. Norton to G. W. Curtis, Dec. 17, 1860, *Letters of Charles Eliot Norton,* ed. Sara Norton and M. A. De Wolfe Howe (Boston and New York, 1913), I, 215–216.

7. *The Diary of George Templeton Strong,* ed. Allan Nevins and Milton H. Thomas (New York, 1952), III, 66.

8. Letter of Horace Binney to D. A. White, March 1, 1861, in Charles Chauncey Binney, *The Life of Horace Binney with Selections from His Letters* (Philadelphia and London, 1903), p. 317.

9. Kenneth Stampp, *And the War Came: the North and the Secession Crisis* (Baton Rouge, La., 1950), p. 247.

10. Moncure Conway, *Autobiography, Memories, and Experiences* (Boston and New York, 1904), I, 322.

11. Wendell Phillips, *Speeches, Lectures and Letters, First Series* (Boston, 1902), pp. 369–370.

12. James Freeman Clarke, *Secession, Concession or Self-Possession: Which?* (Boston, 1861), p. 13. Pamphlet in the Harvard University Library.

13. Quoted in Jeter Allen Isely, *Horace Greeley and the Republican*

Party (Princeton, 1947), pp. 306–307 (from *New York Tribune,* Dec. 17, 1860).

14. For examples, see the *Indianapolis Daily Journal,* Dec. 22, 1860, and the Greenfield, Mass., *Gazette and Courier,* Feb. 11, 1861, in *Northern Editorials,* I, 333–334, 352–353.

15. "The End and the Beginning," *Harper's,* XXII (March 1861), p. 554.

16. *The Collected Works of Abraham Lincoln,* ed. Roy P. Basler (New Brunswick, N.J., 1953–1955), IV, 260; Thomas J. Pressly, "Bullets and Ballots: Lincoln and 'The Right of Revolution'," *American Historical Review,* LXVII (April 1962), pp. 657–658.

17. James Russell Lowell, *Political Essays,* The Writings of James Russell Lowell, V (Boston and New York, 1892), pp. 71, 74.

18. See R. W. B. Lewis, *The American Adam: Innocence, Tragedy, and Tradition in the Nineteenth Century* (Chicago, 1955), pp. 189–191. In 1859, Lowell admitted to an English friend that his *Bigelow Papers,* written in the heat of his earlier more militant abolitionist period, now seemed a little quaint and that he found it hard to write an historical preface to a new edition after "twelve years of more cloistered interests and studies that have alienated me very much from contemporary politics." Letter of James Russell Lowell to Thomas Hughes, Sept. 13, 1859, *Letters of James Russell Lowell* (New York, 1894), I, 295–296.

19. Ralph V. Harlow, *Gerrit Smith: Philanthropist and Reformer* (New York, 1939), p. 428; *Northern Editorials,* I, 359–361.

20. W. P. and F. J. Garrison, *William Lloyd Garrison: The Story of his Life as Told by His Children* (New York, 1885–1889), IV, 21; Whittier quoted in Samuel T. Pickard, *Life and Letters of John Greenleaf Whittier* (Boston and New York, 1894), II, 441; Conway in Mary Elizabeth Burtis, *Moncure Conway* (New Brunswick, N.J., 1952), p. 81.

21. Phillips, *Speeches, etc., First Series,* pp. 413–414.

22. Donald Jordan and Edward J. Pratt, *Europe and the American Civil War* (Boston and New York, 1931), pp. 13, 23, 60–61.

23. George W. Bassett, *A Discourse on the Wickedness and Folly of the Present War,* Speech given at Ottawa, Ill., Aug. 11, 1861 (n.d. or place of publication), pp. 16, 4, 21, 15, 8. For another example of the same point of view, see Joshua Blanchard's undated pamphlet, *The War of Secession.* Both pamphlets are in the Harvard University Library.

24. Phillips, *Speeches, etc., First Series,* pp. 402, 404–405.

25. John L. Thomas, *The Liberator: William Lloyd Garrison* (Boston, 1963), pp. 403–404.

CHAPTER FIVE.   THE SPIRIT OF '61

1. *New York Times,* April 15, 1861, *Erie Weekly Gazette,* May 2, 1861, in *Northern Editorials on Secession,* ed. Howard C. Perkins (New York and London, 1942), II, 735, 756.
2. Quoted from an unpublished lecture of Emerson, given soon after Fort Sumter, in James E. Cabot, *A Memoir of Ralph Waldo Emerson* (Boston and New York, 1887), II, 600.
3. Horace Traubel, *With Walt Whitman in Camden* (New York, 1906–1914), I, 13.
4. See Herbert W. Schneider, *A History of American Philosophy* (New York, 1946), pp. 161–165.
5. *Walt Whitman's Workshop: A Collection of Unpublished Manuscripts,* ed. Clifton Joseph Furness (Cambridge, Mass., 1928), p. 57.
6. Walt Whitman, "Long, Too Long, O Land," *Drum Taps* (New York, 1865), p. 45.
7. "Rise Oh Days From Your Fathomless Depths," *Drum Taps,* pp. 35–37.
8. F. O. Matthiessen, *The James Family* (New York, 1947), pp. 12–13, 50, 55.
9. Henry James, Sr., *The Social Significance of Our Institutions, an Oration Delivered at Newport, R.I., July 4, 1861* (Boston, 1861), p. 27.
10. *Ibid.,* pp. 33–34.
11. Letter of Norton to A. H. Clough, May 27, 1861, *Letters of Charles Eliot Norton,* ed. Sara Norton and M. A. De Wolfe Howe (Boston and New York, 1913), I, 234.
12. Charles Eliot Norton, *The Soldier of the Good Cause* (Boston, 1861), pp. 5–6, 12–13. Pamphlet in the Harvard University Library.
13. Henry W. Bellows, *Duty and Interest Identical in the Present Crisis, Sermon of April 14, 1861* (New York, 1861), p. 16. Sermon in the Harvard University Library.
14. Henry W. Bellows, *The State and the Nation—Sacred to Christian Citizens, Sermon of April 21, 1861* (New York, 1861), pp. 6, 7. Sermon in the Harvard University Library.
15. *Ibid.,* p. 8.
16. *The Works of Orestes Brownson,* ed. Henry F. Brownson (Detroit, 1882–1887), XVII, 121, 139.

17. Oliver Wendell Holmes, "Bread and Newspapers," in *Pages from an Old Volume of Life,* The Writings of Oliver Wendell Holmes, VIII (Boston and New York, 1895), pp. 3, 9.

18. *Harvard Memorial Biographies* (Cambridge, Mass., 1866), I, 306; Edward W. Emerson, *The Life and Letters of Charles Russell Lowell* (Boston and New York, 1907), p. 19; Letter of Lowell to his mother, May 13, 1861, *ibid.,* pp. 207–208.

19. Bliss Perry, *The Life and Letters of Henry Lee Higginson* (Boston, 1921), pp. 183–184.

20. Letter of Theodore Winthrop to George W. Curtis, May 5, 1861, quoted in Ellsworth Eliot, Jr., *Theodore Winthrop* (New Haven, 1938), p. 24.

21. Moncure Conway, *Autobiography, Memories, and Experiences* (Boston and New York, 1904), I, 335; John Murray Forbes, *Letters and Recollections,* ed. Sarah Forbes Hughes (Boston and New York, 1900), I, 227; *Christian Inquirer,* Aug. 10, 1861, clipping in the Charles Eliot Norton Papers, Harvard University Library. *Letters and Journals of Thomas Wentworth Higginson,* ed. Mary Thacher Higginson (Boston and New York, 1921), p. 156.

22. Charles Eliot Norton, "The Advantages of Defeat," *Atlantic,* VIII (September 1861), pp. 361–363.

23. *Ibid.,* p. 364.

24. Letter to *Boston Daily Advertiser,* Sept. 4, 1861, in *Letters of Francis Parkman,* ed. W. R. Jacobs (Norman, Okla., 1960), I, 142–143.

25. Horace Bushnell, *Reverses Needed: A Discourse Delivered on the Sunday after the Disaster at Bull Run in the North Church, Hartford* (Hartford, 1861), pp. 9–10.

26. *Ibid.,* pp. 10–11, 24.

27. *North American Review,* XCIII (October 1861), p. 588.

28. Wendell Phillips, *Speeches, Lectures, and Letters, First Series* (Boston, 1902), p. 348.

29. *Ibid.,* pp. 422–423.

30. Charles Chauncey Binney, *The Life of Horace Binney with Selections from His Letters* (Philadelphia and London, 1903), pp. 346–347; Horace Binney, *The Privilege of the Writ of Habeas Corpus under the Constitution* (Philadelphia, 1862).

31. Phillips, *Speeches, etc., First Series,* p. 424.

CHAPTER SIX. "THIS CRUEL WAR": THE INDIVIDUAL RESPONSE
TO SUFFERING

1. Allan Nevins, *The War for the Union* (New York, 1959–

1960), II, 111; W. Fletcher Thompson, *The Image of War: The Pictorial Reporting of the American Civil War* (New York, 1959), pp. 70–73.

2. Richard H. Shryock, "A Medical Perspective on the Civil War," *American Quarterly*, XIV (Summer 1962), pp. 161–162.

3. Oliver Wendell Holmes, "My Hunt after the Captain," *Atlantic*, X (December 1862), pp. 743–744.

4. Letter of Norton to G. W. Curtis, May 11, 1862, quoted in Kermit Vanderbilt, *Charles Eliot Norton: Apostle of Culture in a Democracy* (Cambridge, Mass., 1959), p. 81.

5. *The Works of Orestes Brownson*, ed. Henry F. Brownson (Detroit, 1882–1887), XVII, 214.

6. Horace Bushnell, *Reverses Needed: A Discourse Delivered on the Sunday after the Disaster at Bull Run in the North Church, Hartford* (Hartford, 1861), pp. 5, 22–23. Sermon in the Harvard University Library.

7. Letter of Emerson to Benjamin and Susan Rodman, June 17, 1863, *The Letters of Ralph Waldo Emerson*, ed. Ralph L. Rusk (New York, 1939), V, 332.

8. William Henry Furness, *A Word of Consolation for the Kindred of Those Who Have Fallen in Battle, a Discourse of September 28, 1862* (n.d. or place of publication), p. 7. Sermon in the Harvard University Library.

9. Hazel Catherine Wolf, *On Freedom's Altar: The Martyr Complex in the Abolition Movement* (Madison, 1952).

10. O. B. Frothingham, *Seeds and Shells: A Sermon Preached in New York, November 17, 1861* (New York, 1862), pp. 3, 6–9. Sermon in the Harvard University Library.

11. Gail Hamilton, "A Call to My Country-Women," *Atlantic*, XI (March 1863), p. 346. Gail Hamilton's real name was Mary Abigail Dodge. For biographical information, see the *Dictionary of American Biography*.

12. Letter of Lydia Maria Child to Henrietta Sargent, July 26, 1861, *The Letters of Lydia Maria Child* (Boston, 1884), p. 154.

13. *The Philanthropic Work of Josephine Shaw Lowell*, ed. William Rhinelander Stewart (New York, 1911), pp. 28, 30.

14. John Greenleaf Whittier, "To Samuel W. Sewall and Harriet W. Sewall," in *Anti-Slavery Poems: Songs of Labor and Reform*, The Writings of John Greenleaf Whittier, III (Boston and New York, 1900), p. 216.

15. Quoted in Eva Ingersoll, Introduction to *The Letters of Robert Ingersoll* (New York, 1951), p. 32.

16. Letter of Robert Ingersoll to Ebon Clark Ingersoll, 1862, *Letters of Robert Ingersoll* (New York, 1951), pp. 119–120.

17. Orvin Larson, *American Infidel: Robert G. Ingersoll* (New York, 1962), p. 67.

18. Holmes to his mother, Dec. 12, 1862, *Touched with Fire: Civil War Letters and Diary of Oliver Wendell Holmes, Jr.*, ed. Mark De Wolfe Howe (Cambridge, Mass., 1946), p. 78; Mark De Wolfe Howe, *Justice Holmes: The Shaping Years 1841–1870* (Cambridge, Mass., 1957), Chapter III, *passim*.

19. There is a good account of De Forest's literary career in Edmund Wilson, *Patriotic Gore: Studies in the Literature of the American Civil War* (New York, 1962), pp. 669–742; the war sketches have been published in book form as *A Volunteer's Adventures* (New Haven, 1946).

20. Letter of De Forest to his brother, Nov. 27, 1863, De Forest Papers, Yale University Library.

21. Louisa May Alcott, *Hospital Sketches*, ed. Bessie Z. Jones (Cambridge, Mass., 1960), pp. 30, 50 (originally published in 1863).

22. *Ibid.*, p. 37.

23. Ishbel Ross, *Angel of the Battlefield: The Life of Clara Barton* (New York, 1956), p. 142.

24. Letter of Clara Barton to her sister Fannie, Jan. 9, 1862, quoted in William E. Barton, *The Life of Clara Barton, Founder of the American Red Cross* (New York and Boston, 1922), I, 42.

25. *Ibid.*, pp. 181–183; Ross, *Angel of the Battlefield*, p. 33.

26. Katherine Prescott Wormeley, *The Other Side of War* (Boston, 1888), p. 102.

27. Gay Wilson Allen, *The Solitary Singer: A Critical Biography of Walt Whitman* (New York, 1955), pp. 270–287.

28. For a version of the sainthood theory, see Oscar Cargill's introduction to *The Wound Dresser* (New York, 1949); the sublimated homosexuality thesis is ably presented in Roger Asselineau, *The Evolution of Walt Whitman* (Cambridge, Mass., 1960), pp. 171–174.

29. Walt Whitman to his mother, April 15, 1863, in *Correspondence*, ed. Edwin H. Miller (New York, 1961), I, 89.

30. Walt Whitman to Nathaniel Bloom and John F. S. Gray, March 19, 1863, *ibid.*, pp. 81–82.

31. *Ibid.*, pp. 112, 213; Walt Whitman, *Complete Poetry and Prose* (New York, 1954), II, 74.

32. *Correspondence,* I, 75, 171–172.

33. *Poetry and Prose,* II, 76.

34. *Loc. cit.*

35. Whitman to his mother, July 7, 1863, and March 22, 1864, *Correspondence,* I, pp. 114, 204; *Poetry and Prose,* II, p. 30.

36. Whitman to Thomas P. Sawyer, April 21, 1863, *Correspondence,* I, p. 92.

37. The manuscript version has been published in *Walt Whitman and the Civil War: A Collection of Original Articles and Manuscripts,* ed. Charles I. Glicksberg (Philadelphia, 1933), pp. 121–123. Drastically altered, it was included in *Drum Taps* (New York, 1865), pp. 55–56.

38. Whitman to his mother, August 23, 1863, *Correspondence,* I, 138.

39. Some examples in *Drum Taps* are "Camps of Green," "Hymn of Dead Soldiers," and "Pensive on Her Dead Gazing, I Heard the Mother of All."

40. An Hegelian interpretation of the Civil War, along the lines suggested by Whitman, was worked out after the Civil War by William T. Harris and Denton J. Snider; see Herbert W. Schneider, *A History of American Philosophy* (New York, 1946), pp. 177–184.

CHAPTER SEVEN.   THE SANITARY ELITE: THE ORGANIZED RESPONSE
TO SUFFERING

1. William Quentin Maxwell, *Lincoln's Fifth Wheel: The Political History of the United States Sanitary Commission* (New York, London, and Toronto, 1956), Chapters I and II.

2. Lucius Pierpont Brockett, *The Philanthropic Results of the War in America* (New York, 1864), p. 119.

3. *Hospital Transports: A Memoir* (Boston, 1863), Introduction, p. ix.

4. Henry W. Bellows, *The Valley of Decision, a Discourse of Sept. 26, 1861, All Souls Church* (New York, 1861), pp. 22–23.

5. Charles J. Stillé, *History of the United States Sanitary Commission* (New York, 1868), p. 70.

6. *The Diary of George Templeton Strong,* ed. Allan Nevins and Milton Halsey Thomas (New York, 1952), III, 272.

7. Stillé, *Sanitary Commission,* pp. 76–77. On Olmsted see Broadus Mitchell, *Frederick Law Olmsted, A Critic of the Old South* (Baltimore, 1924); *Frederick Law Olmsted, Landscape Architect, 1822–1903,* ed. F. L. Olmsted and T. Kimball (New York, 1922–1928), 2 vols.

8. Charles J. Stillé, *The Historical Development of American Civilization* (New Haven, 1863). Pamphlet in the Harvard University Library. See Chapter IX for a full analysis of Stillé's thought; for biographical information on Stillé, see Hampton L. Carson, *A History of the Historical Society of Pennsylvania* (Philadelphia, 1940), II, 78–94.

9. Charles J. Stillé, *A Memoir of Horace Binney, Jr.* (Philadelphia, 1870), p. 9. Pamphlet in the Harvard University Library.

10. *The Journals and Letters of Samuel Gridley Howe,* ed. Laura E. Richards (Boston, 1909), II, 499.

11. Katherine Prescott Wormeley, *The United States Sanitary Commission* (Boston, 1863), pp. 253–254.

12. *Statement of the Object and Methods of the Sanitary Commission,* U.S. Sanitary Commission Document No. 69 (New York, 1863), p. 5.

13. Bellows to Cyrus A. Bartol, April 12, 1861, and Aug. 9, 1861, Bellows Papers, Massachusetts Historical Society.

14. Bellows to his sister and brother-in-law, March 7, 1862, and Bellows to Bartol, April 5, 1862, Bellows Papers.

15. Strong, *Diary,* III, 274–275.

16. *Statement of the Object and Methods,* Sanitary Document No. 69, pp. 55–56.

17. *A Report to the Secretary of War on the Operations of the Sanitary Commission, December 1861,* U.S. Sanitary Commission Document No. 40 (Washington, 1861), pp. 98–107.

18. Strong, *Diary,* III, pp. 253, 278; *A Record of Certain Resolutions of the Sanitary Commission,* U.S. Sanitary Commission Document No. 21 (n.d., n.p.), p. 5.

19. Stillé, *Sanitary Commission,* p. 246.

20. *Ibid.,* pp. 247–248.

21. Henry W. Bellows, "The Sanitary Commission," *North American Review,* XCVIII (January 1864), p. 179.

22. Henry W. Bellows, *Speech at the Philadelphia Academy of Music, Feb. 24, 1863* (Philadelphia, 1863), p. 20.

23. Bellows, "Sanitary Commission," p. 193.

24. Stillé, *Sanitary Commission,* p. 258.

25. Walt Whitman, *Correspondence,* ed. Edwin H. Miller (New York, 1961), I, 110–111.

26. "Hospital Visits," reprinted from *New York Times,* Dec. 11, 1864, in *The Wound Dresser,* ed. Richard M. Bucke (New York, 1897), pp. 33, 44.

27. Maxwell, *Fifth Wheel,* p. 192; *U.S. Christian Commission: Second Annual Report* (Philadelphia, 1864), pp. 17–18.

28. Letter of Stillé to Louisa Lee Schuyler, Louisa Schuyler–Angelina Post Manuscripts, New-York Historical Society.

29. Frederick Law Olmsted, *An Account of the Executive Organization of the Sanitary Commission*, U.S. Sanitary Commission Document No. 60 (Washington, 1862), *passim;* Bellows is quoted in Maxwell, *The Fifth Wheel*, p. 10.

30. See Sanitary Commission Documents 20 and 21.

31. Bellows to C. A. Bartol, Sept. 13, 1861, Bellows Papers, Massachusetts Historical Society.

32. Bellows to Norton, Aug. 21, 1861, Norton Papers, Harvard University Library.

33. Norton to Bellows, Aug. 23, 1861, Bellows Papers, Massachusetts Historical Society.

34. Cited in Helen E. Marshall, *Dorothea Dix, Forgotten Samaritan* (Chapel Hill, N.C., 1937), p. 221.

35. Francis Tiffany, *The Life of Dorothea Lynde Dix* (Boston and New York, 1891), pp. 338–339.

36. Marshall, *Dix,* pp. 225–226.

37. Strong, *Diary,* III, 182.

38. Quoted in Tiffany, *Dix,* p. 339.

39. Allan Nevins, *The War for the Union* (New York, 1959–1960), I, v.

40. Bellows to his son, Sept. 7, 1862, Bellows Papers, Massachusetts Historical Society.

41. See Frank D. Watson, *The Charity Organization Movement in the United States: A Study in American Philanthropy* (New York, 1922), Chapter III.

42. Quoted in Robert H. Bremner, *American Philanthropy* (Chicago, 1960), p. 46.

CHAPTER EIGHT.   THE MEANING OF EMANCIPATION

1. Benjamin Quarles, *Lincoln and the Negro* (New York, 1962), p. 143; W. P. and F. J. Garrison, *William Lloyd Garrison: The Story of His Life as Told by His Children* (New York, 1885–1889), IV, 69–70.

2. Charles J. Stillé, *Northern Interests and Southern Independence* (Philadelphia, 1863), pp. 42–43. Bellows, who was very close to Stillé in his views on the war, did not positively oppose emancipation. His attitude was rather one of indifference to the question. See the letter of Bellows to Thomas Starr King, July 4, 1862, Bellows Papers, Mas-

sachusetts Historical Society, in which Bellows wrote: "my own opinion is that it does not matter what we do, or don't do in reference to that subject."

3. Letter of Binney to J. C. Hamilton, Aug. 4, 1862, Charles Chauncey Binney, *The Life of Horace Binney with Selections from His Letters* (Philadelphia and London, 1903), p. 358.

4. *Works of Orestes Brownson,* ed. Henry F. Brownson (Detroit, 1882–1887), XVII, 155.

5. Theodore Maynard, *Orestes Brownson: Yankee, Radical, Catholic* (New York, 1943), Chapter 14, *passim;* Brownson, *Works,* XVII, 584 (from *Brownson's Quarterly Review,* October 1864).

6. *Ibid.,* p. 176.

7. E. H. Derby, "Resources of the South," *Atlantic,* X (October 1862), pp. 508–509.

8. *The Diary of George Templeton Strong,* ed. Allan Nevins and Milton Halsey Thomas (New York, 1952), III, 344–345, 347; review of Robert Dale Owen's *The Wrong of Slavery, Atlantic,* XIV (October 1864), p. 517.

9. Irving H. Bartlett, *Wendell Phillips: Brahmin Radical* (Boston, 1961), p. 247. Letter of Conway to Charles Sumner, Sept. 17, 1861, Sumner Papers, Harvard University Library; Conway wrote to Sumner that "there is no President of the United States—only a President of Kentucky."

10. Letter of Lydia Child to Whittier, Jan. 21, 1862, *Letters of Lydia Maria Child* (Boston, 1884), p. 160; *Letters and Journals of Thomas Wentworth Higginson,* ed. Mary Thacher Higginson (Boston and New York, 1921), p. 167.

11. Moncure Conway, *The Rejected Stone,* Second Ed. (Boston, 1862), pp. 71–72, 116–118, 128.

12. James Russell Lowell, *Poems,* II, The Writings of James Russell Lowell, VII (Boston and New York, 1892), pp. 297–302.

13. Moncure Conway, *Autobiography, Memories, and Experiences* (Boston and New York, 1904), I, 348–349.

14. Edward E. Hale, *Future Civilization of the South, A Sermon Preached on the 13th of April 1862 at South Congregational* (Boston, n.d.), pp. 12–14, 17. Sermon in the Harvard University Library.

15. William Henry Furness, *A Word of Consolation for the Kindred of Those Who Have Fallen in Battle, A Discourse of September 28, 1862* (n.d. or place of publication), pp. 7, 13. Sermon in the Harvard University Library.

16. Letter of Emerson to Charles Sumner, Dec. 8, 1864, *The Letters of Ralph Waldo Emerson,* ed. Ralph L. Rusk (New York, 1939), V, 391.

17. D. A. Wasson, "The Law of Costs," *Atlantic,* XI (February 1863), pp. 246, 249.

18. Letter of Lydia Child to Mrs. S. B. Shaw, 1863, *Letters of Lydia Maria Child,* p. 171.

19. Letter of Ingersoll to his brother John, Oct. 7, 1862, *Letters of Robert Ingersoll* (New York, 1961), p. 128.

20. See Emerson's journal for August 1862, *The Journals of Ralph Waldo Emerson,* ed. Edward W. Emerson and Waldo E. Forbes (Boston and New York, 1909–1914), IX, 444.

21. Ralph Waldo Emerson, "The President's Proclamation," *Atlantic,* X (November 1862), pp. 638–642.

22. Lowell, *Poems,* II, 345 (originally published in the *Atlantic* for February 1863).

23. James Russell Lowell, *Political Essays,* The Writings of James Russell Lowell, V (Boston and New York, 1892), pp. 183, 185–186.

24. *Ibid.,* p. 191.

25. W. P. and F. J. Garrison, *William Lloyd Garrison,* IV, 61.

26. Gerrit Smith, *Speech on the Country, Delivered at Cooper Institute, December 21, 1862* (New York, 1862), p. 8. Pamphlet in the Harvard University Library.

27. Gerrit Smith, *Speeches and Letters on the Rebellion* (New York, 1864), pp. 23, 39–40.

28. Ralph Harlow, *Gerrit Smith: Philanthropist and Reformer* (New York, 1939), pp. 441–442.

29. Letter of Conway to Sumner, April 22, 1862, Sumner Papers, Harvard University Library.

30. Moncure Conway, *The Golden Hour* (Boston, 1862), pp. 30–32, 34.

31. *Ibid.,* p. 59.

32. *Ibid.,* pp. 157–158.

33. Conway, *Autobiography,* I, Chapter XXIII, *passim;* II, 87–94. The Conway criticism of Lincoln was most fully developed in his "President Lincoln," *Fraser's,* LXXI (January 1865), pp. 1–21. His view that Lincoln was obstructing rather than hastening emancipation, at least in 1863, has found support from modern historians, notably Ralph Korngold, *Thaddeus Stevens* (New York, 1955). There is also evidence to support this theory in Quarles, *Lincoln and the Negro;* and Richard Current in his *Lincoln Nobody Knows* (New York, 1958)

summarizes this interpretation as one possible explanation of Lincoln's actions.

34. Conway, *Autobiography*, I, 367–368.

35. Quoted in Mary E. Burtis, *Moncure Conway* (New Brunswick, N.J., 1952), p. 99.

36. Burtis, *Conway*, pp. 99–107; *Autobiography*, I, 412–425.

37. Quoted in Burtis, *Conway*, pp. 105–106.

38. *Ibid.*, pp. 148–149.

39. *Ibid.*, pp. 115–116; Moncure Conway, *Testimonies Concerning Slavery* (London, 1864).

40. Moncure Conway, *Pine and Palm* (New York, 1887).

41. Wendell Phillips, *Speeches, Lectures, and Letters, First Series* (Boston, 1902), pp. 555–556, 561.

42. Bartlett, *Phillips*, pp. 269–273; T. Harry Williams, *Lincoln and the Radicals* (Madison, Wis., 1960), pp. 314–315.

CHAPTER NINE. THE DOCTRINE OF LOYALTY

1. Wood Gray, *The Hidden Civil War: The Story of the Copperheads* (New York, 1942), Chapter VI.

2. Frank Freidel, *Francis Lieber: Nineteenth Century Liberal* (Baton Rouge, La., 1947), pp. 345–346; and "The Loyal Publication Society: A Pro-Union Propaganda Agency," *Mississippi Valley Historical Review*, XXVI (December 1939), pp. 359–376.

3. Russell N. Bellows, *Henry W. Bellows* (Keene, N.H., n.d.), p. 301 (printed from advance sheets of the "Bellows Genealogy").

4. George Winston Smith, "Broadsides for Freedom: Civil War Propaganda in New England," *New England Quarterly*, XXI (September 1948), pp. 291–312; Ralph L. Rusk, *The Life of Ralph Waldo Emerson* (New York, 1949), p. 419.

5. John L. O'Sullivan, *Union, Disunion or Reunion?* (London, 1862), p. 4.

6. John L. O'Sullivan, *Peace: The Sole Chance Now Left for Reunion* (London, 1863), p. 9.

7. Freidel, *Lieber*, pp. 5–6, 23, 73, 244, 312, 392–393.

8. Francis Lieber, *The Arguments of Secessionists*, Loyal Publication Society Pamphlet No. 35 (New York, 1863), pp. 3–6.

9. Francis Lieber, *No Party Now, but All for Our Country*, Loyal Publication Society Pamphlet No. 16 (New York, 1863), p. 3.

10. Gray, *Hidden Civil War*, pp. 139–140.

11. See the article on Thompson in the *Dictionary of American Biography*.

12. Joseph Parrish Thompson, *Revolution against Free Government Not a Right but a Crime, an Address Delivered at the Union League Club of New York* (New York, 1864), pp. 13, 17–18, 39, 44–45.

13. Henry W. Bellows, *Unconditional Loyalty* (New York, 1863), 15 pp., *passim*.

14. See *Harper's*, XXIV (January 1862), p. 261.

15. Joseph T. Duryea, *Civil Liberty: A Sermon Preached on August 6, 1863* (New York, 1863), pp. 23–25; Perry Miller and Thomas Johnson, *The Puritans* (New York, 1938), p. 206.

16. Horace Bushnell, "Popular Government by Divine Right," a sermon delivered in Hartford on November 24, 1864, in *Building Eras in Religion* (New York, 1881), p. 309.

17. Horace Bushnell, "The Doctrine of Loyalty," *New Englander*, XXII (July 1863), p. 560.

18. Henry James, Sr., *The Social Significance of Our Institutions, an Oration Delivered at Newport, July 4th, 1861* (Boston, 1861), pp. 7–8.

19. Bushnell, "Loyalty," pp. 564–571.

20. *Ibid.*, pp. 571–576.

21. Bushnell, "Popular Government," p. 297.

22. Emerson D. Fite, *Social and Industrial Conditions in the North during the Civil War* (New York, 1910), pp. 308–309.

23. Bushnell, "Divine Right," pp. 287, 314.

24. Horace Bushnell, *Reverses Needed, a Discourse Delivered on the Sunday after the Disaster of Bull Run, in the North Church, Hartford* (Hartford, 1861), p. 15.

25. Bushnell, "Divine Right," p. 298.

26. *Ibid.*, p. 291.

27. William Quentin Maxwell, *Lincoln's Fifth Wheel: The Political History of the United States Sanitary Commission* (Philadelphia, 1956), p. 345.

28. Charles J. Stillé, *How a Free People Conduct a Long War* (Philadelphia, 1863), pp. 3–5, 15.

29. Charles J. Stillé, *The Historical Development of American Civilization, An Address Delivered before the Society of the Graduates of Yale College, July 29, 1863* (New Haven, 1863), p. 9.

30. *Ibid.*, pp. 13, 18–19, 14–15.

31. *Ibid.*, pp. 11–13.

32. Alexis de Tocqueville, *Democracy in America*, ed. Phillips Bradley (New York, 1945), I, 241–244.

33. Stillé, *Historical Development*, p. 33.

34. *The Works of Orestes Brownson,* ed. Henry F. Brownson (Detroit, 1882–1887), XVII, 274, 284 (from *Brownson's Quarterly Review,* July 1862).

35. Stillé, *Historical Development,* pp. 26–27, 19.

36. Stillé, *Long War,* p. 38.

37. Bushnell, "Divine Right," p. 296.

38. "Discipline," *Harper's,* XXIV (January 1862), pp. 259–264.

39. "Institutions and Men," *Harper's,* XXVI (January 1863), pp. 273–277.

40. Walt Whitman, *Correspondence,* ed. Edwin H. Miller (New York, 1961), I, 171.

41. *Walt Whitman's Workshop: A Collection of Unpublished Manuscripts,* ed. Clifton Joseph Furness (Cambridge, Mass., 1928), pp. 127–128.

42. See Gay Wilson Allen, *The Solitary Singer: A Critical Biography of Walt Whitman* (New York, 1955), pp. 339–340; Roger Asselineau, *The Evolution of Walt Whitman* (Cambridge, Mass., 1960), p. 174.

CHAPTER TEN. THE MARTYR AND HIS FRIENDS

1. Benjamin Quarles, *The Negro in the Civil War* (Boston, 1963), pp. 3–8.

2. *Reminiscences of John Murray Forbes,* ed. Sarah Forbes Hughes (Boston, 1902), II, 257–260.

3. Quarles, *The Negro,* pp. 10–12.

4. *Ibid.,* pp. 13–17.

5. See *Memorial: RGS* (Cambridge, Mass., 1864), a privately printed volume of tributes to Shaw, which included thirteen poems and a large number of letters and newspaper and magazine reports. Copy in the Harvard University Library.

6. Lydia Maria Child to Mrs. S. B. Shaw (mother of Robert Gould Shaw), July 1863, *Letters of Lydia Maria Child* (Boston, 1884), p. 176.

7. *Memorial: RGS,* p. 117.

8. Letter of Eliza H. Schuyler to Shaw's mother and father, July 28, 1863, *ibid.,* p. 132.

9. H. W. Beecher to Mrs. Shaw, Sept. 6, 1863, *ibid.,* p. 152.

10. Motley to Mrs. Shaw, Sept. 8, 1863, *ibid.,* p. 156.

11. Ralph Waldo Emerson, *Poems,* Complete Works of Ralph Waldo Emerson, IX (Boston and New York, 1904), p. 207.

12. Walter Mitchell, "Harvard Heroes," *Atlantic*, XII (September 1863), pp. 385–388.

13. Quoted in George Winslow Smith, "Broadsides for Freedom: Civil War Propaganda in New England," *New England Quarterly*, XXI (September 1948), p. 303; W. S. R. Hodson, *Twelve Years of a Soldier's Life in India* (Boston, 1860).

14. Thomas Wentworth Higginson, Introduction to *Harvard Memorial Biographies* (Cambridge, 1866), pp. iv–v.

15. Henry James, *Notes of a Son and Brother* (New York, 1914), p. 374; Leon Edel, *Henry James: The Untried Years* (Philadelphia and New York, 1953), pp. 184–187.

16. Quoted in Edel, *James*, pp. 171–172.

17. Quoted in Henry James, *Notes*, p. 242.

18. Letter of William James to Katherine James Prince, Sept. 12, 1863, *Letters of William James*, ed. Henry James (Boston, 1920), I, 44.

19. Henry James, *Notes*, p. 244.

20. Edel, *Henry James*, pp. 173 ff.; Henry James, *Notes*, pp. 296–298.

21. Quoted in Edel, *Henry James*, p. 46.

22. Letter from Mrs. Tappan to Henry Lee Higginson, quoted in Bliss Perry, *The Life and Letters of Henry Lee Higginson* (Boston, 1921), p. 192.

23. Edel, *Henry James*, p. 172.

24. Henry James, *Notes*, pp. 372, 379–380, 304–305.

25. *Ibid.*, pp. 243–244.

26. *Letters of William James*, I, 56–57, 60.

27. *Ibid.*, pp. 62–63.

28. William James, "Oration," in *Dedication of the Robert Gould Shaw Memorial* (Boston, 1897), pp. 50–51.

29. Letters of Parkman to Abbé Casgran, Sept. 12, 1890, and to Charles Colcock Jones, May 20, 1892, *The Letters of Francis Parkman*, ed. W. R. Jacobs (Norman, Okla., 1960), II, 244–245, 260.

30. Parkman to his cousin Mary, Sept. 27, 1862, *ibid.*, I, 153.

31. Parkman to his cousin Mary, Dec. 6, 1863, *ibid.*, I, 169.

32. Letter of Parkman to the Boston *Advertiser*, Jan. 8, 1862, *ibid.*, pp. 145–146.

33. Parkman to the *Advertiser*, Aug. 12, 1862, *ibid.*, p. 151.

34. Parkman to the *Advertiser*, Oct. 14, 1862, *ibid.*, pp. 154–156.

35. William R. Taylor, *Cavalier and Yankee: The Old South and American National Character* (New York, 1961), *passim*.

36. Parkman to the *Advertiser*, June 30, 1863, *Letters*, I, 159–160.

37. Parkman to the *Advertiser*, July 4 and July 14, 1863, *ibid.*, pp. 162–165.

38. Parkman to the *Advertiser*, July 21, 1863, *ibid.*, pp. 165–167.

39. See Kermit Vanderbilt, *Charles Eliot Norton: Apostle of Culture in a Democracy* (Cambridge, Mass., 1959), pp. 92–96; Charles Eliot Norton, "Abraham Lincoln," *North American Review*, C (January 1865), pp. 1–20, and "American Political Ideas," *North American Review*, CI (October 1865), pp. 550–566.

CHAPTER ELEVEN. THE STRENUOUS LIFE

1. Charles Francis Adams, Jr., to Henry Adams, July 27, 1864, *A Cycle of Adams Letters, 1861–1865*, ed. Worthington Ford (Boston and New York, 1920), II, 168.

2. *Touched With Fire: Civil War Letters and Diaries of Oliver Wendell Holmes, Jr.*, ed. Mark De Wolfe Howe (Cambridge, Mass., 1946), pp. 122, 142–143.

3. John W. De Forest, *A Volunteer's Adventures: A Union Captain's Record of the Civil War*, ed. James H. Croushore (New Haven, 1946), pp. 123–124, *et passim*.

4. One of these letters is printed in Edmund Wilson, *Patriotic Gore: Studies in the Literature of the American Civil War* (New York, 1962), pp. 673–674.

5. See De Forest letters of 1855 from Charleston in the De Forest Papers, Yale University Library; De Forest, *Volunteer's Adventures*, pp. 50–51.

6. John W. De Forest, *Miss Ravenel's Conversion from Secession to Loyalty* (New York, Rinehart edition, 1955), pp. 455–456.

7. Quoted in Mark De Wolfe Howe, *Justice Oliver Wendell Holmes: The Shaping Years, 1841–1870* (Cambridge, Mass., 1957), p. 49. My account of Holmes' war experience relies heavily on Howe's perceptive discussion.

8. *Ibid.*, pp. 65–68.

9. Holmes, *Touched With Fire*, p. 24; quoted in Howe, *Holmes*, p. 109.

10. Howe, *Holmes*, pp. 82–84.

11. Oliver Wendell Holmes, "The Soldier's Faith" (1897), in *Speeches* (Boston, 1913), p. 59.

12. Letter of Holmes, Nov. 16, 1862, *Touched With Fire*, p. 71.

13. Letter of Holmes to his father, Dec. 20, 1862, *ibid.*, p. 79.

14. Charles Francis Adams, Jr., to his father, June 10, 1861,

Adams Cycle, I, 10; C. F. A., Jr., to his father, June 28, 1862, *ibid.,* pp. 160–161; Henry Adams to Charles Francis Adams, Jr., May 16, 1862, *ibid.,* pp. 148–149.

15.   Henry Adams to C. F. A., Jr., July 19, 1862, *ibid.,* p. 167; C. F. A., Jr., to his father, July 28, 1862, *ibid.,* p. 169; C. F. A., Jr., to Henry Adams, July 28, 1862, *ibid.,* p. 171; C. F. A., Jr., to his father, March 11, 1862, *ibid.,* p. 118; C. F. A., Jr., to Henry Adams, April 6, 1862, *ibid.,* pp. 130–131.

16.   *Ibid.,* p. 172. It should be noted that Adams later became converted to the use of Negro troops as an expedient measure, and in 1864 even took command of Negro cavalry; but his observations on the Negroes under his command reflect his unwillingness to credit them with the essential attributes of humanity. It is significant that his plan of reconstruction was to force the Negroes to remain in the army so that they could be taught habits of industry by the military experience. (*Adams Cycle,* II, 195, 215–219.)

17.   Howe, *Holmes,* p. 54.

18.   Lowell to Miss Shaw, June 17, 1863, Edward W. Emerson, *Life and Letters of Charles Russell Lowell* (Boston and New York, 1907), p. 259.

19.   Lowell to Henry Lee Higginson, Sept. 10, 1864, *ibid.,* pp. 341–342.

20.   Bliss Perry, *The Life and Letters of Henry Lee Higginson* (Boston, 1921), pp. 232, 536.

21.   Thomas Wentworth Higginson, *Cheerful Yesterdays* (Boston and New York, 1898), p. 269.

22.   De Forest, *Miss Ravenel's Conversion,* pp. 50, 465, 484.

23.   This commitment to practical life, this rejection of the ideal of the isolated scholar or genius which had been such an important part of Emerson's message, is reflected in another novel written by a soldier, *The Thinking Bayonet* (Boston, 1865), by James K. Hosmer, a New England clergyman who had taken up arms. This novel is more conventional and romantic than *Miss Ravenel's Conversion.* In it, the typical hero of the romance, the melancholy young man who is led by narcissism into a rejection of social obligations, is transformed into a useful citizen by his war service.

24.   Letter of Motley to Oliver Wendell Holmes, Sr., Aug. 31, 1862, *Correspondence of John Lothrop Motley* (New York, 1889), II, 42.

25.   Emerson to James Eliot Cabot, Aug. 4, 1861, *The Letters of Ralph Waldo Emerson,* ed. Ralph L. Rusk (New York, 1939), V, 253.

26. *The Journals of Ralph Waldo Emerson,* ed. Edward W. Emerson and Waldo E. Forbes (Boston and New York, 1909–1914), IX, 412.

27. Ralph Waldo Emerson, *Nature, Addresses, and Lectures,* Complete Works of Ralph Waldo Emerson, I (Boston and New York, 1903), p. 107.

28. Ralph Waldo Emerson, *Miscellanies,* Works, IX (Boston and New York, 1904), p. 302.

29. Ralph Waldo Emerson, "American Civilization," *Atlantic,* IX (April 1862), p. 504.

30. Emerson, *Journals,* IX, 493 (end of March 1863).

31. George E. Woodberry, *Ralph Waldo Emerson* (New York, 1907), p. 105.

32. Stephen E. Whicher, *Freedom and Fate: An Inner Life of Ralph Waldo Emerson* (Philadelphia, 1953), Chapters VII and VIII.

33. Emerson, *Journals,* IX, 577 (November 1863).

34. Emerson, *Journals,* X, 7 (February 1864).

35. Moncure Conway, *Autobiography, Memories, and Experiences* (Boston and New York, 1904), I, 436.

36. Emerson, *Journals,* IX, 513 (May 1863).

37. Ralph L. Rusk, *The Life of Ralph Waldo Emerson* (New York, 1949), pp. 419–424.

38. Emerson to Charles Sumner, Dec. 19, 1864, *The Letters of Ralph Waldo Emerson,* V, 396.

39. *Loc. cit.*

CHAPTER TWELVE. THE TWILIGHT OF HUMANITARIANISM

1. *The Journals of Ralph Waldo Emerson,* ed. Edward W. Emerson and Waldo E. Forbes (Boston and New York, 1909–1914), X, 116.

2. Francis Lieber, "Amendments of the Constitution," in *Miscellaneous Writings of Francis Lieber* (Philadelphia, 1881), II, 147.

3. Samuel Fowler, "The Political Opinions of Thomas Jefferson," *North American Review,* CI (October 1865), pp. 313–334. Fowler's article is discussed at some length in Merrill D. Peterson, *The Jefferson Image in the American Mind* (New York, 1960), pp. 217–218. Peterson has a perceptive discussion of the impact of the Civil War on Jeffersonian ideas.

4. James Russell Lowell, "Ode Recited at the Harvard Commemoration," in *Poems,* IV, The Writings of James Russell Lowell, X (Boston and New York, 1892), pp. 17–31.

5. Herman Melville, *Battle Pieces and Aspects of the War* (Gainesville, Fla., Facsimile Ed., 1960), p. 162.

6. Hennig Cohen, Introduction to *The Battle Pieces of Herman Melville* (New York, London, and Toronto, 1963), p. 21.

7. Melville, "The House Top," *Battle Pieces* (Facsimile Ed.), p. 87.

8. "The Conflict of Convictions," *ibid.*, p. 17.

9. *The Works of Orestes Brownson*, ed. Henry F. Brownson (Detroit, 1882-1887), XVIII, 29.

10. *Ibid.*, p. 7.

11. *Nation*, I (July 27, 1865), p. 105.

12. Eugene N. Curtis, "American Opinion of the French Nineteenth Century Revolutions," *American Historical Review*, XXIX (January 1924), p. 269.

13. Brownson, *Works*, XVIII, 8, 105-106, 179-184, 187.

14. John Alexander, "The Ideas of Lysander Spooner," *New England Quarterly*, XXIII (June 1950), pp. 200-217; Irving H. Bartlett, *Wendell Phillips: Brahmin Radical* (Boston, 1961), p. 210.

15. Lysander Spooner, *No Treason, No. 1* (Boston, 1867), pp. iii, iv. Pamphlet in the Harvard University Library.

16. Lysander Spooner, *No Treason, No. 6* (Boston, 1870), p. 57. Pamphlet in the Harvard University Library.

17. Brownson, *Works*, XVIII, 126-127. This theory was further developed by the conservative legalist John C. Hurd in his *Theory of Our National Existence* (Boston, 1881).

18. Irving H. Bartlett, *Wendell Phillips: Brahmin Radical* (Boston, 1961), p. 305.

19. See the cogent criticism of the Stevens confiscation plan in Fawn Brodie, *Thaddeus Stevens: Scourge of the South* (New York, 1959), pp. 303-305.

20. Carl Schurz, "The True Problem," *Atlantic*, XIX (March 1867), pp. 371-378.

21. Albion W. Tourgée, *A Fool's Errand*, ed. John Hope Franklin (Cambridge, Mass., 1961), pp. 137, 169.

22. Georges Clemenceau, *American Reconstruction* (New York, 1928), pp. 297-298.

23. John W. De Forest, *A Union Officer in the Reconstruction*, ed. James H. Croushore and David M. Potter (New Haven, 1948), pp. 117, 131.

24. William Graham Sumner, *What Social Classes Owe to Each Other* (New York, 1883), pp. 65-66.

25. Paul Buck, *The Road to Reunion* (New York, 1937), Chapter IV.

26. "Indianapolis Speech," *The Works of Robert G. Ingersoll,* ed. Clinton P. Farrell (New York, 1902), IX, 167-170.

27. *Atlantic,* XXIV (November 1869), p. 644.

28. Thomas Wentworth Higginson, "Some War Scenes Revisited," *Atlantic,* XLII (July 1878), pp. 2-9.

29. Jesse H. Jones, *His Last Battle and One of His Greatest Victories, Being the Speech of Wendell Phillips in Faneuil Hall on the Louisiana Difficulties, January 15, 1875* (Boston, 1897).

30. Jesse H. Jones, *The Kingdom of Heaven: What It Is; Where It Is; and the Duty of American Christians concerning It* (Boston, 1871), pp. 204-205, 222-225, 273, *et passim;* for biographical information on Jones see H. H. Loud, "Biographical Sketch of the Reverend Jesse Henry Jones," in Jesse H. Jones, *Joshua Davidson, Christian* (New York, 1907), pp. vii-xiv; and Arthur Mann, *Yankee Reformers in an Urban Age* (Cambridge, Mass., 1954) pp. 86-89.

31. James Dombrowski, *The Early Days of Christian Socialism in America* (New York, 1936), Chapter VII; Mann, *Yankee Reformers,* pp. 86-89.

32. Bartlett, *Phillips,* pp. 349-351; Fine, however, makes no mention of Phillips in his *Laissez Faire and the General Welfare State: A Study of Conflict in American Thought* (Ann Arbor, Mich., 1956).

33. Dombrowski, *Christian Socialism,* p. 83.

34. Bartlett, *Phillips,* pp. 355 and 316-401, *passim.*

CHAPTER THIRTEEN. SCIENCE AND THE NEW INTELLECTUALS

1. John W. Draper, *Thoughts on the Future Civil Policy of America* (New York, 1865), pp. 251-252; quoted in Donald Fleming, *John William Draper and the Religion of Science* (Philadelphia, 1950), p. 109.

2. Draper, *Civil Policy,* pp. 248, 316-317; Fleming, *Draper,* Chapter 14.

3. John W. Draper, *History of the American Civil War* (New York, 1867-1870), I, 20-24, 208-211; III, 636, 669-671.

4. *Ibid.,* III, 669; I, 291.

5. Quoted in Royal Cortissoz, *The Life of Whitelaw Reid* (New York, 1921), I, 256-257.

6. Francis Parkman, "The Failure of Universal Suffrage," *North American Review,* CXXVII (July-August 1878), p. 19.

7. Carroll Wright, "Francis Amasa Walker," *Publications of the American Statistical Association*, V (June 1897), p. 249.

8. James Phinney Munroe, *A Life of Francis Amasa Walker* (New York, 1923), pp. 11–15; on the economic thought of Amasa Walker see Joseph Dorfman, *The Economic Mind in American Civilization* (New York, 1946–1949), III, 49–56.

9. Munroe, *Walker*, pp. 101–102.

10. *Ibid.*, pp. 109–111; Ernest Samuels, *The Young Henry Adams* (Cambridge, Mass., 1948), pp. 173–174.

11. Francis A. Walker, *Oration Delivered at the Soldier's Monument in North Brookfield, Mass., Jan. 19, 1870* (Worcester, Mass., 1870), p. 8.

12. Munroe, *Walker*, pp. 127–149.

13. Sidney Fine, *Laissez Faire and the General Welfare State: A Study of Conflict in American Thought* (Ann Arbor, Mich., 1956), pp. 74–79; Walker's economic thought is contained in *The Wages Question* (New York, 1876) and *Political Economy* (New York, 1883).

14. Munroe, *Walker*, pp. 301–302; Barbara Miller Solomon, *Ancestors and Immigrants: A Changing New England Tradition* (Cambridge, Mass., 1956), pp. 69–81.

15. Dorfman, *Economic Mind*, III, 51–52.

16. Henry Adams, *History of the United States of America during the First Administration of Thomas Jefferson* (New York, 1889), I, 73; *A Cycle of Adams Letters 1861–1865*, ed. Worthington Ford, 2 vols. (Boston and New York, 1920), *passim*.

17. Letter of Henry Adams to Charles Francis Adams, Jr., *Letters of Henry Adams*, ed. Worthington Ford (Boston and New York, 1930), p. 160.

18. Charles Francis Adams, *Autobiography* (Boston and New York, 1916), pp. 166–167, 179.

19. *Ibid.*, p. 170.

20. Adams' writing on railroads started with "The Railroad System," *North American Review*, CIV (April 1867), pp. 476–511, and culminated in *Railroads: Their Origins and Problems* (New York, 1878).

21. Adams, *Autobiography*, pp. 171–174.

22. *Ibid.*, pp. 174–175; *Railroads: Their Origins and Problems, passim*.

23. Charles Francis Adams, *Individuality in Politics: A Lecture*

Delivered in Steinway Hall, New York, April 21, 1880 (New York, 1880), pp. 11–13.

24. Adams, *Autobiography*, p. 190.

25. See Oliver Wendell Holmes, *The Common Law* (Boston, 1881). For a good discussion of Holmes' "realism" as a product of the Civil War, see Edmund Wilson, *Patriotic Gore: Studies in the Literature of the American Civil War* (New York, 1962), pp. 743–796.

26. Mark De Wolfe Howe, *Justice Oliver Wendell Holmes: The Proving Years 1870–1882* (Cambridge, Mass., 1963), pp. 43–44.

27. Edward Chase Kirkland, *Dream and Thought in the Business Community 1860–1900* (Ithaca, N.Y., 1956), pp. 139–140, *et passim.*

28. Dorman B. Eaton, "A New Phase of the Reform Movement," *North American Review,* CXXXII (June 1881), p. 548.

29. John Wesley Powell, *Report on the Lands of the Arid Regions of the United States,* ed. Wallace Stegner (Cambridge, Mass., 1962), pp. 39–42, *et passim.* For the career of Powell see William Culp Darrah, *Powell of the Colorado* (Princeton, 1951), and Wallace Stegner, *Beyond the Hundredth Meridian: John Wesley Powell and the Second Opening of the West* (Boston, 1954).

30. Stegner, *Hundredth Meridian,* Chapter V.

31. The relationship of Powell and Ward is discussed in Darrah, *Powell,* pp. 280–282; on Ward's military experience see *Young Ward's Diary,* ed. Bernhard J. Stern (New York, 1935); on Ward's work as a sociologist, see Samuel Chugarman, *Lester Ward: American Aristotle* (Durham, N.C., 1937).

32. Marjorie Barstow Greenbie, *Lincoln's Daughters of Mercy* (New York, 1944), pp. 55, 65–66; *The Philanthropic Work of Josephine Shaw Lowell,* ed. William Rhinelander Stewart (New York, 1911), pp. 78–79.

33. E. V. Smalley, "A Great Charity Reform," *Century,* 24-2 (July 1882), pp. 401–408.

34. *Philanthropic Work,* ed. Stewart, pp. 8–9.

35. Oliver Wendell Holmes, "Memorial Day," *Speeches* (Boston, 1913), pp. 9–10.

36. Frank D. Watson, *The Charity Organization Movement in the United States: A Study in American Philanthropy* (New York, 1922), pp. 209–211, *et passim; Philanthropic Work,* ed. Stewart, Chapter IX.

37. *Joseph Tuckerman on the Elevation of the Poor* (Boston, 1874), pp. 25, 73–74, *et passim.*

38. *Philanthropic Work*, ed. Stewart, p. 129.

39. *Ibid.*, pp. 161–162, 171.

CHAPTER FOURTEEN. THE MORAL EQUIVALENT OF WAR

1. Francis A. Walker, "Is It a Gospel of Peace?" *Lippincott's Magazine*, IV (August 1869), p. 203.

2. See Edmund Wilson, *Patriotic Gore: Studies in the Literature of the American Civil War* (New York, 1962), pp. 753–754. Letter of Holmes to Harold Laski, May 4, 1924, *Holmes-Laski Letters*, ed. Mark De Wolfe Howe (Cambridge, Mass., 1953), p. 615. See also Holmes to Sir Frederick Pollock, Feb. 1, 1920, *Holmes-Pollock Letters*, ed. Mark De Wolfe Howe (Cambridge, Mass., 1941), II, 36.

3. Moncure Conway, *Autobiography, Memories, and Experiences* (Boston and New York, 1904), I, 222.

4. Mary Elizabeth Burtis, *Moncure Conway* (New Brunswick, N.J., 1952), Chapters 21–23; Conway, *Autobiography*, II, 87–94, 305.

5. Quoted in George R. Farnham, *Justice Holmes—Silhouettes*, pamphlet published by the American Law Book Company, n.d. or place of publication, p. 4.

6. Oliver Wendell Holmes, "Natural Law," *Collected Legal Papers* (New York, 1920), pp. 315–316. Originally published in *Harvard Law Review*, XXXII (1918).

7. Oliver Wendell Holmes, "The Soldier's Faith" (1895), *Speeches* (Boston, 1913), p. 62.

8. Holmes, "Memorial Day" (1884), *ibid.*, pp. 11, 2–3.

9. Holmes, "Soldier's Faith," p. 59.

10. "Soldier's Memorial Services," *Century*, 38-16 (May 1889), p. 157.

11. Holmes, "Soldier's Faith," pp. 56, 62–63.

12. *Ibid.*, p. 56.

13. Hofstadter's theory of "the status revolution" is set forth in Chapter IV of his *Age of Reform* (New York, 1955). I believe that this theory needs modification in the light of Edward Kirkland's suggestion, in *Dream and Thought in the Business Community* (Ithaca, 1956), that the men of the "mugwump" type, whom Hofstadter describes as losing status to the new businessmen, were themselves often men of great power in the business community. It would seem in fact that the "mugwumps" acted as spokesmen for a large segment of that community, articulating the prevailing attitude of businessmen toward government, education, philanthropy, etc. This view gains credence from the study of "The American Industrial Elite in the 1870's," by

Frances W. Gregory and Irene D. New, in *Men of Business: Essays in the History of Entrepreneurship*, ed. William Miller (Cambridge, Mass., 1952), in which it is demonstrated that the business leaders of the age did not fit the Horatio Alger, "rags to riches" pattern, but were generally men who had started their careers with assured social position and family connections.

14. Holmes, "Memorial Day," p. 6.

15. Horace Porter, "The Philosophy of Courage," *Century*, 36-14 (June 1888), p. 253.

16. Holmes, "Soldier's Faith," p. 63.

17. Henry Lee Higginson, "The Soldiers Field," in Bliss Perry, *The Life and Letters of Henry Lee Higginson* (Boston, 1921), p. 535.

18. Francis A. Walker, *College Athletics: An Address before the Phi Beta Kappa Society, Alpha, of Massachusetts at Cambridge, June 29, 1893*, reprinted from *Technology Quarterly*, VI (July 1893), pp. 2–3, 6, 13.

19. *Ibid.*, pp. 7–8.

20. See Theodore Roosevelt, *The Rough Riders and Men of Action*, The Works of Theodore Roosevelt, XI (New York, National Ed. 1926), especially pp. 9, 27–28, 149.

21. Theodore Roosevelt, *The Strenuous Life: Essays and Addresses* (New York, 1901), pp. 4–5, 8.

22. Manuscripts in the Bellamy Papers, Houghton Library, Harvard University.

23. Arthur E. Morgan, *Edward Bellamy* (New York, 1944), pp. 31–32, 41.

24. Edward Bellamy, "The Religion of Solidarity," *Selected Writings on Religion and Society*, ed. Joseph Schiffman (New York, 1955), pp. 6–7, 22–23; Morgan, *Bellamy*, pp. 200–203.

25. Morgan, *Bellamy*, p. 363.

26. Edward Bellamy, "An Echo of Antietam," *The Blindman's World and Other Stories* (Boston and New York, 1898), pp. 42–43, 46.

27. Morgan, *Bellamy*, pp. 322–323.

28. Edward Bellamy, *Looking Backward, 2000–1887* (Boston and New York, 1889), p. 97.

29. Edward Bellamy, *Equality* (New York, 1897), p. 277.

30. James to Holmes, Jan. 3, 1868, Holmes to James, April 19, 1868, James to Holmes, May 15, 1868, in Ralph Barton Perry, *The Thought and Character of William James* (Boston, 1935), I, 507–514; William James to Henry James, Oct. 2, 1869, *ibid.*, p. 307.

31. James to Holmes, May 18, 1868, *ibid.*, p. 517.

32. James to Thomas Ward, Oct. 9, 1868, *ibid.*, p. 287.

33. James to Holmes, May 18, 1868, *ibid.*, p. 515. The Holmes quotation is from a letter to James, March 24, 1907, *ibid.*, II, 460.

34. Entry in James' diary, Feb. 1, 1870, *ibid.*, I, p. 322; William James, *The Will to Believe and Other Essays in Popular Philosophy* (New York, 1897), p. 30.

35. James, *The Will to Believe*, pp. 212–213.

36. William James, "Oration," in *Dedication of the Robert Gould Shaw Memorial* (Boston, 1897), pp. 40–42, 51–52.

37. Perry, *Thought and Character*, II, 250–251.

38. James, "Oration," pp. 50–51.

39. Perry, *Thought and Character*, II, 308.

40. Roosevelt, *Strenuous Life*, pp. 7–8, 18.

41. William James, letter to the *Boston Evening Transcript*, March 1, 1899; Perry, *Thought and Character*, II, 311–312.

42. From an address of 1902, quoted in *ibid.*, pp. 298–299.

43. William James, "The Energies of Men" (1906) and "On a Certain Blindness in Human Beings" (1899), in *Essays on Faith and Morals* (New York, 1943), pp. 235, 279, 232.

44. William James, "The Moral Equivalent of War," *ibid.*, pp. 311, 325.

45. *Ibid.*, pp. 323–325.

46. William James, "The Social Value of the College Bred" (1908), in *Memories and Studies* (New York, 1911), p. 317.

47. William James, "Thomas Davidson," *ibid.*, pp. 102–103.

INDEX

Abolitionism: Garrison's leadership of, 17, 41; Wendell Phillips' role in, 18; Parkman's criticism of, 34; Parker's leadership of, 36–9; issue of pacifism in, 41–4; response to secession, 56–60, to war, 61, 63–4, 78, to suffering, 81; dilemma of emancipation, 116–18, 122–3, and Conway's stand, 123–7; and use of Negro troops, 151; martyrology of, 153–61, 165; Emerson's disillusionment with, 176; war seen as defeat for, 187–8; postwar disinterest in, 195, 215; William James on, 232–3, 234; mentioned, 77, 147, 168, 169, 203

Adams, Charles Francis, Jr.: military realism of, 166, 170–1, 174; scientific approach to postwar career, 205–8, 209; mentioned, 175, 210, 215

Adams, Charles Francis, Sr.: anti-slavery commitment of, 170–1; mentioned, 194

Adams, Henry: scientific elitism of, 205; quoted, 37

Adams, John Quincy, 9

Advertiser (Boston), 162

Agassiz, Ida, 162

Agassiz, Louis, 160

Alcott, Bronson, 12, 49

Alcott, Louisa May, response to suffering, 87–9, 90

American Academy of Arts and Sciences, 179

American Red Cross, 89

American Revolution: Lieber's interpretation of, 133; Stillé's justification of, 145, Bushnell's, 146; mentioned, 36, 38, 43, 61, 64, 135, 136

Anarchiad, republication of, 77

Andrew, Gov. John, 152

Anglo-Saxonism: of Stillé, 142–4, mentioned, 146

Antietam, battle of, 79, 89, 165

Anti-institutionalism: in ante-bellum North, 9–10; Emersonian, 10–12; and Garrison's extremism, 17; of Wendell Phillips, 19; of Whitman, 20; characteristics of leaders, 23; and civil disobedience, 39; and secession, 54; attacked by Bellows, 70, by *Harper's*, 147; postwar decline, 176, 177, of Emerson's, 179–80, of William James', 237

"Antirent rebellion," 20

Anti-Slavery Standard, 153

Appleton, William, on philanthropy, 111–12

Army Medical Bureau, 99

Army Nurse Corps, 89

Army of the Potomac, 178

Atlantic Monthly, 49, 117, 155, 177, 191, 195

Ball's Bluff, 165, 169

Bancroft, George: anti-institutionalism of, 19; mentioned, 146

Barton, Clara: response to suffering, 89; mentioned, 90

269

Bassett, George W.: antiwar position, 62–3, 64; mentioned, 145
Beecher, Henry Ward, 45, 56, 153
Bellamy, Edward: military values of, 225–8; transcendental socialism of, 226; utopianism of, 227–8
Bellows, Henry W.: religious institutionalism of, 26–7, 28; fear of secession, 54; advocacy of coercion, 55, 56; religious support of war, 70–1; Sanitary Commission leadership, 100–1, 106, 108–9, 111; views of suffering as valuable, 103; loyalty efforts of, 131; affirms "divine right," 136, 141, 144; mentioned, 105, 147, 177, 185
Bigelow Papers, 117, 120
Binney, Horace, Jr., 101, 102
Binney, Horace, Sr.: defense of Federalism, 77; attitude toward emancipation, 114; mentioned, 54
Blanc, Louis, 32
Boston Symphony Orchestra, 173
Boston Vigilance Committee, 37
Bowen, Francis, 32
Brahmins, New England: transcendental experiences of, 29–35; response to war, 72–3, to Shaw's martyrdom, 153–6; and Parkman's elitism, 164–5; mentioned, 169, 221
Brook Farm, 226
Brooklyn Eagle, 20
Brown, John: Parker's support of, 38; Emerson's view of, 39–40; effect on Garrison, 41–2, on Phillips, 42–3, on conservatives, 47–8; mentioned, 36, 54, 61, 83, 120, 126; *see also* John Brown's raid
Brownson, Orestes: anti-institutionalism of, 19; conservatism of, 27–8, 144, postwar, 186–8; effect of slavery issue on, 44–5; views on war, 71, on suffering, 80, on emancipation, 114–15; denies right to revolution, 144–5; view of war as defeat for abolitionism, 187–8; fear of Jacobin democracy, 190; mentioned, 26, 103, 133, 198, 200
Brownson's Quarterly Review, 28, 114
Buchanan, James, 45
Buck, Paul, 220

Bull Run, First Battle of, response to, 73–6; mentioned, 79, 84, 103, 104; Second Battle of, 79
Burns, Anthony, 37
Bushnell, Horace: religious conservatism of, 25–6, 28; chauvinistic opposition to slavery, 45–6; response to Bull Run, 75–6, to suffering, 80; "divine right" views, 137–41, 143, 144; mentioned, 103, 133, 185, 200

Calhoun, John C., 28
"Cavalier," concept of Southern, 164, 184
Chancellorsville, battle of, 94
Channing, William Ellery, 33
Channing, William Henry, 13
Charity Organization Society of New York, Social Darwinism of, 213
Chatillon, Henry, 33
Cheever, George B., 45
Child, Lydia Maria: response to suffering, 84, to emancipation, 119; mentioned, 116, 120, 153
Choate, Rufus, 143, 149
Christian Commission, 107
Christian Inquirer, 73
Christian Labor Union, 198
Civilian Conservation Corps, 236
Civil service, postwar reform of, 209, military model for, 209–10
Clarke, James Freeman: support of secession, 58; mentioned, 15, 56
Clemenceau, Georges, 192, 193
Coercion: as issue of secession, 55–6, 57; advocated by Lowell, 59–60
Congress, United States: passes confiscation law, 73; reorganizes Medical Bureau, 99; mentioned, 190
Conservatism: in opposition to anti-institutionalism, 23–4, 147, 149; of Lieber, 24–5; religious, 25–8; New England Brahmin, 29–35; effect of slavery issue on, 44, of secession on, 54–6; and support of war, 69–71; in Sanitary Commission, 100–6, 111; attitude toward emancipation, 114–16; extreme, 2, in promotion of loyalty, 135, in postwar era, 199; "divine right" views of, 136–41, 144; Anglo-Saxon loyalty traditions,

141–4; Brownson's denial of right to revolution, 144–5; postwar nationalistic, 186–8, 190; and Draper's scientific elitism, 199–201

Constitution, relation of loyalty to, 138

Conway, Martin F., 125

Conway, Moncure: transcendentalist reformism of, 14–16; effect of John Brown on, 43; pacifism of, 57, 218–19; support of war, 61; stand on emancipation, 116–17, 118; criticism of Lincoln, 124–5; disenchantment with Northern cause, 123–7, with Emerson, 178; expatriation, 126; mentioned, 22, 23, 26, 68, 73, 157, 233

Cooper, James Fenimore, 33

Copperheads (Peace Democrats): program, 130, 132; belief in right of revolution, 134; in Union Army, 169; mentioned, 126, 131, 136, 168

Crane, Stephen, 95

Curti, Merle, 2

Curtis, George William: abolitionist view of civil service reform, 209; mentioned, 49, 154

Dana, Richard Henry, 81

Darwin, Charles, 74, 192

Darwinism: as justification for war, 75; mentioned, 192, 199; see also Social Darwinism

Declaration of Independence: invoked by millennialists, 7, 19, by transcendentalists, 37, by secession defenders, 58, 132, by abolitionists, 62, 63; criticized by Bushnell, 76, by Brownson, 145, 186; mentioned, 2, 49, 71, 129, 134, 144

De Forest, John W.: stoic response to suffering, 86–7, 90; realistic view of war, 167–8; pessimistic view of Negroes, 168, 193; mentioned, 97, 112, 174, 175, 179

Democracy, mass, as political creed, 19–20; of Whitman, 20

Democratic Party: in Jacksonian era, 20; Whitman's rejection of, 20–1; mentioned, 194

Democratic Review, 132

Discipline, as conservative value of Sanitary Commission, 104–6

Disloyalty: growth of, 130–1; attempts to combat, 131–2, 141; mentioned, 151

Disunionism, as response to secession, 54, 57–9

Divine Providence, deterministic concept of as explanation of suffering, 81–2

"Divine right": doctrine of, 150, 199; revived by Bellows, 136, by Duryea, 137, by Bushnell, 137–41, by Stillé, 143

Dix, Dorothea: humanitarianism of, 109–11; mentioned, 81

Douglass, Frederick, 152

Draper, John W., scientific elitism of, 199–201, 205

Dred Scott decision, 44

Duryea, Joseph T., "divine right" views of, 137

Eaton, Dorman B., use of military model for civil service reform, 209

Edel, Leon, 157

Egalitarianism, in ante-bellum America, 8–10

Elitism: New England, 29–35, 72, 75, 163; conservative, in Sanitary Commission, 99–102; scientific, of Draper, 199–201, of Charles Francis Adams, Jr., 205–8; administrative, 209; in philanthropy, 214

Elkins, Stanley, 9

Emancipation: Boston celebration of, 113; intellectual view of, 113, conservative, 114–16, abolitionist, 116–18, 122–3, 127–9; millennial interpretation of, 118–19; critics of, 119; and support of Lincoln's policy, 120–1; Conway's disillusionment in, 123–7; mentioned, 62, 124, 130, 189, 196, 232

Emerson, Ralph Waldo: view of "American Scholar," 10–12; influence on transcendentalists, 12–13, 15, 29, 30, wartime decline of, 172–3; Parker's criticism of, 13–14; Bellows' criticism of, 26–7; impact of slavery issue on, 38–40, 43; acceptance of secession, 54; effect of Fort Sumter attack on, 65–6, 67, 68; response to suffering, 80–1, to emancipation, 120, 121; joins Union Club of Boston, 132; poem for Shaw's martyrdom, 152, 154; effect of war on philosophy of, 176–80; favorable view of military life, 178–9; postwar commitment to institutions, 179; opinion of war outcome, 183; mentioned, 22, 23, 33, 37, 49, 113, 118, 226

Enlightenment: rejected by Stillé, 140, 142; influence on Draper, 201; mentioned, 64, 134, 187

European revolutions: support of, 135; deplored by Stillé, 142, 145–6; postwar lack of sympathy toward, 187

Federalism, revival of, 76–7, 78

Fine, Sydney, 197

Finney, Charles Grandison, 8, 81, 196

Forbes, John Murray, 152

Fort Hudson, Louisiana, assault on, 167

Fort Sumter: attack on, 63, 73, 103, 123, 217, 225; effect on North, 65, 72, on Emerson, 65–6

Fort Wagner: Negro troops in assault upon, 151–2, 165; mentioned, 156, 157, 161, 212

Fowler, Samuel, 184

Fredericksburg, battle of, 79, 91, 165

Freedman's Bureau, 191, 193

Free-soil doctrine, as conservative basis of abolition, 46, 47, 50

Frémont, John C., 114, 116, 128

Frothingham, Octavius B., response to suffering, 82–3

Fugitive Slave Act of 1850, 28, 34, 36, 39

Fuller, Margaret, 12

Furness, William Henry: explanation of suffering, 82; millennial interpretation of emancipation, 118, 119; mentioned, 15

Garrison, William Lloyd: abolitionism of, 17, 18, and use of force, 41; switch to coercion, 61, 64; reaction

to emancipation, 122, 127; mentioned, 22, 49, 56, 113, 128, 152, 189

Gaskell, Elizabeth, 153

Gettysburg, battle of, 165, 166

Giddings, Joshua, 56

Grant, Gen. Ulysses S.: corrupt administration of, 194, 195, 203; mentioned, 188, 225

Great Britain: views of secession, 62; Stillé's comparison of to U.S., 141–2

Greeley, Horace: support of secession, 58–9; mentioned, 194

Hale, Edward Everett: attitude toward emancipation, 117–18; mentioned, 113

Hamilton, Alexander, 9, 149

Hamilton, Gail, justification of suffering, 83–4

Hampton, Gov. Wade, 195

Harpers Ferry, 40, 41, 42

Harper's Monthly: institutionalism of, 147; mentioned, 59, 137

Harvard Divinity School, 15

Harvard University: war martyrs of, 155, 165; mentioned, 184, 198, 222

Hawthorne, Nathaniel, reaction to war, 1–3

Hay, John, 228

Hegelianism, of Whitman, 97

Higginson, Henry Lee: transcendentalism of, 30–1; volunteer for Union, 72–3; war heroism of, 162; effect of war experience on, 173, 174; promotes collegiate athletics, 223; mentioned, 224, 225

Higginson, Thomas Wentworth: abolitionism of, 37; 42, 168–9; postwar disinterest in, 195; response to Bull Run defeat, 73–4; on Brahmin heroism, 155–6; wartime experiences, 173

Hodson, Maj. W. S. R., 155

Hofstadter, Richard, 221

Holmes, Oliver Wendell, Jr.: response to suffering, 86, 87, 90; military disillusionment of, 167, 168–70, 172, 178; scientific approach to law, 208; stoicism of, 219; realistic view of war, 218, 219–22; relationship with William James, 229–31, 233; mentioned, 97, 174, 175, 212, 215, 224, 227

Holmes, Oliver Wendell, Sr.: elitism of, 33–4; patriotism of, 70, 72; description of Antietam battle, 79; mentioned, 29, 31, 170, 174

Homestead Act, 210

Hosmer, James K., 260

Howe, Samuel Gridley: in Sanitary Commission, 102; quoted, 48–9; mentioned, 56

Howells, William Dean: postwar boredom with Negro question, 195; mentioned, 49

Humanitarianism: of Whitman, 20; opposition to, 34; of James family, 165; decline of, 183, 185, 198; postwar goals of, 189; *see also* Abolitionism

Hunter, Gen. David, 116, 171

Immigration, restriction of, 202

Individualism: Emersonian, 14, general description, 10–12, conservative opposition to, 31, modification of, 65, decline of, 176–80; as antebellum theme, 22; Draper's criticism of, 200–1; of William James, 237

Ingersoll, Col. Robert G.: response to suffering, 85–6, 90, to emancipation, 119; as "bloody-shirt" orator, 194

Institutions: as viewed in ante-bellum America, 7, 8–9; religious, 25; generalized doctrine of, 147; *see also* Anti-institutionalism

Intellectuals, Northern: and antebellum egalitarianism, 10, Emerson's view of, 11–12; De Forest's postwar recommendations to, 174–5; effect of war on, 175, 183–4; views of Reconstruction, 192, 195; Draper's view of, 200; postwar scientific approach of, 202–8

Jackson, Andrew, 8, 9–10, 20

Jacksonians: opposition to "privilege," 8; disillusionment of, 20

James, Henry, Jr.: quoted on impact of Civil War, 1, on Hawthorne's reaction, 1–2; reaction to brother's

heroism, 157–8; failure to participate, 158–9, 162; mentioned, 156, 229

James, Henry, Sr.: millennialism of, 68–9; view of loyalty as sentiment, 137–8; abolitionism of, 156–7; mentioned, 71, 153, 226

James, Robertson, 157, 160

James, Wilkinson: wounded at Fort Wagner, 156, 157; effect on brothers, 159, 160, 161; mentioned, 234

James, William: reaction to war heroism, 157, 161; failure to participate, 158, 159–60, 162; search for emotional equivalent of war, 229–38; relationship with Oliver Wendell Holmes, Jr., 229–31, 233; utilitarianism of, 230–1; moralism of, 231–4; adaptation of "strenuous life," 234–7; democratic values of, 236; anti-institutional defense, 237; mentioned, 156, 212

Jefferson, Thomas, 9, 76, 77, 78, 135

John Brown's raid: effect on transcendentalists, 38, 40, 47, 57; mentioned, 126

Jones, Jesse H.: postwar agitation for Negro rights, 196; political millennialism of, 196–7, 198

Kansas, abolition controversy in, 37, 39, 41, 126, 169

Kansas-Nebraska Act of 1854, 44, 45

Kennedy, John F., 236

Kirkland, Edward, 209

"Knights of the Golden Circle," 130

Kossuth, Louis, 32

Labor Reform Party, 197, 198

Laissez faire, doctrine of, 203, 204, 208, 209, 211

Legree, Simon, 86

Liberal Republicans, 194

Liberator, 17, 122

Lieber, Francis: theory of "institutional liberty," 24–5; effect of John Brown on, 47–8; spokesman for loyalists, 131, 133–4, 135; on impact of war on intellectuals, 184

Lincoln, Abraham: view of legality of secession, 59; pardoning of deserters, 104; cautious view of abolition, 116; and Emancipation Proclamation, 118, 122; James Russell Lowell's defense of, 120–1, 185; criticized by Conway, 124–5, by Phillips, 128; defended by Bellows, 136; mentioned, 49, 53, 61, 66, 98, 108, 113, 150, 225

Lippincott's, 218

Longfellow, Henry Wadsworth, 113

Lovejoy, Elijah, 83, 153

Lovie, Henry, 79

Lowell, Charles Russell: transcendentalism of, 29–30, modified by war, 172–3; volunteer for Union, 72; mentioned, 158, 175, 179, 212, 223

Lowell, James Russell: advocacy of coercion, 59–60; gradualist view of emancipation, 117; support of Lincoln, 120–1; nationalism of, 184–5; mentioned, 29, 49, 179, 245n

Lowell, Josephine Shaw: response to suffering, 84; postwar career in philanthropy, 212–13; Social Darwinism of, 214–15; mentioned, 158, 172

Loyal Publication Society (New York), 131, 133

Loyalty: organized efforts to promote, 131–2; attempts to define, 132–5, 143; "divine right" theory of, 135–47; Bushnell's doctrine, 137–41; Anglo-Saxon tradition of, 141–4; and right to revolution, 144–6; and revival of institutionalism, 147

Madison, James, 9

Mason, James M., 125

Massachusetts Board of Railroad Commissioners, 206

Massachusetts Fifty-fourth Regiment, 151–2, 156

Massachusetts Institute of Technology, 202

Mazzini, Giuseppi, 32

McClellan, Gen. George B., 104, 188

Melville, Herman: nationalism of, 185–6; mentioned, 184

Memorial Day, observance of, 220

Military life: Parkman's belief in values of, 163–4, 166; defeatism in, 166; realistic views of De Forest on, 167–8, of Holmes, Jr., 168–70, 218–20, of Charles Francis Adams, Jr., 161, 170–1; and decline of Emersonian ideals, 172–6; Emerson's view of, 178; influence of on civil service reform, 209, on general reform, 211; heroic values of, as seen by Holmes, Jr., 220–2; competitive athletics as substitute for, 222–4

Mill, John Stuart, 205, 206

Millennialism: in ante-bellum America, 7; of Garrisonians, 17; effect of war on, 68–9, of suffering, 82; and emancipation, 118; postwar, 196–7

Missouri Compromise, 44, 45

Motley, John Lothrop, 153, 175

Mugwumps: crusade against corruption, 194; mentioned, 183, 234, 266n

Napoleon III, 3, 70

National Academy of Literature and Art, Emerson's endorsement of, 179

National Era, 83

Nationalism: of Francis Lieber, 133–4, 184; positive effect of war on, 184–9

Negroes: Norton's view of, 47; Northern conservative attitude toward, 115, 161, 162; in Fort Wagner assault, 151–2, 165; De Forest's contempt for, 168, 193; Charles Francis Adams, Jr.'s pessimism about, 171–2; postwar rights for Southern, 189, 191–2; Darwinian attitudes toward, 192–4; as tools of Republican opportunists, 194; postwar disinterest in, 195; agitation for, 196, 198

Nevins, Allan, 111

New England Loyal Publication Society, 131–2, 155

Newman, Cardinal John, 26

New York State Charities Aid Association, reform principles of, 211–12

North American Review, 77, 105
Norton, Andrews, 31
Norton, Charles Eliot: elitism of, 31–2; free-soil basis of antislavery, 46–7; advocates coercion, 55; view of war, 69–70; response to Bull Run defeat, 74, to suffering, 80; Darwinism of, 73–4; loyalty efforts of, 132; mentioned, 31, 34, 48, 72, 96, 103, 109, 113, 154, 165

Olmsted, Frederick Law: Sanitary Commission leadership of, 101, 104, 108; mentioned, 47
Organicism, social: of Bushnell, 139; mentioned, 144
O'Sullivan, John L., Copperhead spokesman, 126, 132, 144

Pacifism: as abolition issue, 41–4; and response to secession, 56–7, 61; of Conway, 218–19
Parker, Theodore: reformism of, 13–14, 16; advocacy of force in abolition, 36–9, 42; mentioned, 15, 22, 26, 29, 33, 68, 118
Parkman, Francis: elitism of, 33, 34, 35, 163–5, 221; response to Bull Run defeat, 75, to war heroism, 161–5; military values of, 163–4, 166, 225; "new reform" of, 202; mentioned, 31, 113, 154, 175, 176, 222, 236
Patriotism: *see* Loyalty
Peace Corps, 236
Peace Democrats: *see* Copperheads
Peninsula Campaign of 1862, 90, 100
Perfectibility: ante-bellum belief in, 2, 7–8; Garrisonian, 17
Philanthropy, effect of Sanitary Commission on concept of, 111–12
Phillips, Wendell: as abolitionist spokesman, 18, 41, 125; view of American civilization, 18–19; effect of John Brown on, 42–3; moral suasion position on secession, 57–8; switch to coercion, 61, 63–4; response to war, 73, 77–8, to emancipation, 127–8; repudiation of Federalism, 77, of Lincoln, 127–8; proposal for confiscation of Southern

estates, 191; postwar agitation for Negro rights, 196, in politics, 197–8; mentioned, 22, 23, 49, 56, 114, 116, 152, 169, 188, 205, 234, 239n
Porter, Gen. Horace, suggests frontier as moral equivalent to war, 222
Powell, Maj. John Wesley, social planning of, 210–11, 216

"Radical Reconstruction": *see* Reconstruction
Radical Republicans: postwar goals, 190; mentioned, 128, 196
Reconstruction ("Radical"), 191–5
Redpath, James, 93
Reform: transcendentalist, 13–16; moral, 17–18, 198, 233, 236, and response to secession, 57; failure of, 61; postwar apathy toward, 188; mass, 18, 19; humanitarian, 199; "new," or scientific, 202, 204, 207, in legal, 208, in civil service, 209, in charity work, 211–15
Reid, Whitelaw, scientific approach to politics, 202
Republican Party: Northern intellectual support of, 49; postwar opportunism in, 192, 194; liberal desertions from, 194, 196; mentioned, 20, 121, 183, 197
Revivalism, similarity of to Emersonianism, 15
Revolution: right of qualified, by Lieber, 133–4, by Thompson, 134–5, by Stillé, 145–6, by Bushnell, 146; denied by Brownson, 144–5; *see also* American Revolution, European revolutions
Ripley, George, 13
Roosevelt, Franklin D., 236
Roosevelt, Theodore, exemplar of "strenuous life," 222, 224–5, 228, 234, 236

Saint-Simon, Henri, 200
Sanitary Commission, United States: creation of, 98–9; legend of, 99; elitist rule of, 99–102; conservative values of, 102–6; view of volunteerism, 106–11; significance of, 111–12; professionalist influence on

postwar reform, 211, 212, 213; mentioned, 89, 90, 128

Santayana, George, 236

Schurz, Carl, 8, 191, 194

Schuyler, Louisa Lee, leadership in charity reform, 211–12, 213

Science: elitist role of, as viewed by Draper, 199–201, by Adams, 205–8; as postwar tool of politics, 202, of reform, 202, 209–15, of law, 208

Scott, Sir Walter, 167

Secession: ideological questions posed by, 53; Emerson's view of, 54; conservative response to, 54–6, abolitionist, 56–60; viewed as right of self-government, 62–3

"Self-culture": Emersonian doctrine of, 11, 35; reaction against, 13; Lowell's attempt at, 30, disillusionment with, 172–3; Higginson's attempt at, 31; Emerson's departure from, 179

Shaw, Francis George, 84, 153

Shaw, Josephine: see Lowell, Josephine Shaw

Shaw, Robert Gould: commands Negro regimental assault on Fort Wagner, 152; martyrdom, 152–5; effect of on James family, 156, 158, 161, 233, 234, on Parkman, 161; mentioned, 164, 173, 212, 223, 232

Sherman, Gen. William T., 160, 187

Shiloh, battle of, 79, 80, 85, 86, 210

Slavery: Conway's repudiation of, 16; impact of on Emerson, 38–9; wartime role of, as viewed by Draper, 200; mentioned, 220; see also Abolitionism

Smith, Gerrit: support of coercion, 60, of emancipation policy, 122–3, 127; mentioned, 41, 56

Social Darwinism: in Reconstruction, 192–4; in charity work, 213–15; mentioned, 198, 211

Social science, postwar approach to, 202, 205

Spanish-American War, 224, 233

Spencer, Herbert, 192, 211

Spooner, Lysander, 188–9

Sports, as productive of military spirit, 222–4

Stearns, Charles, 41

Stevens, Thaddeus, 191

Stillé, Charles Janeway: Sanitary Commission leadership, 101–2, 105; criticism of Christian Commission, 107–8; opposition to emancipation, 113–14; emphasis on Anglo-Saxon traditions, 141–4; justifies American Revolution, 145; mentioned, 201

Story, Justice Joseph, 143

Stowe, Harriet Beecher, 15, 81, 113

"Strenuous life": of Theodore Roosevelt, 222, 224–5, 234; William James' adaptation of, 234–7; see also Military life, and Chapter Eleven

Strong, George Templeton: conservatism of, 54–5; Sanitary Commission leadership, 101; views of suffering as valuable, 103; mentioned, 105

Suffering: as national discipline, 47, 48; individual responses to, of intellectuals, 80–1, 85–7, of abolitionists, 81–5, of nurses, 87–90, of Whitman, 90–7; organized responses to, of Sanitary Commission, 99–112, of Christian Commission, 107

Sumner, Charles, 56, 123, 179, 194

Sumner, William Graham, 192

Sydney, Sir Philip, 169

Taylor, Nathaniel, 81

Taylor, William R., 163

Thompson, Joseph Parrish, on right to revolution, 134–5

Thoreau, Henry David: reaction to war, 73; mentioned, 12, 189

Tocqueville, Alexis de, view of patriotism, 143

Tourgée, Albion, criticism of Reconstruction, 192

Transcendentalism: influence of Emerson on, 12; reformism of, 13–16; of New England Brahmins, 29; anarchist trends in, 39–40; wartime decline of, 172; of Bellamy, 226

Tuckerman, Joseph, views of philanthropy, 213

Twain, Mark, 194

Uncle Tom's Cabin: influence on Conway, 15; mentioned, 81, 86

Union League Club (New York), 131, 134

Union League Club of Boston, 132, 179

Unionism: democratic, of Whitman, 66–8; conservative, 69–71, 114; organized attempts to combat disloyalty, 131–2; postwar triumph of, 188; mentioned, 147, 150, 187

Union Pacific Railroad, presidency of Charles Francis Adams, Jr., 207

Unitarian Church, conservative wing of, 26–7

United States Geological Survey, 210, 211

Utilitarianism, of William James, 230–1

Vallandigham, Clement: Copperhead leader, 130, 134; arrest and banishment, 131

Vicksburg, battle of, 166

Virginia, reaction to John Brown crisis, 43

Volunteerism, opposed by Sanitary Commission, 106–11

Walker, Amasa, ante-bellum intellectual, 203, 204

Walker, Gen. Francis A.: "scientific" approach to reform, 202–5; criticism of warmongers, 217–18; support of collegiate athletics, 223–4; mentioned, 210, 215

War: spirit of in peacetime values, 217; qualified justification of by Walker, 218, by Holmes, 218, 219–20; rejection of by Conway, 218; heroic values of, as seen by Holmes,

220–2; competitive athletics as moral substitute for, 222–4; "strenuous life" as, 224–5; Bellamy's militarism, 225–8; William James' search for equivalent of, 229–38

Ward, Lester: "scientific" planning theories of, 211; mentioned, 216

Wasson, David A.: millennial interpretation of emancipation, 119; mentioned, 15

Webster, Daniel, 149

Weiss, John, 15

Weld, Theodore, 81

Whicher, Stephen E., 12, 177

Whitman, George, 91

Whitman, Walt: anti-institutionalism of, 20–2, 24; initial attitude toward war, 66–8; response to suffering, 90–7; criticism of Sanitary Commission, 106–7; patriotic dilemma of, 148–9; mentioned, 23

Whittier, John Greenleaf: support of war, 61; response to suffering, 84–5; mentioned, 56, 83, 113

Winthrop, Theodore: martyrdom, 73; mentioned, 34, 83, 175

Women's Central Association of Relief for the Sick and Wounded of the Army, 98, 211

Wormeley, Katherine Prescott: response to suffering, 89–90; description of Sanitary Commission, 102; mentioned, 104

Wright, Chauncey, 231

Wright, Henry Clarke, 57

Wright, Silas, 20

"Yankee," concept of, 164

Yale University, 202, 222

Young Men's Christian Association, 139

GEORGE M. FREDRICKSON is Edgar E. Robinson Professor of United States History at Stanford University. His other major publications include *The Black Image in the White Mind*, which won the Annisfield-Wolf Award for a book on race relations, and *White Supremacy: A Comparative Study of American and South African History*, runner up for the Pulitzer Prize, and winner of the Ralph Waldo Emerson Award from Phi Beta Kappa and the Merle Curtis Award from the Organization of American Historians.